キリスト教・ユダヤ教・イスラム教の知識と英語を身につける

Toward a good knowledge and better understanding of
Christianity, Judaism and Islam in English

石井隆之 [著] ● Ishii Takayuki
土井清孝 [監修] ● Doi Kiyotaka

ベレ出版

監修にあたって

　異なる文化、生活習慣や言語的背景を持つ人々の国境を超えたビジネスや交流が、加速するインターネット上の交流や情報交換ツールなどの発達と相俟って、一般庶民的なレベルにまで及んでくる時代となりました。日本に上陸する外国企業や、日本に在住する外国人の数も、ますます増える一方で、日本企業の海外進出や海外貿易も増大し、様々な国々の人との貿易・交渉など、異文化に生きる人々との協働の機会や仕事上の業務も日常化するようになりました。

　それに伴い、ビジネス交渉やインターネット上の圧倒的な「国際共通語（リンガ・フランカ）」となった英語の学びはもとより、文化を異にする人々とのソーシャライゼーションやコミュニケーションを、よりスムーズに行うことが求められています。この国際共通語を使用して意思疎通をする際に、むしろ大切になってきたことは、他の文化圏に生きる人々の価値観や発想・歴史的背景などを、より深く知っておく必要があるということでしょう。それはまた同時に、自分自身や、自分がそこで生まれ育った文化を、より国際的な視点から客観的に把握することにもつながります。

　「文化」についてはいろいろな定義がありますが、異文化間コミュニケーションの分野では、「何世代にもわたる個人や集団の努力によって、多くの人々により受け継がれた知識、経験、信念、価値観、態度、意味、階級、宗教、時間の観念、役割分担、空間の使い方、世界観、物質的な財産などすべてを包含したものである」（サモーバー他『異文化間コミュニケーション入門』）といった定義が一般的によく用いられるようです。

　さらにまた、「文化」を、日常的な習慣・行動といった表層部分から、次第にその深層にまで掘り下げて考えていくとき、習慣・行動→価値→信念といった内面的領域へと進み、最後に、中心部分で、「文化」の型を規定している「世界観」に行き着きます。そして、この世界観は、何らかの究極の実

在（リアリティ）や人生の意味、この世界が何であるかといった考え方と結びついているために、各人のバックグラウンドや居住地にかかわらず、その深層において、宗教的に決定されていると言えます。

　表面的な日常生活上の違いを知ることはもとより、内容のあるコミュニケーションや異文化交流をする上で、その背後にあって、意識の深層を刺激し、普段の生活や言動からビジネス現場の問題や価値観・人生観に至るまで影響を及ぼしてくる「宗教」について知っておくことは、よりよい相互理解や共生共栄のためには、さらに大切な事柄となるでしょう。

　かつてフランスの数学者・物理学者・哲学者のパスカルは、「すべての人は、幸福になることを探し求めている。それには例外がない。どんな異なった方法を用いようと、みんなこの目的に向かっている。…これこそすべての人間のすべての行動の動機である。首を吊ろうとする人たちまで含めて」…と、その著書の『パンセ』の中で書いています。見方を変えれば、小さな日常的な事柄や行動についても、宗教的か無宗教かにかかわらず、そのつど自分の幸福のありかや、生存の意味・根拠を求め、あるいは素朴に感じ、確かめながら、他人と世界とのかかわりの中で、人は生きていると言えます。その意味では、パスカルの言葉は、その信奉の対象がどのような形であれ、すべての人はみんな、宗教的な存在として生きており、それには例外がない、と言い換えられるかもしれません。

　こうした宗教的な意識が、システムとなり世界観をかたちづくるとき、1つの宗教が形成されるとも言えるでしょう。時代や場所を問わず、人が生存しているということは、自分の人生に何らかの究極的な意味・根拠を与えるもの（あるいは神的存在）へのかかわり、対人、対世界（または対自然）という3つの関係について、自分なりの応答をしつつ生の営みを続けています。そしてこれがシステムとして成立し、この3つの関係に対する特徴が明らかに認められるようになったとき、宗教的世界観が成立すると言えます。

　宗教哲学者の稲垣久和は、日本の伝統的世界観における、自我の対神・対

人・対自然関係の独自性の構造について多角的に分析し、言及しています（『知と信の構造』）。この見方に従えば、金山宣夫も指摘するような…日常生活から国家行事まで、日本人の深層心理のすみずみに入り込んだ宗教性としての…シャーマニズム的神観念、祖先崇拝とアニミズム《対神》、村落共同体と"ミディアモクラシー"（媒体本位主義）、あるいは浜口恵俊のいう「間人（かんじん）主義」等として指定されるようなエートス・システム《対人》、また、西欧の力学的自然に対する、「内在的な産霊（むすび）の霊力によって不断に成りゆく世界」としての生物学的自然観《対自然》と、これらの特徴を含む日本の精神風土も、一種のユニークな宗教的世界観を形成していると見ることもできます。

　前世紀の終わりごろから現代にかけても、世界の動きは、日常的な習慣・行事から国家間の外交レベルの事柄に至るまで、深く宗教がかかわってくる例も多く見られるようになりました。また、しばしばそれは、政治とも連動する形で新たな形態をとって表れてきます。例えばキリスト教では、アメリカのファンダメンタリズムやエバンジェリカリズム、ポーランドやフィリピンのローマ・カトリック、特に後者では近年台頭したINC（イグレシア・ニ・クリスト）との対立など、イスラム教では、シーア派とスンナ派の対立（先のイラン・イラク戦争やイラク戦争後の内部対立、最近のシリアの国内問題など）、イスラム原理主義の台頭やインドネシアにおける多様なイスラムの競合などがあげられます。またインドやスリランカなど、ヒンズー教徒とシク教徒、仏教徒との対立や、パレスチナ地方のユダヤ教徒とイスラム教各派の複雑な関係など、数多くの例も見られます。

　宗教は、古代から現代に至るまで、人類の歴史・生活・思想・芸術・政治・社会・経済・国際関係などの全般にわたって、大きな影響を与え、また今も与え続けています。こうした宗教、とりわけ、キリスト教・イスラム教・ユダヤ教の基本的な概要を学べるように本書は工夫されています。それぞれの宗教の知識を、英語との対訳で理解しつつ、情報交換やビジネス交流、また自己発信できるようになることは、単に言葉としての英語学習にとどまらず、国境や文化の違いを超えて、より実りある国際コミュニケーションや

相互協力を円滑にする上で、重要な事柄となってくるでしょう。

　なお、本書の内容や記述に関して、神学、信仰、歴史上の論争の対象となりうる事項についても、できるだけ公平で一般的な記述を試みているつもりですが、神学者、教派、歴史学者の間で意見の異なる解釈、表記、見解や、各項目のさらに詳しい専門的知識については、本書の最後にあげた参考文献や論文等を参照していただければ幸いです。

　キリスト教の項目について、聖書の引用和訳文については、主として新共同訳に統一し、よく知られた引用句については、口語訳聖書の訳を参照引用しています。

監修者　土井 清孝

はじめに

　最近、言葉としての英語ができる人は増えてきましたが、西洋文化の基礎となっているキリスト教を理解して英語コミュニケーションができる人は、まだまだ少なく、また、ユダヤ教がわかってユダヤ社会の方々と英語で会話できる人は、もっと少ないのが現状です。イスラム教について熟知した上で、コミュニケーションができる人は、さらに少ないかもしれません。

　そこで、本書は、西洋文化やユダヤ社会そしてイスラム世界を理解するのに不可欠なキリスト教やユダヤ教、さらにイスラム教に着目し、これらの宗教を全体的に理解し、世界の人とのコミュニケーション能力を向上させることを目的としています。

　キリスト教の説明に多くのページを割きますが、ユダヤ教やイスラム教についても幅広く説明している点が、本書の特長の1つです。

　但し、日本古来の宗教である神道や、日本人の生活に密接にかかわっている仏教、また、日本社会に定着している儒教（的発想）などについては、本書では扱っていません。これらの宗教については、前著『日本の宗教の知識と英語を身につける』を参照ください。

　本書の監修は、世界の思想や宗教など、比較文化に詳しい兵庫県立大学教授の土井清孝先生にお願いしました。土井先生は専門の英語教育とともに、キリスト教文化を含め、比較生活文化、異文化間コミュニケーションなどの研究家です。

　英文校閲はベルリッツ講師およびコーディネーターのJoe Ciunci先生にご担当いただきました。Ciunci先生は、聖書歴史学者（biblical historian）でもあり、ユダヤ教とイスラム教にも詳しい方です。

　本書を手にした方々が、世界の宗教についての基礎知識を学ぶとともに、英語コミュニケーション能力を身につけることに、本書が少しでも貢献できれば、著者として望外の喜びです。

著者　石井　隆之
近畿大学総合社会学部教授

本書の特長と使い方

■**本書の12大特長**

その１：日英対照（左ページに日本語、右ページに英語）の形式を中心としている。

その２：基本的情報として注意すべきものがあれば、「注」として添えている。注には英訳がある。尚、日本語の本文中に注１、注２のように注マークを入れている場合、下に1. 2. …と示して簡単な説明を施している。

その３：英語ページには、英語表現において注意すべき情報がある場合、「注目」として特記している。

その４：補助的な情報や理解を助ける知識などは「参考」として添えている。参考には英訳はないが、必要に応じ、日本語の右に（　）を設け英訳が示される場合がある。

その５：必要に応じ、TIPSを設けて、内容を面白くしている。TIPSは英訳をつけている。

その６：必要に応じ、「関連情報」を追加し、本文の内容をわかりやすくしている。これには英訳はないが、和文の（　）内に英訳を示す場合がある。

その７：必要に応じ、監修者の執筆による「補足情報」を追加し、内容を奥深いものにしている。

その８：図表やイラストを使って、内容をわかりやすくしている。

その９：英語ページには、必要に応じUseful Usage（表現力拡充のヒント）がある。

その10：索引（日本語と英語）で重要な表現や専門語を確認できる。

その11：巻末に参考図書をあげている。

その12：巻末に「世界の宗教制覇表」をつけている。

　＊「世界の宗教制覇表」は、本書読破または理解の目標を立て、それ

がどの程度達成されたかをチェックするシステム。

■本書の対象：次のような10種類の人たちに最適な本です。
① 英語学習の中・上級者
② 世界の宗教、特にキリスト教のことを英語で学びたい人
③ 英語圏の文化の基礎知識となるキリスト教を学びたい人
④ ユダヤのことをもっと知りたいという人
⑤ イスラムのことをもっと理解したいという人
⑥ 世界の宗教の概略と相違点を知りたいという人
⑦ 中身のある英語コミュニケーションを身につけたい人
⑧ 中身のある英語コミュニケーションを教える立場にある教師
⑨ 世界にも目を配る必要を感じている通訳ガイド
⑩ 世界を舞台に活躍しているビジネスパーソン

■本書の使い方：本書は次のように6つの方法で使用することができます。
(1) 左ページの日本語のパラグラフを見て、それに相当する英語のパラグラフを読む。
(2) 英語でどう言うかわからない日本語をチェックし、その英語を右ページで調べる。
(3) 右ページの英文をざっと読んで、日本語の意味を考え、左ページで確認する。
(4) 右ページの英文を音読し、わかりにくい箇所を左ページで確認し、再度音読する。
(5) 日本語の文章の中から重要と思う箇所を選び、それに対応する英語を書き取る。
(6) 日本語の文章の中から英訳に挑戦する箇所を選び、独力で作文し、右ページの英文で確認する。

CONTENTS

監修にあたって……………………………………………………… 3
はじめに …………………………………………………………… 7
本書の特長と使い方 ……………………………………………… 8

第1章 宗教の基礎知識 …………………………… 13

第1節　宗教とは？ ……………………………………………… 14
第2節　宗教の分類 ……………………………………………… 16
第3節　日本の宗教と世界の宗教 ……………………………… 18

第2章 キリスト教を知る …………………………… 27

第1節　日本にキリスト教徒が少ない10の理由 ……………… 28
第2節　キリスト教の基礎知識 ………………………………… 34
　① キリスト教とは？　34
　② キリスト教の宗派と信者数　38
　③ キリスト教の教義　42
　④ キリスト教の歴史Ⅰ　世界編　48
　⑤ キリスト教の歴史Ⅱ　日本編　54
　⑥ キリスト教の教祖と聖典　60
　⑦ イエス・キリストの弟子　64
　⑧ キリスト教の影響　70
　　（1）美術・建築への影響　70
　　（2）文学・音楽への影響　72
　　（3）哲学・科学への影響　74
　　（4）生活・社会への影響　78
　⑨ キリスト教徒の生活　80
　⑩ キリスト教の習俗　84

- 第3節　キリスト教と他の宗教を比べてみる ……………………… 94
  - ① キリスト教と仏教　類似点と相違点　94
  - ② キリスト教とユダヤ教　類似点と相違点　100
  - ③ キリスト教とイスラム教　類似点と相違点　104

第3章　聖書を知る ……………………………………………… 109

- 第1節　聖書の基礎知識 ……………………………………………… 110
- 第2節　旧約聖書の世界 ……………………………………………… 116
  - ① 天地創造　116
  - ② エデンの園　118
  - ③ 原罪と楽園追放　120
  - ④ ノアの箱舟　124
  - ⑤ バベルの塔　126
  - ⑥ 民族の祖となった族長たち　130
  - ⑦ 出エジプト　136
  - ⑧ 約束の地　138
  - ⑨ 士師記　140
  - ⑩ サムエル記　144
  - ⑪ ダビデとソロモン　146
  - ⑫ 王国の分裂と北王国滅亡　148
  - ⑬ ユダの興亡とバビロン捕囚　152
  - ⑭ 現代に通じる人生の教訓書　154
- 第3節　新約聖書の世界 ……………………………………………… 160
  - ① 聖誕前夜　160
  - ② 受胎告知　162
  - ③ イエス誕生と少年時代　164
  - ④ 洗礼者ヨハネ　168
  - ⑤ 荒野の誘惑　170
  - ⑥ 十二弟子　172
  - ⑦ イエスの奇跡と救い　174
  - ⑧ 山上の説教　176
  - ⑨ たとえ話　180

⑩　受　難　184
　　　⑪　最後の晩餐と十字架磔刑　186
　　　⑫　復活と昇天　192
　　　⑬　聖霊降臨と弟子の伝道　194
　　　⑭　黙示録　200

第4章　ユダヤ教を知る　207

第1節　ユダヤ教の基礎知識　208
　　　①　ユダヤ教とは？　208
　　　②　ユダヤ教の教義：戒律とタルムード　214
　　　③　聖地・エルサレム　218

第2節　ユダヤ教の影響　224
　　　学問・芸術分野：ユダヤ人学者と芸術家　224

第5章　イスラム教を知る　229

第1節　イスラム教の基礎知識　230
　　　①　イスラム教とは？　230
　　　②　イスラム教の教祖：ムハンマドとその生涯　232
　　　③　イスラム教の教えとコーラン　236
　　　④　イスラム教の六信五行　244
　　　⑤　イスラム教徒の風習と生活　254
　　　⑥　イスラム教史　268
　　　⑦　現在のイスラム教　280

第2節　イスラム教の影響　288
　　　建築・美術分野：イスラム建築と三大聖地　288

図書紹介　292
世界の宗教制覇表　295
索引　日本語索引　298
　　　英語索引　304

第1章

宗教の基礎知識

第1節

宗教とは?

■ **宗教はいつ始まったのか?**

　宗教は、人類が「人は死んだらどこへ行くのだろう？」と疑問を持ったときに始まったと言われることがあります。

　宗教の起こりは非常に古いと思われます。実際、旧人の遺跡からも宗教的行為の名残が見受けられるのです。イラクのシャニダール遺跡では、約6万年前に滅びたネアンデルタール人の人骨の下から多数の花粉が発見されました。これは、花を飾って死者を送り出した跡だと推察されています。

　この例からもわかるように、宗教の起源は、人類の起源とともに極めて古いと言えます。地球上に人類誕生後、まもなくヒトは直立歩行をするようになり、脳が高度に発達しました。すると「死んだらどうなるのか？」といった根源的な問題に興味や不安を持つようになり、そうした疑問に答えを出し、また、心を安定させるシステムとして宗教が成立したのではないかという学者もいます。

　雷や嵐、そして地震といった自然の猛威や、植物の生成に必要な光を与える太陽に見られる自然の恵みに対して、人類は畏敬と感謝の念を抱き、次第に自然崇拝を始めました。次第に、自然界のすべてのものに精霊が宿るというアニミズムが起こりました。また、精霊と交信できるとされるシャーマンを中心とするシャーマニズムも各地に見られます。

> **関連情報**　「宗教」とreligionの違い
> 　日本語の「宗教」は「宗の教」＝「宗たる教え」、つまり中心の教えということであり、必ずしも超越者の存在を暗示しません。
> 　一方、religionの語源は、reが「再」を表し、ligの部分は「つなぐ」を意味すると言われています。＜「超自然の神」とつなぐということを、再び行う＞という意味が元来の意味であると考えられるのです。いったん神から離れた人間が、また、神のもとに向かうというキリスト教的な思想が浮かび上がってきますね。

Section 1

What is religion?

■ When did religion begin?

It is sometimes said that religion began when men had questions about where they would go after death.

The beginning of religion is thought to be very old. In fact, religious artifacts are found with the remains of ancient people. In the Shanidar Cave in Iraq, the remains of flower pollen were found in large amounts under the bodies of Neanderthals, who perished about 60,000 years ago. This is thought to be evidence of the burying of the dead with flowers.

As we understand from the above story, the origin of religion is as old as that of humans. Soon after the emergence of the human race, men came to walk upright and their brains developed to a high degree. After developing higher self-awareness, they came to have thoughts and anxieties about what would happen to them after they died. Some scholars say religion came into existence as a system that seeks to answer questions about our mortality and grants peace of mind.

Men developed a feeling of awe and gratitude for natural threats like thunderstorms, earthquakes, and natural blessings such as the sun which radiates light necessary for the growth of plants and the sustainment of life. Thus began nature worship. Gradually animism took root where people believed spirits exist in all things. Shamanism, which centered on a Shaman believed to be capable of communicating with spirits, also became widespread.

第2節

宗教の分類

■ 宗教分類の2方法

　宗教は、一般に神や仏などの超越者が存在すると主張します。その数で宗教を二分できます。超越者は唯一であるという宗教を一神教、唯一ではなく多く存在するとする宗教を多神教と言います。

　一方、ある特定の民族のための宗教と全人類のための宗教の2つに分けることもできます。前者は民族宗教、後者は世界宗教に分類されます。

　世界の宗教を、これらの視点から分類すると、次のようになります。

	民族宗教	世界宗教
一神教	ユダヤ教 シク教	イスラム教 キリスト教
多神教	神　道 道　教 ヒンドゥー教 ＊バラモン教 ＊古代エジプト宗教 ＊古代ギリシャ宗教	仏　教 ＊マニ教

＊印は古代宗教、そのほかは現代宗教

注1：仏教は万物に神的なものが内在しているとする「汎神教」に分類されることがある。また、現在、主にイラン・パキスタンに信者がいるゾロアスター教は、善と悪の「二神教」とされるのが普通である。
注2：マニ教は、ゾロアスター教・ユダヤ教・キリスト教、さらには、仏教や道教の影響も受け、かつてはスペインから中国にまで広がった古代の世界宗教とされている。

Section 2

Classification of religion

■ The two ways in which religion is classified

In general, religion argues that there exist supreme beings such as God and Buddha. The object of worship causes religion to fall into two distinct groups. A religion which argues there is only one supreme creator falls under the category of monotheism and a religion in which many gods or spirits are worshipped is considered polytheism.

We can also divide religion in two other main categories: religions relegated to a particular place or culture and religions which spread globally. The former is classified as ethnic religions and the latter, world religions.

The main religions in the world are as follows if we classify them from these points.

	Ethnic religions	World religions
monotheism	Judaism Sikhism	Islam Christianity
polytheism	Shinto Daoism (Taoism) Hinduism ＊Brahmanism ＊Ancient Egyptian religion ＊Ancient Greek religion	Buddhism ＊Manichaeism

Marks (＊) denote ancient religions and the others are modern religions.

Note1: Buddhism is sometimes classified into pantheism, which says something divine dwells in everything. Zoroastrianism, which has believers mainly in Iran and Pakistan, is now commonly bitheism with virtue and vice in its system.

Note2: Manichaeism was influenced by Zoroastrianism, Judaism, and Christianity, and even by Buddhism and Taoism. It is now in limited practice but is said to have been an ancient world religion spread from Spain to the borders of China.

17

第3節

日本の宗教と世界の宗教

■ 日本の宗教と宗教人口の不思議

　日本の古来の宗教と言えるのは、土着の神道と538年（または552年）に公式に伝来したとされる仏教の2つです。

　日本では神仏習合という考え方が起こり、神道と仏教が共存し、神道の神と仏教の仏が関連づけられた歴史があります。このことも影響し、平均的日本人は神道の神社と仏教のお寺の両方を参詣することを不思議なこととは感じません。

　だから、日本の宗教人口が、全人口を大きく上回るという妙なことになっているわけです。『宗教年鑑』（平成18年版）によると、2005年12月現在で、日本の宗教人口は、神道系が1億725万人、仏教系が9,126万人となっています。ちなみにキリスト教徒の人口は260万人、その他いずれにも属さない人口は992万人となっています。

TIPS：ある調査での日本人の宗教観に関するアンケート回答結果(%) [2000年]

	存在する	存在しない	わからない	無回答
A) 神	35.0	31.6	33.4	─
B) 死後の世界	31.6	30.5	37.9	─

（調査対象55カ国）

＊日本人は「信じる」「信じない」「わからない」がほぼ同じ割合であるのが興味深い。キリスト教を中心とした国では、神を信じる割合は増え、60％から95％程度、イスラム教国では、さらに増え、90％からほぼ100％である。一般的傾向として、日本人のように「わからない」という回答は少ない。

Section 3

Japan's religions and world's religions

■ The mystery of Japanese religions and the number of followers

Japan has two main ancient religions: the native Shinto and Buddhism, which is said to have come to Japan in 538（or 552）.

One reason Shinto and Buddhism are able to exist dualistically is the history of both religions having become intertwined over the course of many years so that the gods of Shinto and the Buddhas and Bodhisattvas of Buddhism have similar aspects to each other. The average Japanese do not think it strange to visit both shrines of Shinto and temples of Buddhism.

Therefore, the number of Japan's followers surprisingly surpasses that of its entire population. According to "the religion yearbook" published in the 18th year of the Heisei era, as of December, 2005, there were 107,250,000 followers of Shinto and 91,260,000 followers of Buddhism. By comparison, the number of followers of Christianity is 2,600,000 and those who don't believe in any religion is 9,920,000.

TIPS：Results of the Japanese attitude toward the existence of A and B（%）[in 2000]

	I think it exists	I think it dosen't exist	I don't know	No answers
A）God, a god	35.0	31.6	33.4	—
B）Life after death	31.6	30.5	37.9	—

（55 countries surveyed）

第3節　日本の宗教と世界の宗教

> **TIPS：世界の人口TOP 10（2008年時点、WHO加盟国193カ国を対象）**
> 1位　中国・・・・・・・　1,344,920,000
> 2位　インド・・・・・・　1,181,412,000
> 3位　アメリカ・・・・・　311,666,000
> 4位　インドネシア・・・　227,345,000
> 5位　ブラジル・・・・・　191,972,000
> 6位　パキスタン・・・・　176,952,000
> 7位　バングラデシュ・・　160,000,000
> 8位　ナイジェリア・・・　151,212,000
> 9位　ロシア・・・・・・　141,394,000
> 10位　日本・・・・・・・　127,293,000
> ・世界の総人口は6,737,480,000人（約67億人）。
> ・世界の5人に1人は中国人。
> ・中国とインドだけで世界人口の約37.5％（4割近く）を占める。
> ＜2010年5月10日WHO発表の「World Health Statistics 2010」による＞

■ 世界の代表的宗教

　民族や国境を超えて広がった宗教は、世界宗教と呼ばれます。代表的世界宗教に、キリスト教・イスラム教・仏教があります。これらは世界三大宗教と呼ばれます。

　キリスト教の教祖はユダヤ人のイエスでしたが、彼はユダヤ人指導者の間では受け入れられず、その教えはまず地中海世界からヨーロッパ全域に広がりました。

　イスラム教は、その発祥地のアラビア半島をはるかに超えて、北アフリカから中央アジア、そして東南アジアまで勢力を拡大しました。

　仏教は、インドで生まれた宗教ですが、インドでの信者は少数で、むしろ、その周辺地域に広がり、世界的に受容される素地を持っています。

Section 3

> TIPS : The world's population (in 2008, covering 193 WHO member countries)
> NO.1　China 1,344,920,000
> NO.2　India 1,181,412,000
> NO.3　U.S.A 311,666,000
> NO.4　Indonesia 227,345,000
> NO.5　Brazil 191,972,000
> NO.6　Pakistan 176,952,000
> NO.7　Bangladesh 160,000,000
> NO.8　Nigeria 151,212,000
> NO.9　Russia 141,394,000
> NO.10　Japan 127,293,000
> ・The overall world population is 6,737,480,000 (about 6.7 billion)
> ・One out of five people in the world is Chinese.
> ・Just China and India account for about 37.5% (about four out of ten).
> <According to "World Health Statistics 2010" announced by WHO on May 10th, 2010>

■ The world's typical religions

　The religions which transcend nations and borders are called the world religions. The typical world religions are Christianity, Islam, and Buddhism. They are the three largest world religions.

　The founder of Christianity was the Jewish Jesus Christ, but he wasn't accepted among the mainstream Jews. Christianity first spread in the Mediterranean world and then in the whole Europe.

　Islam extended its influence from North Africa to Central Asia and Southeast Asia far beyond its birthplace in the Arabian Peninsula.

　Buddhism originated in India, where there were few followers, spread peripherally instead and has gained ground to become accepted worldwide.

第3節　日本の宗教と世界の宗教

　キリスト教は、発祥より2000年を超えて現代に生きており、イスラム教は後発ではありますが、それでも約1400年の歴史を有し、仏教に至っては約2500年間も続いています。

　つまり、これらの世界宗教は、時空を超えて、その存在を際立たせていることになります。ちなみに、時空を超えず、特定の民族のために存在し、独自の文化に制限される宗教を民族宗教と言います。

■ 三大世界宗教の人口

　『ブリタニカ国際年鑑2009』によると、2008年現在で、キリスト教は22億5,400万人、イスラム教は15億人、仏教は3億8,400万人の信者がいるとしています。

　これらをすべて足し算すると41億3,800万人となり、この人口を三大宗教が占めることになります。現在の世界の人口が約67億5,000万人なので、全世界の61.3%、すなわち、3分の2近くが、これらの宗教の信者ということになります。

関連情報　**他の著名な世界の宗教**

　ユダヤ人の民族宗教であるユダヤ教、インド人の民族宗教と言えるヒンドゥー教、主に中国人の宗教と言える道教、中国や韓国で著名な儒教、ペルシャの宗教であったゾロアスター教などがあります。

■ 日本の宗教と世界の宗教の総合比較

　日本の宗教（神道と仏教）と世界の宗教の主なもの（キリスト教・イスラム教・ユダヤ教）の5つを種々の観点から比較してみましょう。

Section 3

Christianity has been around for about 2000 years since its birth. Islam follows, with a history of about 1400 years, and Buddhism has outdated them all with a history as long as about 2500 years.

In short, these religions have been pushing their views and spreading across time and space. By comparison, religions which exist for certain peoples and usually remain confined to its culture of origin are called ethnic religions.

■ The population of the world's three greatest religions

"The Britannica International yearbook of 2009" says that as of 2008, the followers of Christianity number 2,254,000,000 with 1,500,000,000 members of Islam and 384,000,000 followers of Buddhism.

The total number of these followers is 4,138,000,000, which means the three greatest religions account for 61.3% of the world population because the world population at present is about 6,750,000,000 so it means that nearly two thirds of the world population are followers of these religions.

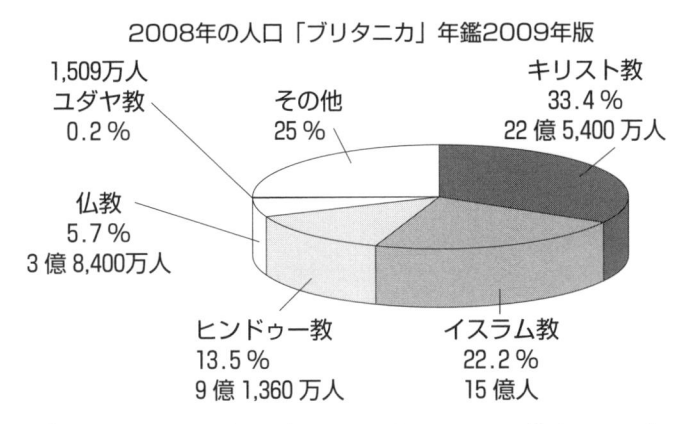

2008年の人口 「ブリタニカ」年鑑2009年版

- ユダヤ教 0.2% 1,509万人
- その他 25%
- キリスト教 33.4% 22億5,400万人
- 仏教 5.7% 3億8,400万人
- ヒンドゥー教 13.5% 9億1,360万人
- イスラム教 22.2% 15億人

■ Comprehensive comparison between Japanese religions and religions of the world

Let us compare Japanese religions (Shinto and Buddhism) with major religions of the world (Christianity, Islam and Judaism).

第3節　日本の宗教と世界の宗教

	キリスト教	イスラム教	ユダヤ教	神道	仏教
成立	1世紀	7世紀	紀元前13世紀ごろ*1	自然発生	紀元前5世紀ごろ
創始者	イエス	ムハンマド	（モーセ）	なし	釈迦
信仰対象	神 イエス 聖霊	アラー	ヤハウェ	八百万の神	如来・菩薩・明王・天
聖典	旧約聖書 新約聖書	コーラン 旧約聖書と新約聖書の一部	旧約聖書 タルムード	古事記*2 日本書紀	般若心経 法華経など多数
信仰施設	教会	モスク	シナゴーグ	神社	寺
聖地	エルサレム バチカンなど	エルサレム メッカ*3 メディナ	エルサレム	各神社	ルンビニー ブッダガヤなど多数
主要宗派	カトリック プロテスタント 東方正教会	スンニ派（スンナ派） シーア派	正統派 保守派 改革派	神社神道 教派神道 皇室神道	大乗仏教 上座部仏教
聖職者	神父 牧師	ウラマー*4	ラビ	神主	僧侶
信者	キリスト教徒	イスラム教徒	ユダヤ教徒	氏子	仏教徒

*1　前5世紀以前は、ユダヤ教は古代イスラエル宗教（ヤハウェ信仰）と呼ばれていた。
*2　これらの書は、厳密な意味で聖典ではなく、日本神話を含む歴史書ともされる。
*3　サウジアラビアは、1980年代に通称である「メッカ」（Mecca）の英語の正式名称を「マッカ」（Makkah）に改めた。
*4　厳密には階層を嫌うイスラムには聖職者はいない。Ulamaはイスラムにおける知識人で、聖職者の役割をする側面がある。
注1：ルンビニーは釈迦の誕生地、ブッダガヤは釈迦の悟りの地である。
注2：教派神道には天理教・金光教・黒住教・御嶽教などがある。
注3：神父はカトリックの、牧師はプロテスタントの聖職者の呼び方である。

Section 3

	Christianity	Islam	Judaism	Shintoism	Buddhism
Founded	1st cen. AD	7th cen. AD	13th cen. BC*1	Not known	5th cen. BC
Founder	Jesus	Muhammad	(Moses)	No founder	Gautama
Pray	God, Jesus, Holy spirits	Allah	Jehovah	a myriad of deities	Buddha, Bodhisattva, Myoo, Ten
Holy books	the Bible (Old & New Testaments)	the Koran, parts of Old & New Testaments	the Old Testament, the Talmud	Kojiki*2, Nihonshoki	Heart Sutra, Lotus Sutra, and others
Pray at	a church	a mosque	a synagogue	a shrine	a temple
Sacred places	Jerusalem, the Vatican, etc.	Jerusalem, Mecca*3, Medina	Jerusalem	each shrine	Lumbini, Bodhgaya, etc.
Major Sects	Catholicism, Protestantism, Eastern Church	Sunni, Shiah	Orthodox, Conservative, Reform	Jinja, Sectarian, Imperial Shinto	Mahayana, Hinayana
Clergy	a priest, a clergyman	an ulama*4	a rabbi	a Shinto priest	a Buddhist priest
Followers	a Christian	a Muslim	a Jew	a Shintoist	a Buddhist

*1 Before 5th cen. B.C., Judaism was called Yahweh worship (Israelite monotheism).

*2 Another theory is that these are not exactly holy scriptures but historical books containing Japanese mythology.

*3 Saudi Arabia changed the popular name Mecca into Makkah, which is regarded as the formal name in English, during the 1980's.

*4 Strictly speaking, there is no clergy in Islam, which negates hierarchy. Ulamas are Islamic intelligentsia who are said to function as clergy.

Note 1 : Lumbini is the birthplace of Sakyamuni, Bodhgaya being the place of his enlightenment.

Note 2 : Sectarian Shinto sects include Tenri-kyo, Konko-kyo, Kurozumi-kyo, and Ontake-kyo.

Note 3 : "Shimpu" is for Catholicism, while "Bokushi" is for Protestantism.

宗教の基礎知識

キリスト教を知る

聖書を知る

ユダヤ教を知る

イスラム教を知る

第2章

キリスト教を知る

第1節

日本にキリスト教徒が少ない10の理由

■ どうして日本にはキリスト教徒が少ないの？

　宗教年鑑によると、日本のキリスト教徒の総数は260万人ということですが、現実には異端ではないキリスト教徒で正会員として登録されている人たちは日本の人口の1％ぐらいであると考えることもできます。いずれにせよ、世界の人口の3分の1近くがキリスト教徒である現状を考えると、日本のキリスト教徒の数は極めて少ないということになります。日本人にキリスト教徒が少ない理由として、一般に、次のようなものがあげられています。

① 改宗を迫ることに対して、日本人はそこまでしなくてもと思う傾向があります。また、日本人は改宗を迫る宗教はどうも性に合わないというイメージを持っています。
② 仏教は外来宗教ですが、日本になじもうとし、自らが日本文化に溶け込みました。つまり日本化しました。しかし、キリスト教は自らを変えることなく、日本的な精神や文化とは関係なく、日本人に神道や仏教からの改宗を勧めるという側面があります。
③ 日本が文化的に未開ではなく、未開の国を改宗してきたキリスト教が日本に伝わる以前に、成熟した仏教という世界宗教が日本に浸透していたことも重要な要因であると思われます。未開の地域においては、キリスト教の教えや考え方を素直に受け容れる側面があります。
④ キリスト教が広まらない国で、有名な国は他にもあります。例えば、中国とタイがそうです。日本とこれらの国に共通するのは、近代に他国により完全な植民地化を経験していない国です。植民地化とキリスト教の伝播とは関係があり、植民地化されると普及率が高まった経緯があります。
⑤ 日本の歴史上、神のもとでの平等を説くキリスト教は、江戸幕府にとっては危険な思想となると判断され、禁止されたという歴史的な経緯も無視できない要因です。

Section 1

Ten reasons why the Christian population is small in Japan

■ **Why is the Christian population so small in Japan?**

It is recorded in the yearbook of religions that the number of Christians in Japan is 2.6 million. However, in reality, about 1% of people living in Japan are registered as true Christians. Given the fact that nearly one third of the world's population is Christian, the number of Christians in Japan is very small. Generally, it is because:

① Many Japanese don't think it necessary to make people convert to another religion. Japanese view religions which force conversion as antithetical.

② Although Buddhism is foreign, it adapted well with Japanese culture. In other words, it was Japanized. On the other hand, Christianity has a more rigid, non-conforming system which asks Japanese to convert from their native Shinto/Buddhism to Christianity with no regard to Japanese spirit and culture.

③ Buddhism had been well-established in a refined Japan before missionaries came after the people in the countries perceived barbarian were converted to Christianity. In places of unrefined or barbaric peoples, they tend to accept the Christian message without much protest.

④ In countries such as China or Thailand, Christianity didn't take root as well. The similarity between Japan and such countries is they haven't been entirely colonized by other countries in the modern era. There is a correlation between the rate of colonization and the rate of spread of Christianity.

⑤ The hierarchal Edo Shogunate regarded Christianity as dangerous to its rule and prohibited it because people are supposed to be equals under God according to Christianity.

第1節　日本にキリスト教徒が少ない10の理由

⑥ 日本人の国民的性格として、熱心に宗教行為を行うことには抵抗があることも1つの要因と言えるでしょう。周りの人の顔をうかがう性格の日本人が多いので、少数派のすることに抵抗があります。それゆえ、キリスト教がすでに広まっていたら、キリスト教の宗教行為には抵抗を感じないでしょう。

参考：これは論理的不可能な現象となる。キリスト教が広がる（＝キリスト教徒が多くなる）ためには、キリスト教がすでに広がっていなければならない（＝はじめから多くの人がキリスト教徒でないといけない）ことになるからである。

⑦ 日本人は、宗教的信仰の行為そのものよりも、宗教的習俗（初詣、七五三、その他の祭りなど）の行動を重視する傾向があります。だから、クリスマスやバレンタインデーのようなお祭り的なものは受け容れるのです。
⑧ キリスト教徒は真面目で、妙に真面目だと仲間はずれにされるという不思議な現象が日本では見られます。
⑨ キリスト教の一神教的側面が、そもそも多神教的な信仰心を持つ日本人になじめなかったとも言えるでしょう。日本人は古来、森の宗教と言える神道のやや曖昧な宗教的行為に慣れています。交通安全にはこの神、安産にはこの神というように、目的により神が異なることに違和感を感じないという精神性も、一神教が浸透しない原因となっていると思われます。その証拠に、極めて一神教的要素の強い（キリスト教よりもその傾向が強い）、イスラム教徒に至っては、日本人の信者は5,000人ほどしかいません。

注：日本にいるイスラム教徒の数は5万人ぐらいと言われるが、ほとんどが外国人である。日本人のイスラム教徒は5千人ぐらいと推定され、多くがイスラム教徒と結婚した日本人女性であると思われる。

⑩ 価値観が多様化された現代の忙しい日本人には、1つの価値観（3つにして1つである神の唯一性や原罪の存在など）が大きなインパクトを与えることは少ないということも大きな要因でしょう。言い換えれば、これらの教義は、たいていの人たちの人生には些細なことのようです。

とはいっても、キリスト教は、日本に影響を与えていないのではなく、むしろ、多大な影響を与えています。キリスト教系の学校や病院があり、教会もあちこちに存在し、無宗教的で商業的な側面がありますが、クリスマスはもちろん、バレ

Section 1

⑥ As part of the cultural identity, Japanese generally don't feel comfortable performing religious rites with ardor. Because many Japanese are self-conscious and tend to worry about how others look at them, they will not easily follow the actions of a minority of the population. Therefore, if Christianity had already spread among people, Japanese would have less of a problem engaging in Christian acts.

> ●Useful Usage● **ANTITHETICAL**
> 1. Her ideas are antithetical to mine. （彼女の考えは私の考えとは相容れない）
> 2. Are religion and science inherently antithetical? （宗教と科学は本来両立しないか）

⑦ Many Japanese think religious traditions in its own are more important than firmly believing in a religion (such as the New Year's visit to a shrine, the Seven-Five-Three Celebration and other festivals, etc.). Therefore, Japanese accept the festive events such as Christmas or Saint Valentine's Day.

⑧ Christians are seriously devoted in many cases. However, in Japan, if their devotedness causes them to become a curiosity (as it often does), they are cut out of the loop.

⑨ It can be considered that Christianity couldn't adapt to Japanese who originally believe in a polytheistic religion, because Christianity is a monotheistic religion. Japanese are accustomed to the slightly esoteric religious acts of Shinto, which can be considered "a religion of the woods," from ages past. Monotheistic religions can't adapt to Japan, because they don't feel a sense of discomfort in having many gods/spirits which people rely on for purposes such as road safety or safe child birth. This is evidenced by the fact that there are only 5000 Japanese believers in Islam, which has very strong monotheistic factors (more demanding than Christianity).

Note: It is said that the number of followers of Islam is about 50,000 people in Japan. But most of them are foreign nationals. It is considered that Japanese

第1節 日本にキリスト教徒が少ない10の理由

ンタインデーなども大きな位置を占めているのが現状です。この章では、キリスト教をゼロから学ぶことにします。

参考：森の宗教は自然の恵みを享受できる環境に生まれた宗教で、日本の宗教では神道が代表的。多神教的な傾向が見られる。これに対し、キリスト教やイスラム教は「砂漠の宗教」で、自然が厳しい環境に生まれ、一神教的傾向が強い。仏教では、密教が「森の宗教」的で、浄土教（阿弥陀仏のみの信仰を重視）が「砂漠の宗教」的であるとされる（『森林の思考・砂漠の思考』［NHKブックス312］鈴木秀夫 著 参照）。

参考：④に関して
　中国については、キリスト教信者の数は、『ブリタニカ国際年鑑』の最新データや、在米中国人活動家などの最新データによると、現在では人口の7〜10％を超え、9,000万人から1億3,000万人に至るものと考えられる。

●●●補足情報●●●

　キリスト教やイスラム教は「砂漠の宗教」で、厳しい自然環境に生まれた宗教は一神教的傾向が強い、異なる「風土」に育った人には理解しにくいといった説については、反証もあげられている。例えば、古代イスラエル宗教史専門の浅見定雄氏は、もしこうした厳しい砂漠の風土で旧約聖書や一神教が生まれ、またそれゆえ、違う風土に育った人はこれらを理解しにくいと仮定すれば、欧米人はおろか、ユダヤ人自身も旧約聖書を理解できないという結論が生じる、と指摘する（『聖書と日本人』）。

　つまり、ユダヤ人、特に旧約聖書を生み出した階層は、すでに紀元前6世紀初頭には、バビロニアのユーフラテス川のほとりに在住し、紀元後7世紀のイスラム時代までそこに宗教上の拠点を置いていた。紀元前から早々とパレスチナの「砂漠」的風土を去って、中東から欧州全域等に散り、現在まで全くの「非砂漠」的風土に暮らしている。

　旧約聖書の大部分は、厳しい砂漠ではなく、河と麦の農耕文化地帯であるバビロニアで成立した。神が当時約束したパレスチナは「砂漠」とは対照的な、緑豊かな「乳と蜜の流れる地」であった。旧約の人々は、アブラハムの時代からキリスト時代の約2000年の間に、「砂漠」（荒野）はわずか40年しか経験しておらず、しかもこの40年もイスラエルが神を疑ったため罰とし

Section 1

Muslims number about 5,000 people and many of them are Japanese women who are married to Muslims.

⑩ At the present day, key factors in the reason why Christianity can't spread further include the fact that the doctrine of God being three beings in one and that of the existence of original sin do not make such an impact on the lives of the diverse and busy people of Japan. In other words, these seem to be trivialities at best to most people.

****

Aspects of Christianity are found quite easily in Japan, however. Japan has Christian schools or hospitals and also has churches here and there. Moreover, Christmas and Saint Valentine's Day are important days in Japan, albeit in a non-religious and more commercial sense. In this chapter, we will start a study of Christianity from scratch.

て与えられた否定的意義のみを持つ期間であった。さらに旧約の人々にとって、砂漠と海のどちらが身近であるかを調べると、旧約聖書には、ミドバール(「荒野」を表す)が、250回出てくるのに対して、ヤーム(「海」を表す)が、350回出てくる。荒野より海が身近であったことは、地理的にも裏付けられる。

すなわち、キリスト教やイスラム教などの一神教は、「砂漠」という厳しい自然に生まれた宗教で、異なる風土に生まれた人はこれらを受容しにくいという説は、両方とも事実に反している、という指摘である。ユダヤ教、キリスト教などの一神教が生まれたイスラエルの地も、日本列島の平均よりは多少乾燥した地域だが、ギリシャと比べると大差がない。しかも古代ギリシャは最後まで、多神教文化の地であった。

あるいは、イスラム以前のアラビア世界は、確かに大部分「砂漠」であったが、そこは一神教とは正反対の、まさに百鬼夜行の世界であった。逆に、イスラム教が起こったのは、この砂漠ではなく、メッカ、メディナのような商業都市である。また、このイスラム教は「砂漠」とは対照的な熱帯雨林地帯のインドネシアで熱心に受け入れられているし、キリスト教も砂漠とは反対の森林地帯である北欧にまで広がり定着してきた。この他にもいろいろと反証例があげられている。

第2節　キリスト教の基礎知識

❶ キリスト教とは?

■ キリスト教とは？

　キリスト教とは、イエスを救世主として信じる宗教のことです。紀元1世紀、イスラエルはローマ帝国の傀儡［かいらい］政権でした。この時代に、ローマ人と彼らの取り巻きになったユダヤ人に抑圧されていたユダヤ民族の前にイエスが現れ、救いへの道を説きました。彼のメッセージは単純明快です。世界は近く終末を迎え、（神と民への愛を通して表明される）唯一神ゴッドに対する信仰が揺るぎない人たちは、永遠の命を授かることになり、結果として救われるというものでした。

　キリスト教は、発生時点においてはユダヤ教内の一分派とみなされていました。しかし、イエスの死後、弟子たちによる宣教活動が始まった際、ユダヤ教主流派によってこの信仰は認められなかったため、キリスト教は1世紀後半にはユダヤ教と分離して、独自の教会組織を形成していきました。そして、4世紀にキリスト教はローマ帝国の国教になったことを契機に、広い地域に広まりました。

　11世紀になると、キリスト教はローマ教皇を首長とするカトリック教会（西方教会）と、東方正教会とに分裂しました。そして、16世紀には、マルティン・ルターによる宗教改革によって、ローマ・カトリック教会の中からプロテスタント諸教会が成立しました。

　現在では、キリスト教は世界三大宗教の１つになっています。残りの2つは、イスラム教と仏教です。

キリスト教の派生図

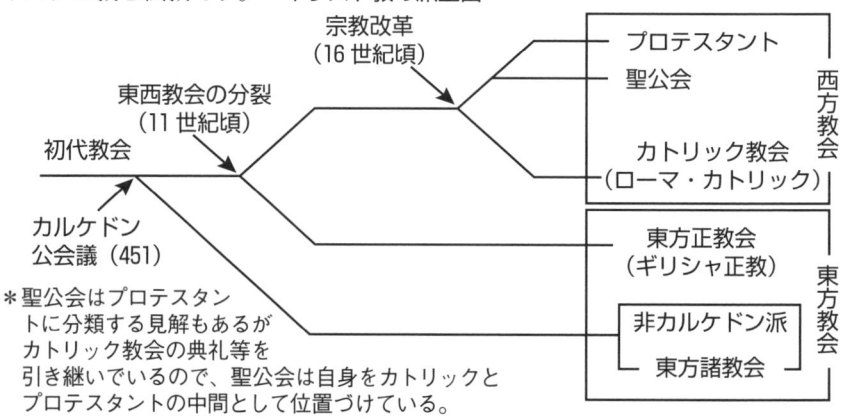

```
                            宗教改革              ┌─ プロテスタント
                           (16世紀頃)            │                     西
              東西教会の分裂  ╱────────────────┤─ 聖公会              方
              (11世紀頃)                         │                     教
  初代教会 ───╱                                  └─ カトリック教会      会
              ╲                                     (ローマ・カトリック)
   ↑          ╲                                  ┌─ 東方正教会
  カルケドン    ╲                                 │   (ギリシャ正教)    東
  公会議(451)   ╲────────────────────────────┤                     方
                                                 │  ┌ 非カルケドン派   教
  *聖公会はプロテスタン                           └──┤                 会
   トに分類する見解もあるが                          └ 東方諸教会
   カトリック教会の典礼等を
   引き継いでいるので、聖公会は自身をカトリックと
   プロテスタントの中間として位置づけている。
```

Section 2

What is Christianity?

■ What is Christianity?

Christianity is a religion in which Jesus, an aspect of God, is believed to be the Messiah. In the first century of the Christian era, Israel was a puppet state of the Roman Empire. During this time, Jesus began preaching salvation to those Jewish people who were being oppressed by the Romans and their Jewish lackeys. His message was simple: The world was soon to end and those who put their faith and belief in the one true God (expressed through love for God and people) would be rewarded with eternal life and therefore saved.

When Christianity originated, it was regarded as a cult offshoot of the main Jewish religion. After the death of Jesus, his apprentices, known as apostles, began to spread his teachings. Their views were not approved by mainstream Jews. This nascent religion eventually separated from the Jewish religion in the late 1st century and formed its own church. Once Christianity became the official religion of the Roman Empire in the 4th century, it spread quickly throughout the Roman lands.

In the 11th century, Christianity split into the Catholic Church (the Western Church) with the Pope at the top and the (Eastern) Orthodox Church. In the 16th century, various churches seceded from the Roman Catholic Church as a result of the Reformation by Martin Luther. These became the Protestant Churches.

Christianity is now one of three major world religions. The other two religions are Islam and Buddhism.

第2節　キリスト教の基礎知識

　キリスト教は聖書に基づいています。聖書は、神とイスラエル民族とのかかわりの歴史をつづった旧約聖書（39巻）と、イエス・キリストの生涯と言葉や、彼の弟子たちの伝道記録や手紙などが記された新約聖書（27巻）の2部から構成されています。

　キリスト教には様々な宗派がありますが、大きく分けると、ローマ‐カトリック教会・東方正教会・プロテスタント諸教会の3つに分かれます。

....

注：キリスト教の中心的教義の1つには、三位一体（the Trinity）というものがある。
　　これは、キリスト教は一神教であり、神は本質においては1つであるが、「父」「子」「聖霊」の3つの位格（ペルソナ）があるという教え。

主要宗教の派生図

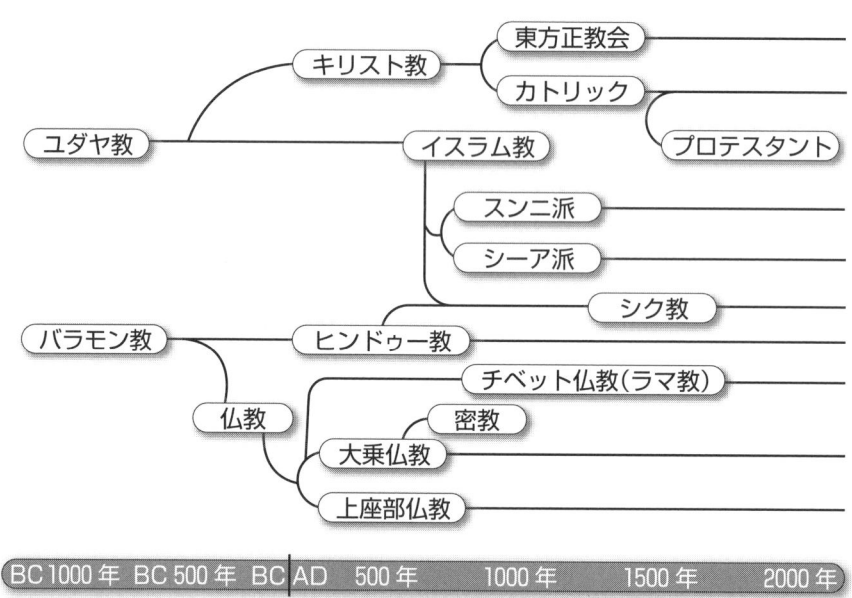

```
                    ┌─ 東方正教会 ──────────────
         ┌─ キリスト教 ─┤
         │          └─ カトリック ──────────
ユダヤ教 ─┤                      └─ プロテスタント ───
         └─ イスラム教 ─┬─ スンニ派 ──────────
                       └─ シーア派 ──────────
                                  └─ シク教 ────
バラモン教 ─┬─ ヒンドゥー教 ──────────────────
           └─ 仏教 ─┬─ チベット仏教（ラマ教） ──
                    ├─ 密教 ───────────
                    ├─ 大乗仏教 ─────────
                    └─ 上座部仏教 ────────
```

BC1000年　BC500年　BC｜AD　500年　　1000年　　1500年　　2000年

Section 2

Christianity is based on the Christian Bible. The Bible consists of two parts. The first is the Old Testament, which in 39 volumes tells the history of the relations between God and the nation of Israel. The second part is the New Testament, which describes the life and sayings of Jesus Christ as well as the record of the mission made by his disciples and their letters in 27 volumes.

There are a variety of denominations in Christianity, but it is divided into three main branches: the Roman Catholic Church, the Orthodox Church and the various Protestant churches.

注目：denomination は「(貨幣・銀行券などの)単位名」以外に「宗派」の意味もある。なお、日本語で言う「デノミ(＝通貨の呼称単位の切り下げ)」は、英語では redenomination と言う。

Note：One of the major doctrines of Christianity is the Trinity. This is a doctrine which means that Christianity is a monotheistic religion and God is one in essence, but exists in three Persons: "the Father," "the Son," and "the Holy Spirit."

第2節　キリスト教の基礎知識

❷ キリスト教の宗派と信者数

■ キリスト教の宗派

　キリスト教は、大きく分けると、ローマ・カトリック教会、東方正教会、プロテスタント諸教会の3つに分かれます。ローマ・カトリック教会とプロテスタント諸教会を総称して、「西方教会」と呼ぶこともあります。東方正教会は、ギリシャ正教とも呼ばれ、主にロシア、スラブ系民族の国々で信仰されています。

　ローマ・カトリック教会は、法王（正式には教皇）と呼ばれる皇帝のような指導者を頂点とする教会組織です。これは全世界的な組織を持つ教会ですが、その名は体を表しています。というのは、catholicとは「普遍的」の意味だからです。特にヨーロッパとアメリカ大陸に信徒が多く存在します。ヨーロッパの中では、イタリア・フランス・スペイン・ポルトガルなどラテン系の国々、アメリカ大陸では特に南アメリカに信徒を有しています。

　プロテスタント諸教会は、16世紀に、マルティン・ルターによる「宗教改革」によって、ローマ・カトリック教会から分かれた諸教派です。主な宗派として、ルーテル教会・改革派教会・会衆派教会・メソジスト教会・バプテスト教会などがあります。

参考1：ギリシャ正教会・ロシア正教会・ルーマニア正教会・ブルガリア正教会などは、組織名であって、宗派名（教派名）ではない。なお「ギリシャ正教」は、これらの組織をカバーする宗派名である。

参考2：「東西教会の分裂」とは、11世紀にキリスト教教会が、カトリック教会（西方教会）と東方正教会とに二分されたことを言う。

■ キリスト教の信者数

　世界におけるキリスト教の信者数は、『ブリタニカ国際年鑑2007』によると、2006年時点で、21億7,318万人です。このうち、11億3,000万人がカトリックの信者です。キリスト教の信者数は、イスラム教徒、ヒンズー教徒を超えて世界最大と言われています。

　日本国内においては、熱心なキリスト教信者は総人口の1%未満です。一方、

Section 2

Christian denominations and the number of Christians

■ Christian denominations

Christianity is divided into three main branches: the Roman Catholic Church, the Orthodox Church and the various Protestant Churches. The Roman Catholic Church and the Protestant Churches are collectively known as "the Western Church." The Orthodox Church is also called the Greek Orthodox Church and is mainly worshipped in Russia and Slavic countries.

The Roman Catholic Church is led by an imperial-like leader known as the Pope, or the Holy Father. It is a church with a global organization which suits its name well, for "Catholic" means "universal." In particular, there are many believers in Europe and America. In Europe, believers can be found in Latin countries such as Italy, France, Spain, and Portugal. In America, they can be found especially in South America.

The various Protestant Churches are a variety of sects that split from the Roman Catholic Church as a result of the religious reformation by Martin Luther in the 16th century. The major denominations are the Lutheran Church, the Reformed Churches, the Congregational Church, the Methodist Church (Methodism), and the Baptist Church (Baptists).

■ The number of Christians

According to the "2007 Britannica Book of the Year," the number of Christian believers in the world is 2.17318 billion as of 2006. Of this, 1.130 billion people are Catholic believers. The number of Christian adherents is said to be the largest in the world exceeding the number of believers in Islam and Hinduism.

The number of pious Christians is less than 1 percent of the total population in Japan. On the other hand, in South Korea, about 30 percent of the total population is Christian.

39

第2節　キリスト教の基礎知識

韓国では、総人口の約3割がキリスト教信者です。

> **関連情報　アメリカの3割を占める福音派（Evangelicalism）**
>
> ニューヨーク市立大学によると、アメリカの宗教人口は次の通りです。
> 　福音派（30％）、カトリック（25％）、リベラル派プロテスタント（20％）、黒人プロテスタント（8％）、ユダヤ（2％）、その他（15％）
> 　聖書を文字通り信じる(それゆえ進化論［revolutionism］を否定する）福音派は、2,000人以上収容できる教会（＝メガチャーチ）を有し、賛美歌も現代風にアレンジ（例えばロック調）して、若者の信者を増やしてきました。人口比率が大きいので政治家も無視できません。福音派は独自のテレビ局（ネットワークも充実）を有し、アメリカ社会を動かす力を持っているのです。

参考：福音派とは、プロテスタント系の一派で、特にルーテル教会にその名を冠したもの（例えば、ドイツ福音主義教会・アメリカ福音ルーテル教会・福音ルーテル宗教会議など）が多い。従来は、福音主義のプロテスタントの宗派のことを指していたが、プロテスタント各教派を横断する保守派の総称として用いられることが多い。中絶や同性愛について反対を表明することが多いグループである。英語では、evangelicalism と言う。

　キリスト教では、「超教派」(interdenominationalism［直訳：：教派間における主義］) という考え方があり、キリスト教において、教派（宗）を超えて協力し、伝道や神学教育などを行い、交わりを持つことを言う。

　世界教会主義とも言われ、キリスト教の教会一致促進運動のことであるエキュメニカル運動（ecumenism）が超教派の例と言える。このエキュメニカル運動では、世界教会協議会（WCC＝the World Council of Churches）を意識し、カトリック教会、プロテスタント諸教会、正教会を含み、場合によっては、他宗教との対話も含まれる。なお、WCCには、現在、120カ国以上、340を超える教会と教派が属している。

　福音派でも超教派という発想があるが、福音主義（カトリックとは異なり、より聖書的なものに立ち戻ろうとする考え方）と聖書信仰（聖書を誤りのない神の言葉と信じる信仰）に同意するプロテスタントのキリスト教徒に限定される。

Section 2

● **Useful Usage** ● **EXCEED**
1. The section chief exceeded his authority.
  （課長は越権行為を行った）
2. The middle-aged woman exceeds him in knowledge.
  （その中年女性は知識では彼を凌駕［りょうが］している）

福音派の教会はコンサートホールのようなものまである！

第2節　キリスト教の基礎知識

❸ キリスト教の教義

■ キリスト教の教義

　キリスト教の教義は、ユダヤ教の律法に基づいたイエスや使徒の言行から発展していきました。キリスト教の主な教義として、三位一体・原罪・終末論があげられます。教義には教派ごとに若干の変異が見られます。例えば、正教会[注1]・東方諸教会[注2]・カトリック教会・聖公会[注3]・プロテスタントでは三位一体が受け入れられていますが、ユニテリアン・非カルケドン派[注4]などは三位一体を認めていません。

1　正教会は、正確には、東方正教会またはギリシャ正教と呼ばれる。
2　東方諸教会は、ヨーロッパから見て東方に位置する地域にその信仰が広がっていて、東方正教会に属さない宗派である。この東方諸教会と（注1の）正教会をまとめて東方教会と呼ぶ。
3　聖公会は、イギリス国教会に属する世界各地の教会のことである。ちなみに、カトリック教会・聖公会・プロテスタントは西方教会に属する。
4　非カルケドン派とは、カルケドン公会議［＝ the Council of Chalcedon］（451年）で制定されたカルケドン信条を拒否し、それぞれ独立した道を歩んだ教会群のことを言う。

■ 三位一体

　三位一体の「三位」とは、父・子・聖霊の3つを指します。つまり、三位一体とは、神は、父なる神、子なる神（イエス・キリスト）＊、聖霊という3つの位格を持ちながら、実体は同一であるという意味です。この「三位一体」という表現は、3世紀初め、カルタゴの教父テルトゥリアヌスにより初めて用いられました。
　イエスは神か人かをめぐり大論争があったため、教義の分裂がローマ帝国の混乱を招くことを懸念したコンスタンティヌス帝は、325年に第1ニカイア（ニケーア／ニケア）公会議を招集しました。この会議では、イエスと神が同質であることが宣言され、これを否定したアリウス派が異端として排除されました。

Section 2

Christian Doctrine

■ Christian Doctrine

Christian doctrine developed from the words and deeds of Jesus and his apostles based on Jewish Law. The main doctrine of Christianity includes the Trinity, the original sin, and eschatology. The doctrine slightly differs from one denomination to another. For example, neither the Unitarian nor the non-Chalcedon faction admits the Trinity though it is accepted in the Orthodox Church, the various Eastern Churches, the Catholic Church, the Anglican Church, and the Protestant Church.

■ The Trinity

The "three Persons" of the Trinity refers to "the Father," "the Son" and "the Holy Spirit." That is, the Trinity means that God is one and the same in essence though God has three Persons: God the Father, God the Son, and God the Holy Spirit. In the early 3rd century, the expression "Trinity" was used by Tertullianus, who was an early Christian author from Carthage.

There was a controversy as to whether Jesus is God or was just a human being. Therefore, Constantine the Great, who worried that the division of the doctrine could cause confusion in the Roman Empire, called the Nicene Council (the First Council of Nicaea) in 325. At the conference, it was declared that Jesus and God were homogeneous, and Arianism, which denied this doctrine, was excluded as heretical.

注目：教父とは「教会の父」の略で、古代および中世初期のキリスト教思想家・著作家のうち教会の模範となる人について用いられるが、実質的には著作家なので上記では Christian author（5行目）と訳している。

第2節　キリスト教の基礎知識

＊「子なる神」はイエスの神性を強調した表現で、神との関係を強調するとイエスは「神の子」となる。「子なるイエス・キリスト」としてもキリスト教的には同義。
参考：アウグスティヌス（Aurelius Augustinus, 354年11月13日〜430年8月28日：古代キリスト教の神学者）は、三位格の関係を、父＜言葉を出すもの＞・子＜言葉＞・聖霊＜言葉によって伝えられる愛＞と捉えた。

■ 三位一体の確立

　381年の第1コンスタンティノポリス公会議で、「三位一体」の教理が確立しましたが、これ以降も論争は続きました。451年には、「キリスト単性論」（単性説＝イエス・キリストの人性は神性に吸収されて1つの性［＝神性］となったとする説）を判定するために、カルケドン公会議が開かれました。イエスの人性を認めない単性論派は異端とされ、イエスは人であると同時に神でもあるとする両性論派が正統とされました。

■ 原罪

　原罪とは、人類が最初に犯したとされる罪のことです。失楽園の物語において、アダムとイブ（エバ）は蛇の誘惑に駆られて神が禁じた善悪を知る木の実を食べ、神との約束を破ってしまいました。彼らが罪を犯して以降、神と人間とのあるべき正しい関係が失われ、その子孫である人類は、死すべき運命を持ち、神の裁きを受けるべき存在となりました。

Section 2

●**Useful Usage**● **REFER TO**
1. She never once referred to her notes during her speech.
（彼女は演説の最中にメモに一度も頼らなかった）（参照する）
2. The author refers to Chomskey's theory many times.
（その著者はチョムスキーの理論を何度も引用している）（言及する）
3. This regulation refers only to people under 20.
（この規則は20歳未満の人のみに当てはまる）（適用される）
4. This graph refers to the sharp increase in crimes committed by adolescents.
（このグラフは若者による犯罪件数の急増を示す）（…を指す）
＊本文の refer to（The Trinity の１行目）の用法は４番。

■ Establishment of the Trinity

The doctrine of the "Trinity" was established at the First Council of Constantinople in 381. However, controversies continued after this. In 451, the Council of Chalcedon was held to debate "Monophysitism" (the theory that the human nature of Jesus Christ was absorbed into the divine nature and Christ was left with only one nature, the Divine). Monophysites, who did not admit Jesus's human nature, were regarded as heretical, and Dyophysites, who believed Jesus to be at once human and God, were looked upon as orthodox.

■ Original sin

Original sin is the name used to describe the first sin committed by humans. In the story of *Genesis*, the first humans Adam and Eve, upon ignoring God's command, ate the fruit of the Tree of the Knowledge of Good and Evil. They were tempted by a serpent to do this and therefore blatantly went against God's will. After they committed the sin, the ideal relationship between God and human beings was lost, and the human race and their descendants became mortal and subject to the judgment of God.

注目：失楽園とは創世記第３章の物語であるが *Paradise Lost* と訳すとミルトン（John Milton）の著作と混同するので Genesis という表現が用いられている。

第2節　キリスト教の基礎知識

　新約聖書の中のパウロの「ローマの信徒への手紙」において、原罪についての思想が述べられていますが、「原罪」という概念を確立したのは古代キリスト教の教父アウグスティヌスであると考えられています。彼は原罪をアダムから遺伝された罪と捉えました。彼によれば、人間はアダムが犯した罪によって、罪を犯さずにはいられない性［さが］を受け継ぎ、自由を失ったとされます。

　原罪の理解は、キリスト教の教派によって大きな差があります。さらに、ペラギウス主義のように、原罪を否定する教義もあります。

■ 終末論

　終末論とは、人間社会と世界の終末についての宗教思想のことを言います。終末思想とも言われています。人間の死後の運命を研究する神学の一部で、キリストの再臨、人類の復活、最後の審判などを説き、重要な教説となっています。

関連情報　キリスト教の終末論と仏教の末法思想との違い

　キリスト教の終末論（eschatology）は、ギリシャ語の ta eschata（最後のこと：キリスト教では四終［＝死、審判、天国、地獄］を指す）からきており、イエスの復活と最後の審判が重要テーマとなっています。

　一方、仏教の末法思想は、仏の教えが次第に伝わらない時代になることを指し、本来、天変地異や政情不安を指すものではありません。したがって、末法思想はこの世の終わりを説いているわけではないのです。

　しかし、日本では、鎌倉期への転換期で政情不安も手伝って、末法思想が終末思想的に展開していきました。その結果、阿弥陀仏に救いを求める浄土教が発達し、日蓮もこの世が末法であるとし、法華経への帰依を説きました。禅宗にも末法思想が存在しますが、曹洞宗の開祖、道元は末法思想を否定しています。

Section 2

Detailed thinking about the original sin is described in Paul's 'Letter to the Romans' in the New Testament, and it is considered that Augustine, an early Church Father of ancient Christianity, established the concept of "original sin." He interpreted original sin as the sin that was inherited from Adam. According to him, human beings accepted the destiny that they cannot help committing a sin due to the sin that Adam committed, and so lost their freedom.

The understanding of original sin varies greatly by Christian denominations. In addition, there is a doctrine like Pelagianism which denies original sin.

■ Eschatology

Eschatology is the religious belief about the end of humanity and the world. It is also known as eschatological thought. It is a part of a theology that studies the human fate after death and is an important doctrine that explains the Second Coming of Christ, the regeneration of the human race, and the Last Judgment.

●Useful Usage●　VARY

1. The opinion varies from person to person.
   (その意見は人により異なる)
2. Aquatic animals vary in size and shape.
   (水生動物は大きさや形が様々である)

❹ キリスト教の歴史Ⅰ　世界編

■ 古代のキリスト教

　キリスト教は、イエスの磔刑［たっけい］のあと、イエスの弟子たちがガリラヤ地方とユダヤ地方で伝道活動を始めた紀元1世紀の30年代に起こりました。

　当初キリスト教はユダヤ教の一派と考えられていたため、キリスト教徒の皇帝礼拝は免除されていました。しかし、別の宗教であることが明らかになり、しかもキリスト教徒は皇帝礼拝も拒んだため、反社会的集団であるとされ迫害が始まりました。キリスト教は、ネロ帝（ローマ帝国第5代皇帝）の代からディオクレティアヌス帝までの約250年間迫害を受け続けてきましたが、313年コンスタンティヌス1世とリキニウス帝によるミラノ勅令によって、他のすべての宗教とともに公認されました。そして、380年にテオドシウス帝はキリスト教をローマ帝国の国教と宣言しました。

■ 中世のキリスト教

　395年のローマ帝国の分裂後、東西両教会の交流が次第に衰退していきました。そして、両教会の教義の解釈に相違が生まれ、フィリオクェ問題[注1]など幾度かの対立が起こりました。1054年に、コンスタンティノープル総主教ミカエル・ケルラリオスとローマ教皇レオ9世は相互破門するに至り、東西両教会は、東方正教会とローマ・カトリック教会に分裂しました。

Section 2

Christian History I World

■ Ancient Christianity

Christianity began in the third decade of the 1st century of the Christian era when Jesus's apprentices started evangelizing in the Galilean regions (Galilee) and Judean regions (Judea) after the execution of Jesus by crucifixion.

Since Christianity was considered to be a sect of Judaism at first, Christians were exempt from emperor worship. However, when it became obvious that Christianity was a different religion from Judaism, and Christians refused emperor worship, it was regarded as an anti-social group and the persecution of Christians started. Christianity was persecuted for about 250 years from the time of Emperor Nero to that of Emperor Diocletianus. However, it was recognized officially with all other religions by the Edict of Milan signed by Emperors Constantine I and Licinius. Emperor Theodosius declared Christianity to be a state religion of the Roman Empire in 380.

注目：「伝道する」は evangelize、gospelize、missionize、propagate などの英語を用いる。

■ Christianity in the Middle ages

The relationship between the churches in the east and the west declined gradually after the partition of the Roman Empire in 395. Then, a difference in the interpretation of the doctrine of both churches arose, which led to several conflicts such as Filioque. Patriarch Constantine Michael Keroularios (Cerularius) and Pope Leo IX came to excommunicate each other in 1054, and both east and west churches split into the Orthodox Church and the Roman Catholic Church.

第2節　キリスト教の基礎知識

　古代末期以来、国王をはじめとする世俗領主たちは、自分の領土に聖堂や修道院などを建てるようになり、やがて聖堂の聖職者あるいは修道院長の任命も自らが行うようになりました。教会内部では、このような世俗化を食い止めようという気運が高まり、聖職者の任命権をめぐる教皇と世俗領主との対立抗争が起こりました。1076年、教皇グレゴリウス7世が世俗領主による叙任を禁じたため、神聖ローマ皇帝ハインリヒ4世と衝突した結果、教皇は皇帝を破門しました（叙任権闘争[注2]）。1077年、ハインリヒ4世は自らの政治的地位が危うくなることを恐れ、教皇グレゴリウス7世の許しを請い、破門が解かれることとなりました（カノッサの屈辱[注3]）。

....

1　フィリオクェ問題（Filioque）とは、ニカイア・コンスタンティノポリス信条の解釈・翻訳をめぐる、キリスト教神学上の最大の論争の1つ。
2　叙任権闘争（Investiture Controversy）とは、中世初期において神聖ローマ皇帝がローマ教皇との間で、司教や修道院長の任命権（＝叙任権）をめぐって争ったこと。
3　カノッサの屈辱（Walk to Canossa）とは、神聖ローマ皇帝ハインリヒ4世が教皇による破門の解除を願って、自ら北イタリアのカノッサ城へ赴き、許しを願ったこと。

■ 近世のキリスト教

　十字軍の失敗による教皇権威の衰えや教会の混乱などにより、14世紀から15世紀にかけて、カトリック教会批判運動が起こりました。イギリスのジョン・ウィクリフは、ローマ・カトリックの教義は聖書から離れていると批判しました。また、ウィクリフの影響を受けて、ボヘミア地方の宗教改革者ヤン・フスは、聖書中心の教説を唱え、免罪符を販売する腐敗した教会を批判しました。その結果、コンスタンツ公会議によって有罪とされ、火刑に処されました。
　そして、16世紀初頭、ドイツのマルティン・ルターによる宗教改革へと発展していきました。それまではドイツではカトリック教会が唯一のキリスト教でしたが、ルターにより「プロテスタント」と呼ばれる諸教会が生まれました。ドイツで起こった宗教改革は、ツヴィングリ、カルヴァンらによりヨーロッパ各地に広がりました。

Section 2

Since the end of the ancient times, secular feudal lords including kings had come to build cathedrals and monasteries in their own territories. In due course, they came to appoint a cathedral clergy or a Superior in their own right. The momentum to halt such secularization increased within the church, and a conflict between the Pope and the secular feudal lords over patronage rights occurred. When Pope Gregorius VII prohibited the investiture by secular feudal lords in 1076, he clashed with the will of the Holy Roman Emperor, Henry IV. As a result, the Pope excommunicated the Emperor (Investiture Controversy). Since Henry IV feared that his political position might be in danger, he asked Gregorius VII for forgiveness and the excommunication was absolved in 1077 (Walk to Canossa).

■ Modern Christianity

The decline of the Pope's authority due to the failure of the crusade and the confusion of churches triggered a movement which criticized the Catholic Church from the 14th to the 15th century. John Wycliffe in England criticized the doctrine of the Roman Catholic Church as being out of sync with the Bible. Under the influence of Wycliffe, Jan Hus, a religious reformer in the Bohemia district promulgated the Bible-centric doctrine and criticized the corrupt church which sold indulgences (forgiveness of sins). As a result, he was judged guilty at the Council of Constance and executed by being burned at the stake.

This movement developed into the Religious Reformation by Martin Luther in Germany in the early 16th century. Until then, the Catholic Church was one unified Christian church in Germany. However, several churches called "Protestant" churches were created by Luther. Zwingli and Calvin spread the Religious Reformation throughout Europe from Germany.

第2節　キリスト教の基礎知識

　宗教改革以降、カトリックとプロテスタントは、国内でも、国家間でも激しく対立し、フランスのユグノー戦争や、ドイツの三十年戦争といった宗教戦争が勃発しました。17世紀になると、西ヨーロッパの植民地化に伴い、カトリック教会とプロテスタント教会による海外宣教が始まりました。

■ 近代以降のキリスト教

　19世紀後半から20世紀初頭、プロテスタントを中心とするキリスト教の教会一致運動（エキュメニカル運動）が起こりました。1937年、この教会一致運動を推進するために、教会指導者たちは、世界教会協議会（WCC）の設立に合意しました。この協議会はスイスのジュネーブを本拠地とし、120カ国以上からの340を超える教会の会員が所属しています。

　また、教皇ヨハネ23世の呼びかけで第２バチカン公会議が、1962年に始まり、1965年に教皇パウロ6世によって終結しました。教会内での一連の会議が議論を通じ、カトリック教会の将来にも影響する16の公的な決定がなされました。この会議以降、プロテスタント諸派とカトリックとの対話および和解が促進されました。

参考：教会一致運動

　教会一致促進運動、エキュメニカル運動、エキュメニズム（Ecumenism）とも言い、「世界教会主義」や「世界教会一致運動」と訳されることが多い。キリスト教の超教派による結束を目指す運動のことである。

Section 2

After the Religious Reformation, the Catholic Church and several Protestant Churches conflicted with each other intensely both within and between countries, which triggered religious wars such as Huguenot Wars in France (French Wars of Religion) and the Thirty Years' War in Germany. In the 17th century, overseas missionary work by the Catholic Church and several Protestant Churches started along with Western European colonialism.

注目1：indulgence（通例「耽溺」「甘やかし」）に「免罪符」の意味がある。（Modern Christianityの7行目）
注目2：colonialismは「植民地化政策」、colonizationは「植民地化」。（Modern Christianityの最終行）

■ Christianity after modern age

From the latter half of the 19th century to the early 20th century, Christian ecumenical movements arose among several Protestant Churches. The church leaders agreed to the establishment of the World Council of Churches (WCC) to promote these ecumenical movements in 1937. Geneva in Switzerland is home to this council and more than 340 church members in over 120 countries belong to it.

The Second Vatican Council opened under Pope John XXIII in 1962 and closed under the Pope Paul VI in 1965. During this series of meetings and discussions within the Church, 16 public decisions were made which affected the future of the Catholic Church. After this council, conversation and reconciliation between the Protestant Churches and the Catholic Church were encouraged.

●Useful Usage● SYNC ［口語］（= synchronization）
1. Your heart is in sync with mine.
   （気持ちがぴったり合うね）
2. His ideas seem to be out of sync with hers.
   （彼と彼女の考えは相容れないみたいだね）

第2節　キリスト教の基礎知識

❺ キリスト教の歴史Ⅱ　日本編

■ 戦国時代から安土桃山時代

　1549年、カトリックのイエズス会の宣教師フランシスコ・ザビエルによって、日本に初めてキリスト教が伝えられました。キリスト教徒は日本では吉利支丹（切支丹＝キリシタン）と呼ばれていました。ザビエルは鹿児島に上陸したのち、天皇の宣教許可を得ようと平戸・山口を経て京都にたどり着きましたが、当時の京都は戦乱で荒廃しており、天皇の拝謁を果たせませんでした。そのため、彼は平戸へ戻り、まず大名などの支配者を改宗させました。彼らはキリシタン大名と呼ばれ、特に有名な人物に大友宗麟［そうりん］・大村純忠・有馬晴信らがいます。

　豊臣秀吉は、織田信長と同様に当初はキリシタンを保護していましたが、やがて国の統一が進むと「バテレン追放令」を発し（1587年）、宣教師を追放しました。さらに、1596年に「サン・フェリペ号事件[注1]」が起こると、秀吉はキリスト教宣教の危険性を認識し、キリスト教の本格的な弾圧を開始しました。そして、26人のカトリック信徒が長崎で処刑されました（日本二十六聖人の殉教）。

1　土佐の浦戸にスペイン船が漂着した際、「スペインの領土拡大のためにキリスト教を布教していた」という航海士の発言が問題に発展した事件。

Section 2

Christian History II Japan

■ **From the Sengoku period to the Azuchi-Momoyama period**

　Christianity was first introduced to Japan by Francis Xavier, a Catholic missionary belonging to the Society of Jesus in 1549. A Christian was called Kirishitan in Japan. After Xavier landed on Kagoshima, he reached Kyoto through Hirado and Yamaguchi to obtain the Emperor's permission for propagation. However, Kyoto in those days was devastated by wars and he was not able to meet the Emperor. Therefore, he returned to Hirado and worked on recruiting the ruling elite such as the feudal lords. They were called Christian feudal lords and particularly famous among them are Otomo Sourin, Omura Sumitada, and Arima Harunobu.

　Toyotomi Hideyoshi protected Christians at first as Oda Nobunaga did before him. However, as the national unification proceeded, he issued the "Edict Expelling Christian Missionaries" and prohibited Christian missionaries from spreading their religion in Japan by expelling them from the country. In addition, when the "San Felipe Incident" happened in 1596, Hideyoshi recognized the danger of the propagation of Christianity and seriously clamped down on Christianity in Japan on a full-scale basis. As a result, 26 Catholics were executed in Nagasaki (the Martyrdom of the 26 Saints of Japan).

注目：recruit（入会を勧める）を「改宗させる」の意味で用いている。英語の convert を用いると、やや強制的なイメージがあり当時の状況に合わない。（7行目）

第2節　キリスト教の基礎知識

■ 江戸時代

　徳川家康は当初キリスト教宣教を黙認していましたが、1609年から1612年にかけて岡本大八［だいはち］事件[注2]が起こると、諸大名と幕臣へキリスト教の禁止令を発布しました。1637年には、島原と天草でキリシタンの農民が中心となって「島原の乱」を起こしました。幕府は1639年に鎖国令を発し、キリシタンを根絶するため、禁書令・宗門改・寺請制度・踏絵といった施策が強行されました。また五人組の連帯責任制や密告奨励のための報奨金制度なども実施されました。江戸時代の末まで、日本では隠れキリシタンと呼ばれる人々を除き、キリシタンは日本全土から姿を消すこととなりました。

2　本多正純［まさずみ］の与力（＝有力武将に従う下級武士）であった岡本大八が、有馬晴信の旧領回復を幕府に働きかけると言って、晴信から収賄したことが発覚し、大八は火刑に処せられ、晴信も死刑に処された事件。大八はキリシタンだった。

■ 幕末から明治時代

　1853年、江戸幕府はアメリカからの要求を受けて、開国に踏み切ることとなりました。そして、1858年に大老・井伊直弼とハリスの間で、日米修好通商条約が結ばれました。この条約が結ばれたことで宣教師の入国が可能になり、ジラールは1862年に横浜に開国以来最初のカトリック教会を建てました。

　また、プロテスタント宣教師も続々と来日し、横浜バンド・熊本バンド・札幌バンドと呼ばれる、日本におけるプロテスタント派の3つの源流を形成しました。横浜バンドはヘボン、ブラウン、バラらアメリカ人宣教師の指導を受けてプロテスタントとなった集団で、1872年には日本で最初のプロテスタント教会である「日本基督公会」を設立しました。そして、井深梶之助・植村正久らを日本人指導者として生み出しました。

Section 2

■ Edo period

Tokugawa Ieyasu tolerated the propagation of Christianity at first. However, when the Okamoto Daihachi Incident occurred between 1609 and 1612, he promulgated the ban on Christianity against feudal lords and vassals of the shogun. In 1637, Christian farmers rebelled in an uprising called the "Shimabara Rebellion" in Shimabara and Amakusa. In 1639, the feudal government initiated the national isolation law, and other measures such as the edict of banning books, *shumon aratame* (religious investigation), *terauke seido* (temple guarantee system), and *fumie* (a plate with a crucifix or other Christian symbol used to search out Christians) were carried out aggressively. Also, the joint responsibility system called Goningumi and a bounty rewarded to those who betray the identity of Christians to authorities were put in place. Until the end of the Edo period, Christians eventually vanished throughout Japan, except for those who practiced their religion in secret.

■ From the end of the Edo period to the Meiji period

In 1853, the Edo government accepted the request from the United States and decided to end its policy of isolation. In 1858, the Treaty of Amity and Commerce between the United States of America and Japan was signed between *Tairo* (Chief Minister) Ii Naosuke and Townsend Harris. The conclusion of the treaty enabled missionaries to enter Japan. In 1862, Girard built Japan's first Catholic Church in Yokohama since the opening of the country.

Protestant missionaries also came to Japan one after another and formed three sources of protestant denominations in Japan: the Yokohama Band, the Kumamoto Band and the Sapporo Band. The Yokohama band is a group that became Protestants with guidance from American missionaries such as Hepburn, Brown, and Ballagh. In 1872, the group established the "Church of Christ in Japan," which was the first Protestant Church in Japan. It produced Ibuka Kajinosuke and Uemura Masahisa as Japanese pastors.

第2節　キリスト教の基礎知識

1861年にはロシア正教会のニコライ・カサートキンが函館のロシア領事館の司祭として来日し、1872年には東京に日本ハリストス正教会を樹立しました。

■ 明治から大正時代

明治中期以降、日本が富国強兵政策をとって、国粋主義的思想が強まる中、1889年に「大日本帝国憲法」が発布されました。この中で信教の自由は許されていたものの、天皇に忠実な臣民にのみ許されるという限定的なものでした。さらに1890年には、「教育勅語」が政府により発布され、天皇制教育体制が確立し、キリスト教に対する風当たりが強まっていきました。

■ 昭和から平成時代

第二次世界大戦後は国家神道が廃止され、1946年に公布された日本国憲法の第20条では、信教の自由が保障されました。これにより、不自由のないキリスト教の宣教が開始されました。

関連情報　熊本バンドと札幌バンド

熊本バンドは、アメリカの教育者ジェーンズ（Janes）によって導かれた学生によって結成されたグループで、徳富蘇峯［とくとみそほう］、海老名弾正［えびなだんじょう］らを輩出しました。

札幌バンドは、アメリカの農学者、教育家であるクラーク（Clark）およびメソジスト教会宣教師のハリス（Harris）に導かれて入信した札幌農学校（現在の北海道大学）の学生たちの通称で、ここから内村鑑三や、『武士道』による日本紹介など、国際人として活躍した新渡戸稲造［にとべいなぞう］らが出ました。いずれも日本社会の様々な方面に大きな影響を与えました。

Section 2

Nikolai Kasatkin of the Russian Orthodox Church (Nicholas of Japan) came to Japan as a priest as part of the Russian consulate in Hakodate in 1861, and he set up the Orthodox Church in Japan in Tokyo in 1872.

■ From the Meiji period to the Taisho period

With the rise of nationalism as a result of policies which sought for the increase of wealth and military power after the middle of the Meiji period, the "Constitution of the Empire of Japan" was promulgated in 1889. Though the freedom of religion was permitted in this constitution, it was limited to the people who were loyal to the Emperor. In addition, the "Imperial Rescript on Education" was issued by the government in 1890 and the educational system based on Japanese Imperialism was established. After this, Christianity came under heavier scrutiny from the government.

■ From the Showa period to the Heisei period

After World War II, State Shinto was abolished, and freedom of religion was guaranteed in Article 20 of the Constitution of Japan, which was issued in 1946. As a result, unrestrained propagation of Christianity began.

●Useful Usage●　SCRUTINY

All sorts of goods undergo a careful scrutiny before they are sold in the store.
（あらゆる商品は店頭に出る前に入念な検査を受ける）

❻ キリスト教の教祖と聖典

■ キリスト教の教祖

　キリスト教の教祖とされているイエス・キリストは、今から約2000年前にユダヤのベツレヘムで生まれました。大工であるヨセフの婚約者であったマリアは、あるとき、天使ガブリエルから、彼女が神の子を身ごもるであろうと告げられました（受胎告知）。この神の子こそイエスでした。

　青年になったイエスは洗礼者ヨハネにより、ヨルダン川のほとりで洗礼を受けました。荒野での試練に耐えたあと、イエスはガリラヤで伝道を始めました。イエスの伝道期間はおよそ3年間でありましたが、ガリラヤとエルサレムの2カ所を中心に行われました。イエスは彼の伝道活動に加わった弟子たちの中から12人の弟子を選び、彼らに特権を与えました。この弟子たちは十二使徒と呼ばれました。

　イエスは、ユダヤ教体制を激しく批判したため、当時のユダヤの宗教指導者たちの要請により、ローマ帝国当局がイエスを十字架刑に処したのです。3日後に、イエスは復活し、墓は空になっていました。復活したイエスは、40日間にわたり弟子たちに教えを説いたあと昇天したとされています。

■ キリスト教の聖典

　聖書はキリスト教の聖典であり、「旧約聖書」（39巻）、「新約聖書」（27巻）から成っています。

　旧約聖書は、元来ユダヤ教の聖典として成立し、のちにキリスト教でも聖典となりました。旧約聖書は、ユダヤ教ではヘブライ語聖書と呼ばれています。ヘブライ語の原典では、旧約聖書は「律法」「預言者」「諸書」の3つに分類されています。

Section 2

Founder of Christianity and the Bible

■ Founder of Christianity

Jesus Christ, the founder of Christianity, was born about 2000 years ago in Bethlehem in Judea. Mary, who was the fiancé of Joseph, a carpenter, was told by the angel Gabriel that she was to carry the Child of God (the Annunciation). This child was to be Jesus.

When Jesus reached adolescence, he was baptized by John the Baptist near the Jordan River. After having endured a trial of temptations in the wilderness, Jesus began his mission in Galilee. Jesus preached for about three years and his mission was mainly carried out in two places, Galilee and Jerusalem. Jesus chose 12 disciples from the group who joined his mission, and accorded a privilege to them. These disciples were called the 12 apostles.

Because of his harsh criticisms of the Jewish religion and leadership of the day, Jesus was arrested, put on trial, and executed by crucifixion by the Roman authorities at the request of the Jewish religious leaders. After three days, he was resurrected and his tomb was found to be empty. Jesus is said to have eventually appeared before his apostles and others to preach for 40 days before finally joining His Father in heaven.

■ Christian Bible

The Bible is a sacred text of Christianity and it consists of the "Old Testament" (39 volumes) and the "New Testament" (27 volumes).

The Old Testament is made up of the Jewish scriptures which became a sacred text of Christianity. From a Jewish standpoint, the Old Testament is known as the Hebrew Bible. In the original text in Hebrew, the Old Testament is classified into three sections: the "Laws," the "Prophets" and the "Writings."

第2節　キリスト教の基礎知識

　新約聖書の編纂は、紀元1〜2世紀にかけて行われました。その構成は以下の通りです。
- 『マタイ』『マルコ』『ルカ』『ヨハネ』の4つの福音書
- 『使徒言行録』
- 『パウロ書簡』
- 『他の書簡』
- 『ヨハネの黙示録』

参考：マリアが処女のまま聖霊によって神の子を身ごもったという処女懐胎の物語の記述は、「マタイによる福音書」第1章18〜25、「ルカによる福音書」第1章26〜56、第2章1〜7に見られる。この記述をめぐる謎に言及する学者もいるが、聖書に見る様々な超自然的出来事の史実性については、合理的認識の範囲内で再解釈するか、信仰の対象とするかは意見の分かれるところである。

Section 2

 The New Testament was compiled from the 1st to the 2nd century of the Christian era. The basic composition is as follows:
- the Four Gospels of "Matthew," "Mark," "Luke," and "John"
- "the Acts of the Apostles"
- "Paul's Letters"
- "Other Letters"
- "the Book of Revelation"

第2節　キリスト教の基礎知識

❼ イエス・キリストの弟子

■ イエス・キリストの弟子
　イエス・キリストとともに宣教活動をした12人の高弟を「十二使徒」と呼びます。十二使徒とは、ペトロ（ペテロ）・アンデレ・ゼベダイの子ヤコブ（大ヤコブ）・ヨハネ・フィリポ・バルトロマイ・トマス・マタイ・アルファイの子ヤコブ（小ヤコブ）・タダイ・シモン・イスカリオテのユダのことを言います。この十二使徒の他に、ある意味で最も有名な弟子として、パウロがいます。

■ ペトロ
　ペトロは、イエスと出会う前のヘブライ名をシモンといい、ガリラヤで漁師をしていましたが、イエスに帰依して十二使徒の中で最初の弟子となりました。十二使徒のうちの1人であるアンデレはペトロの弟です。ペトロは、イエスが逮捕されたとき、イエスのことを知らないと3度も言い放ち（このことはイエスがすでに預言していましたが）、イエスとのかかわりを否定したという有名なエピソードが残っています。ペトロはローマ教会の最初の司教であったと言われています。ネロ皇帝の迫害下にローマで殉教したとも伝えられています。

■ ゼベダイの子ヤコブ
　ヤコブは弟子のヨハネの兄弟で、アルファイの子ヤコブと区別して「大ヤコブ」とも言われます。彼は気性が荒いことから、ヨハネとともにイエスから「ボアネルゲス（雷の子）」と呼ばれていました。ヤコブは、ヘロデ・アグリッパ1世によって斬首刑に処され、十二使徒の中で最初の殉教者となりました。

Section 2

The Disciples of Jesus

■ The Disciples of Jesus

The 12 leading disciples, who did missionary work with Jesus Christ, are called the "Twelve Apostles." The twelve apostles are Peter, Andrew, James the son of Zebedee (=James the Greater), John, Philip, Bartholomew, Thomas, Matthew, James the son of Alphaeus (=James the Lesser), Thaddaeus, Simon, and Judas Iscariot. Paul, while not of the original twelve, is in some ways the most famous of the disciples.

■ Peter

Simon (name in Hebrew), known as Peter, was a fisherman in Galilee when he met Jesus. He converted to Jesus' teachings and became the first disciple among the 12 apostles. Andrew, who is one of the twelve apostles, is Peter's younger brother. The following is a famous episode about Peter: When Jesus was arrested, Peter was questioned by the authorities and denied knowing Jesus three times, something Jesus had predicted and told Peter he would do. It is said that Peter was the first bishop of the Roman church. It is said that Peter was martyred in Rome under Emperor Nero.

■ James the son of Zebedee

James was a brother of John the Apostle and also called "James the Greater" to distinguish him from James, son of Alphaeus. Due to his fiery temper, he was called "Boanerges (Sons of Thunder)" by Jesus together with John. James was executed with a sword by order of King Herod Agrippa I and became the first martyr among the apostles.

第2節　キリスト教の基礎知識

■ ヨハネ

　ヨハネはゼベダイの子ヤコブの兄弟で、「ヨハネによる福音書」では自分のことを「イエスの愛しておられた弟子」と呼びました。イエスが十字架にかけられたとき、母マリアを託したのがこのヨハネであるとされています。イエスの死後、ヨハネはマリアを連れエルサレムを去り、やがてエフェソス（現在のトルコの都市）の地にたどり着きました。マリアはその最期をそこで終えたと言われています。

■ トマス

　トマスが「私は、主の手に釘の跡を見、この指を釘跡に入れてみなければ、また、この手をそのわき腹に入れてみなければ、私は決して信じない」と言ってイエスの復活を信じず、証拠を求めたという話は有名です。彼は、西ヨーロッパでは「疑い深いトマス」と呼ばれています。

■ マタイ

　マタイは、もとは徴税人で、ローマの管轄下にあったカファルナウム収税所に座っているときにイエスが通りかかり、「私に従いなさい」と声をかけたとされています。マタイは、「マタイによる福音書」の著者と考えられています。彼はエチオピアで伝道しているときに剣で殺されたと伝えられています。

■ イスカリオテのユダ

　ユダは使徒団の会計係を務めていました。「イスカリオテ」には「カリオテ出身の男」または「刺客」という意味があるとされます。ユダは、イエスを裏切り、ローマ兵によるイエス逮捕の手引きをしましたが、彼はそれを後悔し、自殺しました。

Section 2

■ John

John was the brother of James the son of Zebedee and called himself "the disciple whom Jesus loved" in the "Gospel of John." It is considered that it was John to whom Jesus entrusted the care of his mother when Jesus was put on the cross. After the death of Jesus, John left Jerusalem with Mary and reached Ephesus (a city in modern day Turkey). It is thought that Mary lived out her remaining days there.

■ Thomas

Thomas is famous for the following story: He said, "I refuse to believe unless I see the nail marks in his hands and put my finger where the nails were, and put my hand into his side," as he didn't believe in the resurrection of Jesus and requested empirical evidence. He is called "Thomas the Doubter" (doubting Thomas) in Western Europe.

■ Matthew

It is assumed that Matthew was originally a tax collector and when he sat at the tax office in Capernaum that was under the jurisdiction of Rome, Jesus walked by and said, "Follow me." He is considered to be the author of the "Gospel according to Matthew." It is said he was killed by a spear when he preached the Gospel in Ethiopia.

■ Judas Iscariot

Judas served as a treasurer of the disciples. It is considered that "Iscariot" means "a man from Kerioth" or "an assassin." He betrayed Jesus and helped the Roman soldiers to arrest Him. Later he regretted what he had done and killed himself.

第2節　キリスト教の基礎知識

■ パウロ

　パウロは、イエスの死後に信仰の道に入ってきたため、イエスの直弟子ではなく、十二使徒の中には数えられません。彼は、キリキアの都市タルソス（タルスス）で生まれ、ヘブライ名をサウロと言いました（のちにパウロと改名）。もとは熱心なユダヤ教信者で、キリスト教徒を迫害していましたが、ダマスコへ向かう途中、復活したキリストに出会い、突如として熱心なキリスト教徒になったとされています。アンティオキア教会を起点にキリスト教の布教を開始しました。3回に及ぶ世界伝道旅行を行い、地中海沿岸の地域に数多くの教会を建てたと伝えられています。

関連情報　十二使徒の日本語訳は、通常の名前の訳とは異なる

　十二使徒の名前でわかりますが、聖書に出てくる人名は、日本語訳が異なっています。[　]内が通常の呼び名です。

　Peter → ペテロ［ピーター］　　　James → ヤコブ［ジェームズ］
　John → ヨハネ［ジョン］　　　　Thomas → トマス［トーマス］
　Matthew → マタイ［マシュー］　　Paul → パウロ［ポール］

　この単語を英語で発音するときは[　]内の発音になります。なお、ペテロはペトロとも表記されます。なお、Peterはフランス語では「ピエール」、イタリア語では「ピエトロ」、スペイン語では「ペドロ」、ドイツ語では「ペーター」、ロシア語では「ピョートル」と発音されます。

Section 2

■ Paul

Paul did not learn directly from Jesus and is not included in the twelve Apostles because he began his religious career after the death of Jesus. He was born in Tarsus (Tarsus), a city in Cilicia and his Hebrew name was Saul (Later, he changed his name to Paul). He was originally an ardent Jew and persecuted Christians. However, it is assumed that he met the risen Jesus on his way to Damascus and suddenly became a devoted Christian. He began his teachings of Christianity in the Antiochia church. It is said that he went on mission trips around the known world three times and established many churches along the Mediterranean.

●Useful Usage●　BETRAY

1. He betrayed military secrets to the enemy.
   （彼は軍事機密を敵に漏らした）（暴く）
2. Her red eyes betrayed the fact that she had not slept well.
   （彼女の眼が赤かったので、よく眠れなかったことがわかった）（示す）

第2節　キリスト教の基礎知識

❽ キリスト教の影響

(1) 美術・建築への影響

■ 美術への影響

　初期キリスト教美術は、2世紀末から3世紀初頭、ローマ美術をもとに始まったと言われています。この時代のキリスト教信者たちは、地下に集会所（現在は、「カタコンベ」と呼ばれている場所）を作り、祈りを捧げていました。ローマには、カタコンベのフレスコ壁画や石棺の浮彫りなどが数多く残っています。

　313年のキリスト教の公認後は、布教の目的で聖堂が建てられるようになり、その聖堂の内部にはキリストの教えの絵解きが飾られました。このころに、東西の美術が融合したビザンティン美術が誕生します。絵画では、教会堂のモザイクや、フレスコ画、イコン（聖画像）などにその特色が見られます。

　12世紀ころになるとロマネスク美術に続いてゴシック美術が北フランスから起こり、建築技術が向上したため、窓が多くなりステンドグラスが発達しました。このころの代表的なステンドグラスに、フランスのシャルトル大聖堂のものがあります。

■ 建築への影響

　初期キリスト教時代に、集中式教会堂とバシリカ式教会堂注1という、2つの教会堂の形式が生まれました。集中式の建築は、洗礼の建物として多く採用されました。一方、バシリカ式の建築は、キリスト教が公認されたのち、大勢のキリスト教徒が集まって典礼注2を行うための建物として適用されました。

　やがて、集中式は主に東方で発展し、バシリカ式は西方で栄えました。西方におけるキリスト教建築は、中世のロマネスク建築から、ゴシック建築、ルネサンス建築、バロック建築を経て今日に至るまで、すべてにおいてバシリカ式が基本となっています。バシリカ式の代表的な建築物としては、ローマの旧サン・ピエトロ大聖堂などがあります。

Section 2

Influence of Christianity

(1) Christian influence on art and architecture
■ Christian influence on art

It is said that early Christian art began between the end of the 2nd century and the early 3rd century based on findings of Roman art. Christian believers in this age built underground catacombs to hold services in secret. Many fresco wall paintings and reliefs on stone coffins in catacombs remain in Rome.

After Christianity was recognized officially in 313, shrines came to be built for the purpose of propagation, and the illustrations of the teachings of Jesus decorated the interior of the shrines. At this time, Byzantine art, which integrated the art of the east with that of the west, was born. The characteristics of Byzantine art can be seen in the mosaic of churches, fresco paintings, and icons.

In the 12th century, Gothic art appeared in northern France following Romanesque art. The number of windows was increased by the advancement of architectural technology, which also developed stained glass. Stained glass typical of this time can be found in the Chartres Cathedral in France.

注目：「カタコンベ」は、ローマおよび付近のキリスト教徒の地下墓所のこと。英語では、特に the Catacombs と表記する。

■ Christian influence on architecture

In the early Christian era, two styles of church, the central plan style church and the basilica style church arose. Central plan architecture was largely adopted as the building for baptism. On the other hand, basilica architecture was applied as the building where many Christians gathered and conducted a liturgy after Christianity was recognized officially.

第2節　キリスト教の基礎知識

1　集中式教会堂とバシリカ式教会堂
集中式教会堂が、円形・多角形・十字形などを基本とする平面を持つのに対し、バシリカ式教会堂は、東西に長い平面を持っている。
2　典礼
典礼とは定まった儀礼や儀式のこと。一般にキリスト教で用いる用語。

(2) 文学・音楽への影響
■ 文学への影響

　キリスト教初期の最も重要な作品として、アウグスティヌスの『告白』があげられます。この作品は、キリスト教への回心や母モニカの死などについてつづられた彼の自伝であり、『神の国』とともに、彼の最も有名な代表作となっています。
　また、ダンテの『神曲』は、中世からルネサンス期において最高の作品と言われており、その作品の中では、彼から見た中世ヨーロッパのキリスト教的世界観が語られています。
　ダンテの『神曲』とともに、キリスト教文学の代表作として知られ、また、長編叙事詩の代表作とも言われる作品は、ミルトンの叙事詩『失楽園』です。アダムとイブが楽園にある禁断の木の実を食べて楽園から追放される、という『旧約聖書』の「創世記」を題材としています。

●●●補足情報●●●
　この他にもキリスト教の思想は、イギリス、アメリカ、フランス、ドイツの文学や、トルストイ、ドストエフスキーらのロシア文学等、数多くの文学者に影響を与えた。また日本では、遠藤周作や三浦綾子・曽野綾子らのキリスト教作家の優れた現代作品があり、19〜20世紀の白樺派の文学者たちや、賀川豊彦・島崎藤村・有島武郎をはじめ、芥川龍之介・太宰治の文学にもキリスト教の影響が認められる。

Section 2

Before long, the central plan developed mainly in the east, and the basilica style flourished in the west. Christian architecture in the west is based on the basilica style in all periods from medieval Romanesque architecture to the more modern styles of Gothic, Renaissance, and Baroque architecture. St. Peter's Basilica in Rome is a building typical of the basilica style.

(2) Christian influence on literature and music
■ Christian influence on literature

The most important work of early Christianity includes "The Confessions" of St. Augustine (Augustinus). This work is St. Augustine's autobiography about his conversion to Christianity and the death of his mother Monica, and it is his most famous masterpiece together with "God's Country."

Moreover, Dante's "The Divine Comedy" is said to be the greatest work from the Middle ages to the Renaissance period. This work deals with the Christian perspective of Europe in the Middle ages seen from his viewpoint.

Milton's epic poem, "Paradise Lost," is representative of the full-length epic poems. It is based on 'Genesis' of the "Old Testament," which tells the tale of Adam and Eve eating the forbidden fruit in the paradise of Eden before being banished for their sin.

第2節　キリスト教の基礎知識

■ 音楽への影響

　キリスト教の教会では礼拝のときに独特の音楽が用いられ、これを教会音楽と言いました。カトリック教会では、正式な典礼聖歌としてグレゴリオ聖歌と呼ばれる単旋律（モノフォニー）の聖歌が作られました。

　17世紀のバロック時代には、ミサ曲やモテット[注1]、レクイエム[注2]などが生まれました。ミサ曲の中で真の傑作に位置づけられているのは、バッハによるミサ曲ロ短調と、ベートーベンの『荘厳ミサ曲（ミサ・ソレムニス）』です。19〜20世紀には、ベルリオーズ、ベルディ、ブルックナーらにより、名作が多数生まれました。

　19世紀初頭のロシアでは、ボルトニャンスキーがイタリア様式の聖歌を導入しました。さらにロシアは、チャイコフスキー、ラフマニノフ、アルハンゲルスキーといった著名なキリスト教徒の作曲家を輩出しました。

1　モテットとは、宗教的声楽曲のジャンルの1つ。ミサ曲を除くポリフォニー（多声）による宗教的声楽曲の総称。
2　レクイエムとは、死者のための典礼で歌われるミサ曲のこと。

(3) 哲学・科学への影響
■ 哲学への影響

　中世のヨーロッパでは、キリスト教の教理を研究する神学が、最高の学問とされており、このことは、「哲学は神学の婢女［はしため］」ということわざからも示されています。

　11世紀になると、西ヨーロッパではスコラ学が興隆しました。スコラ学とは、一般に教会や修道院付属の学校で形成された神学・哲学などの学問の総称です。トマス・アクィナスは、神学とのつながりを欠いたアリストテレス哲学を、キリスト教神学に融合させたとされる学者です。彼の最も有名な著作は『神学大全』です。やがて、ウィリアム・オッカム[注1]が信仰と学問の分離を説いたことにより、スコラ学は崩壊しました。

1　ウィリアム・オッカムの「オッカム」とは、姓ではなく、彼の出身地である。彼は、イングランドのオッカム村に生まれた。

Section 2

■ Christian influence on music

A distinctive type of music was used in Christian churches at worship services which came to be called church music. In the Catholic Church, a monophonic chant called the Gregorian chant was produced as a formal liturgical chant.

A mass, a motet, and a requiem arose during the Baroque period in the 17th century. The true masterpieces are "Mass in B minor" by Bach and "Missa Solemnis" by Beethoven. A multitude of masterpieces were produced by Berlioz, Verdi, and Bruckner in the 19th and the 20th centuries.

Bortniansky introduced the chant in the Italian style to Russia in the early 19th century. In addition, Russia produced famous Christian composers such as Tchaikovsky, Rachmaninoff, and Arkhangelsky.

●Useful Usage● **PRODUCE**
1. Texus produces oil. （テキサスは石油を産出します）（産出する）
2. The tree produces well. （その木は実がよくなります）（実を結ぶ）
3. Please produce your ticket. （切符を拝見します）（[何かの証明のために]示す）

(3) Christian influence on philosophy and science
■ Christian influence on philosophy

Theology, the study of Christian doctrine, was believed to be the pinnacle of learning in Europe in the Middle Ages. This is pointed out in the proverb, "philosophy is the servant of theology."

Scholasticism flourished in western Europe in the 11th century. In general, scholasticism is a collective term which includes studies of theology and philosophy done at churches and convent schools. Thomas Aquinas was a scholar who is considered to have united non-theological Aristotelian philosophy (Aristotelianism) to Christian theology. His best known book is "Summa Theologica." Eventually, scholasticism itself collapsed due to William of Ockham advocating the separation of worship and learning.

第2節　キリスト教の基礎知識

■ 科学への影響

　古代、多くの学者が宇宙の構造について考えを述べました。プトレマイオスは、彼らの学説の中からより確かと思われるものを集めて体系化し、「天動説」（すべての天体が地球の周りを公転しているとする説）を考案しました。中世のキリスト教神学では、人間の住む地球は宇宙の中心であるのにふさわしいと考えられていたため、天動説がカトリック教会に公認された世界観となっていました。

　しかし、16世紀に、カトリック教会の司祭であったニコラウス・コペルニクスが『天球の回転について』を著し、従来のキリスト教的宇宙観をくつがえす「地動説」を唱えました。

　コペルニクスは、この著書で自己の地動説を発表することによる影響を恐れ、その販売を、死期を迎えるまで許さなかったと言われています。彼の著書の発表後も、宗教的な迫害を恐れたため、地動説に賛同する天文学者はなかなか出てきませんでした。

　しかし、17世紀に、ドイツの数学者で天文学者のヨハネス・ケプラーが「ケプラーの法則」を発見すると、天動説に対する地動説の優位が決定的になりました。

●●●補足情報●●●　**オッカムの思想とその影響**

　オッカムの思想は、一方では、16世紀を中心とする宗教改革への途を、他方では、14～16世紀のルネサンス運動と、それに伴う近代理性主義の諸哲学展開への途を用意したと言える。デカルトやカント、ヘーゲルに代表される近代の理性主義哲学も、人間主義を主流として発展の一路をたどるが、19世紀後半ごろから破綻があらわれ始め、2つの大戦を契機に破局へと進んだ。人間の不安や絶望などの宗教的テーマが、実存主義の祖と言われるキェルケゴールやニーチェによって初めて、まともに哲学の主題とされ、これが20世紀のヤスパースやハイデッガーらの哲学思想に受け継がれることとなる。キリスト教の神やキリスト教精神の追求であれ、またこれらに対する反発であれ、キリスト教の思想は、西洋の哲学の展開に深い影響を与えてきたと言える。

Section 2

■ Christian influence on science

In ancient times, quite a few scholars circulated their ideas about the mechanism of the universe. Ptolemy collected what seemed to be the more logical of the theories and systematized them. As a result, he invented the "Ptolemaic System" (the theory that all celestial bodies orbit around the earth). The Ptolemaic System was the view officially recognized by the Catholic Church since it was considered in Christian theology in the Middle Ages that the earth was the center of the universe.

However, Nicolaus Copernicus, who was a priest in the Catholic Church, wrote "On the Revolutions of the Heavenly Spheres" in the 16th century, and advocated the "Copernican System," which overturned the conventional Christian outlook on the universe.

It is said that Copernicus feared the blowback of publishing his book about the Copernican System so he did not permit its sales until the arrival of his death. The astronomers who agreed with the Copernican System stayed out of the limelight for fear of religious persecution even after the announcement of his book.

However, when Johannes Kepler, who was a mathematician and an astronomer in Germany, revealed "Kepler's Laws" in the 17th century, the superiority of the Copernican theory to the Ptolemaic theory became definite.

注目：天動説は地球を中心とする理論なので geocentric theory、地動説は太陽を中心とする理論なので heliocentric theory とも言える。

●●●補足情報●●●　ニュートンやガリレオへの影響

ケプラーと同じ世紀に活躍したニュートンやガリレオ・ガリレイも近代科学の発展に大きく貢献した人々だが、2人とも敬虔なキリスト教徒であった。聖書のどこにも地動説が誤りで天動説が正しいという記述はなく、ガリレオは、科学的立場からコペルニクスの地動説に賛同し、聖書は天文学について教える書物ではなく、人間の魂の救いについて教えている書物であると述べた。彼の言葉として有名な「それでも地球は動く」(Eppur si muove) については伝説と言われている。

第2節　キリスト教の基礎知識

(4) 生活・社会への影響
■ 生活への影響
　4世紀ごろ、より徹底したキリスト教徒の生活を求めた人々の間で修道院での生活が盛んになりました。修道院とは、修道士や修道女が修道会の会規を遵守しながら共同生活を行う施設です。6世紀半ばには、イタリアの修道僧聖ベネディクトゥスが、「祈り、働け」をモットーとする聖ベネディクトゥス会則を作りました。そのため、修道院では、自給自足の生活が行われており、生活に必要な物はすべて修道士の労働によって作り出されていました。つまり、修道士たちは、農業から印刷・大工仕事・医療に至るまですべてを行っていたので、そうした中から、新しい技術や医療・薬品が生まれてきました。医療・病院のルーツは修道院にあると言えます。

■ 社会への影響
　キリスト教がローマ帝国の国教になると、聖職者の社会的地位が高く評価されるようになりました。
　中世西洋においては、教皇を最上位とする上下の段階的組織、ヒエラルキーによって社会は成り立っていました。教会では、聖職者と平信徒の順位を分け、また聖職者においては、教皇を最上位として司教・司祭・助祭という段階が設けられていました。
　16世紀のドイツ国内において、ルターによる宗教改革が起こると、彼は、「信仰のみ」「聖書のみ」「万人祭司」というプロテスタントの3大原理を説きました。そして、「万人祭司」の原理において、人間の職業はすべて神より与えられたものであることを強調しました。この考え方は、職業に聖と俗があるという偏見からの解放につながるものとなりました。

> **関連情報　宗教改革の3大原理**
> 　本文では「信仰のみ」「聖書のみ」「万人祭司」をあげましたが、別の言い方に「聖書のみ」「恵みのみ」「信仰のみ」があります。このことが意味するのは、神様の前にすべての人が平等であるということ、お金とか見せかけの努力ではなく、聖書を信じ、イエスの十字架と復活を信じることにより、人は救われるということ、そして救いは神の恵みのみによって達成できるものということです。

Section 2

(4) Christian influence on life and society
■ Christian influence on life

Monastic life began to flourish among the people who pursued a life as a more committed Christian about the 4th century. The monastery is a facility where monks or nuns live in conformity to the rules of an order. In the middle of the 6th century, the Italian monk Saint Benedict created the Rule of Saint Benedict with the motto, "pray and work." Therefore, the monks lived self-sufficient life in the monastery and all things necessary for life were produced by the labor of the monks. In a word, the monks were doing everything from agriculture to printing, carpentry, and medical care. Therefore, new technology, medical care, and medicine arose from their labor. It can be said that the root of medical care and hospitals is in the monastery.

■ Christian influence on society

When Christianity became the official religion of the Roman Empire, clerical social positions came to be highly evaluated.

In the West during the Middle Ages, Christian society was hierarchal, a top-to-bottom organization with the Pope at the top. In the church, the rank of the clergy and the layman was separated, and the levels of clergyman ranked from the Pope down to the bishops, the priests, and finally the deacons.

When the Reformation by Luther took root in Germany in the 16th century, he advocated the three principles of Protestantism: "by faith alone," "by scripture alone" and "priesthood of all believers." He emphasized the principle of "priesthood of all believers" in that every human occupation was given by God and denied the idea of class based relationship between a saint and a lay at that time where one held God-given authority over the other.

第2節　キリスト教の基礎知識

❾ キリスト教徒の生活

■ キリスト教徒の生活

　プロテスタントの中には洗礼を行わない教派もありますが、カトリックでは、洗礼を受けて信者になります。洗礼を受ければ、キリストの贖罪［しょくざい］の功績にあずかることになり、それまでに犯したすべての罪が赦されるとされています。

　信者は、司祭や牧師らにより執行される公祈祷注・典礼などにおいて、公の祈祷行為（礼拝）を行います。礼拝は、キリストが人々の救いのためにいけにえとなって成し遂げた十字架上の死と復活を記念したものです。その記念行事がミサと呼ばれるものです。ミサはカトリック教会での呼び名で、正教会（ギリシャ正教）では聖体礼儀、聖公会では聖餐式に相当します。カトリック教会では、イエスの最後の晩餐の逸話をもとに、一般に、聖職者はぶどう酒を、信者はパンを分け合うことがミサの中心となっています。ここでのパンはキリストの体、ワインはその血を表しています。ミサは、教会の初期から「主の日」と呼ばれる日曜日にキリスト教徒が集まって祝われてきました（土曜日を公の礼拝の日とする教派も存在します）。

　また、公の祈祷の他に、私的な祈りを共同で行う祈祷会や勉強会なども開かれています。その中の1つに、日曜学校（教会学校）というものがあり、これは、キリスト教会が、日曜日や祝祭日に青少年を集めて宗教教育や一般教育を行うというものです。

Section 2

The Christian life

■ The Christian life

In the Catholic Church, a person becomes a member after being baptized, though there are some denominations among the Protestant Churches where no baptism is conducted. It is assumed that a person receives the achievement of the atonement made by Jesus Christ and all the sins committed up until then are absolved, once baptized.

Believers take part in services where they engage in public prayer, a liturgy and the like, all of which are overseen or delivered by priests and clergymen. The service features the commemoration of the death on the cross that Christ suffered, which is a symbolic sacrifice for the misdeeds of all humans in order for humanity to be saved, and Christ's Resurrection. The memorial event for the crucifixion is the so-called Mass. The Mass is the common name in the Catholic Church and it corresponds to the Eucharist, (also described as Divine Liturgy,) in the Orthodox Church and to Communion in the Episcopal Church. In the Catholic Church, the Mass generally centers on the ritual that clergymen share wine and other believers share bread, based on the anecdote of the Last Supper of Jesus. Here the bread is considered to be the actual body of Christ and the wine, his blood. Christians gathered and celebrated Mass on Sundays, called "the Lord's Day," since the early days of the church. There are some sects which consider Saturday the correct day for public service.

Moreover, meetings where believers conduct private prayer together or study the Bible are often held. One of these events is Sunday school where the Christian church invites the youth and conducts religious education or general education on Sunday or a national holiday.

第2節　キリスト教の基礎知識

「マタイによる福音書」第25章31節から40節に、「私（＝イエス）の兄弟であるこの最も小さい者の1人にしたのは、私にしてくれたことなのである」という一節があります。これは、最も小さい者（社会的弱者）の1人に対して何かをすることは大切なことであるという意味です。このような教えをもとに、キリスト教では、病人や旅行者または貧者を対象にした慈善活動を古来より盛んに行っていました。慈愛・慈善という意味の英語「チャリティー」は、ラテン語で愛を意味する「カリタス」が英語化したものです。現代における社会福祉活動は、このようなキリスト教文化の影響を少なからず受けていると言えるでしょう。

....

参考：「公祈祷」は「こうきとう」と読む。カトリックと正教会において、聖堂などにおいて行われる公式の礼拝のこと。

> **関連情報**　**2進法を発見したライプニッツ（Leibniz）の驚き**
>
> ライプニッツが発見した二進法をよく見ると、「1（＝唯一で全知全能）である神は0（＝無）からすべてを創造された」ということがよくわかると、彼は大いに感動したと言われています。というのは、二進法では、0と1からすべての数が表せるからです。つまり、0である「無」と1である「神」が存在するだけで、すべての数（＝全宇宙）がつくれるというわけです。

参考：聖公会とは、イギリス国教会を母教会とする世界各地の教会の名称で、英語名称は Anglican Church である。「聖公会」という言葉は、「使徒信条(The Apostles' Creed)」にある「聖なる公同の教会」を中国語に翻訳して成立し、1887年に日本聖公会が発足したとき、在日宣教師が正式名称として採用した。

> ●●●**補足情報**●●●
>
> 口語訳聖書の記述の中に、「彼(神)は、…地を何もないところに掛けられる」（ヨブ記第26章7節）、「水のおもてに円を描いて、光とやみとの境とされた」(同、10節)、「主は地球のはるか上に座して、地に住む者をいなごのように見られる」（イザヤ書第40章22節) などがあります。約3千年前に書かれた聖書ですが、地球が宇宙空間に浮かぶ球体の惑星であることがすでに示されているようで興味深いですね。（『科学の説明が聖書に近づいた』[レムナント出版] 久保有政著参照）

Section 2

Following the Gospel According to Matthew 25:31-40, there is a passage attributed to Jesus: What was not done for one of the poorest of people was also not done for me. This means that it is important that people actively help people deprived of the necessities of life. In Christianity, charitable activities intended for sick people, travelers or the poor were done actively based on such teaching from ancient times. The English word "charity," which means generosity towards the needy, is an anglicized word of "caritas" which means love in Latin. It can be said that social welfare activity in the modern period is influenced by this Christian culture in no small part.

●●●補足情報●●●

明治時代のキリスト教の布教家、教育者として、同志社の創始者の新島襄（1843〜1890）が有名である。新島は、初代文部大臣で一橋大学の創設者、森有礼や、慶應義塾の創設者の福沢諭吉などとならんで、明治六大教育家の1人に数えられている。渡米してアーモスト大学等に学び、アメリカに来た岩倉具視大使一行の知遇を受け、ともに欧米を巡歴、教育事情を視察した。日本において、キリスト教精神に基づく大学設立の構想と理念のもとに、残る生涯を同志社の発展に尽くして奔走し、その途次に倒れた。この遺志を引き継いだのが、妻の新島八重という人である。幕末のジャンヌ・ダルク、日本のナイチンゲールなどと呼ばれ、襄の死後、日本赤十字社に入り、看護学校で指導をしながら、篤志看護師として日清・日露戦の際に、救護活動に従事した。明治という時代にあって、先駆的な近代的女性として周囲の圧力や偏見に立ち向かい、不屈のキリスト者レディとして時代を生きた生き様は、数々の著書やテレビの歴史番組、ドラマでも取り上げられている。

第2節　キリスト教の基礎知識

⑩ キリスト教の習俗

● クリスマスの基礎知識
■ クリスマスの語源
　クリスマスはイエス・キリストの誕生を記念する祝日です。クリスマスという言葉の語源は、「キリストのミサ（Christ's Mass）」にあります。

■ クリスマスとミトラス教の関係
　キリスト教がローマ帝国に公認されたころ、ミトラス教（ミトラ教）も栄えていました。ミトラス教では、12月25日に、「ナタリス・インウィクティ」と呼ばれる祭典が行われていました。この祭典は不滅の太陽神の生誕を祝うものでした。キリスト教はこの習慣を取り入れ、イエス・キリストの生誕祭をこの日に行うようになったとされています。12月25日の生誕祭は、345年ころ、西方教会で始まりました。

■ クリスマスツリーとサンタクロース
　クリスマスツリーは、古代ゲルマン民族の「ユール」と呼ばれる冬至祭で使われていた樅（もみ）の木が原型であると言われています。クリスマスツリーを飾る習慣は、15世紀にドイツから広がり始め、イギリスでは1800年ころ、ビクトリア女王の夫であるアルバート公がウィンザー宮でクリスマスツリーを飾りつけたのが始まりとされています。アメリカに最初にツリーを伝えたのはドイツの移民で、1746年に伝わったとされています。また、日本では、1860年、プロイセンの使節オイレンブルクが公館に飾ったのが最初で、一般に浸透したのは1900年代になってからのことです。

Section 2

Christian Customs

● Basic knowledge about Christmas
■ Origin of the word Christmas

Christmas is a holiday to commemorate the birth of Jesus Christ. The word Christmas comes from Christ's Mass.

■ The relationship between Christmas and Mithraism

Mithraism also prospered when Christianity was recognized officially by the Roman Empire. The festival called "Natalis Invicti" was held in Mithraism on December 25th. This festival was held in celebration of the birth of the immortal sun god. It is assumed that Christianity incorporated this custom and the birth festival of Jesus Christ came to be held on this day. The birth festival held on December 25th started in the Western Church about 345.

■ Christmas Tree and Santa Claus

The Christmas tree is said to have originated from the fir tree burned in the Winter Solstice Festival called "Yule" of ancient Germanic peoples. It is believed that the custom of decorating the Christmas tree began to spread from Germany in the 15th century. In England, the custom originated in about 1800 when Prince Albert, the husband of Queen Victoria, decorated a Christmas tree in Windsor Castle. It is considered that it was German immigrants who brought with them the tradition of the Christmas tree to America in 1746. Moreover, in Japan, it originated in 1860 when the Prussian envoy Eulenburg decorated a Christmas tree in the official residence. The act of keeping and dressing a tree didn't reach the masses until the 1900s.

第2節　キリスト教の基礎知識

　サンタクロースは、小アジア（トルコ）の司教であった聖ニコラスの伝説が起源とされています。ニコラスは、殺された子供を生き返らせたり、船乗りを嵐から救ったりなど数々の伝説や奇跡が残っています。このように、聖ニコラスは様々な奇跡を起こし、船乗りや商人・子供など様々な人たちの守護聖人とされていました。

● バレンタインデーの基礎知識
■ バレンタインデーとは？
　バレンタインデーは、2月14日に祝われ、世界各地で、男女間で愛の誓いや贈り物をする日で、日本においては、もっぱら女性が男性にチョコレートを渡す日となっています。

■ バレンタインデーの起源
　ローマ帝国の時代、2月14日は女神ユノの祝日でした。ユノはローマ神話に登場する女神で、結婚や家庭を司る女神でした。ユノの祝日の翌日である2月15日は、豊穣を願うルペルカリア祭が行われる日でした。当時の若い男性たちと女性たちは、別々に生活していました。この祭りの前日（2月14日）に女性が名前を書いた札を桶の中に入れておき、15日に男性は桶から札を1枚ひき、その札に書かれた名前の女性と祭りの間のパートナーとして一緒に過ごす決まりとなっていました。そして、多くはそのまま恋に落ちて結婚したとのことです。これが、バレンタインデーの起源とされる、女神ユノの祝日の話です。
　バレンタインという言葉の語源は、269年にローマ皇帝の迫害を受けて殉教した聖バレンティヌスにあるとされています。当時のローマ皇帝クラウディウス2世は、士気が下がるという理由から、兵士の結婚を禁止していました。しかし、キリスト教の司祭であったバレンタティヌスは、兵士とその恋人を密かに結婚させ、それが明るみに出てしまい、処刑されました。ヴァレンティヌスが処刑された日がユノの祝日（2月14日）であったため、この日が男女の愛の誓いの日となりました。

Section 2

It is assumed that Santa Claus originated from the legend of St. Nicholas, who was a bishop in Asia Minor (Turkey). A number of legends and miracles about Nicholas remain such as him reviving a deceased child and saving a sailor from a storm. Thus, St. Nicholas performed various miracles and is worshipped as the patron saint for various people such as sailors, merchants, and children.

● Basic knowledge about Valentine's Day
■ What is Valentine's Day?

Valentine's Day is celebrated on February 14, when men and women around the world express their love with the exchange of gifts. In Japan, women almost exclusively give chocolates to men on that day.

■ Origin of Valentine's Day

In the age of the Roman Empire, February 14th was the feast day of the goddess Juno. Juno was the goddess of marriage and family in Roman mythology. On February 15th, the next day of the feast dedicated to Juno, the Lupercalia festival took place where people would pray for a good harvest. At that time in Roman culture there was a certain degree of segregation between men and women and it was unlikely that men and women would share the same quarters. However, on the day before this festival (February 14), the women put cards with their names written on them into a tub from which each man picked a card on February 15th. The man was supposed to get acquainted with and spend time with the woman whose name was written on the card for the duration of the festival. Many of these impromptu couples are said to have fallen in love naturally and married. This is the story of the feast day of the goddess Juno, which is believed to be the origin of Valentine's Day.

The origin of the word Valentine is believed to be derived from St. Valentinus, who was persecuted and martyred under the Roman Empire in 269. Claudius II, the Roman Emperor at that time prohibited soldiers from marrying for marriage was believed to lower morale. However, Valentinus who was a Christian priest, allowed a soldier to marry his

第2節　キリスト教の基礎知識

● ハロウィーンの基礎知識
■ ハロウィーンとは？
　ハロウィーンとは、秋の収穫を祝い、悪霊を追い出す祭りのことを言います。

■ ハロウィーンの語源
　ハロウィーンの語源は、キリスト教の「万聖節の前夜祭」を意味する"All Hallows' Eve"にあり、それが短縮され、Halloweenと呼ばれるようになりました。万聖節とは、毎年11月1日にあらゆる聖人を祭るキリスト教の祝日のことです。

■ ハロウィーンの起源
　ハロウィーンは、古代ケルト・古代ローマ・キリスト教の3つの慣習が融合した結果生まれました。

　ハロウィーンの起源となる1つ目の慣習として、ドルイド教を信仰する古代ケルト人の「サーウィン祭」（サムハイン祭）と呼ばれる収穫感謝祭があります。古代ケルト人の1年の暦では、11月1日が新年であり、前日の10月31日が大晦日でした。この日の夜には、死者の魂が家族のもとに戻り、悪霊や魔女がさまよい歩くと信じられていました。そのため、人々はかがり火を焚いて悪霊を追い払おうとしました。

　2つ目の慣習として、古代ローマの「果実の収穫祭（果実の女神ポモナの祭り）」があります。ケルト人の住んでいたブリテン島は1世紀ころ、ローマ帝国による侵略を受けたため、上記ケルト人の祭りに古代ローマの収穫祭が融合していきました。その後、ローマにキリスト教が伝わると、ケルト人の祭りと、古代ローマの祭り、そしてキリスト教の万聖節前夜祭（3つ目の慣習）が混ざり合い、現在のハロウィーンの行事となりました。

Section 2

lover in secret. After the secret wedding was revealed, he was tried and executed under Roman law. Because the day Valentinus was executed was the feast day of Juno (February 14th), this day became the day when men and women declared their love for one another.

● Basic knowledge about Halloween
■ What is Halloween?

Halloween is a festival that celebrates the autumn harvest and drives out evil spirits.

■ Origin of the word Halloween

The word Halloween is derived from the term "All Hallows' Eve" which means the eve of All Saints' Day of Christianity. It was shortened and came to be called Halloween. All Hallows' Day is a holiday of Christianity that celebrates all saints on November 1st every year.

■ Origin of Halloween

Halloween grew from a combination of three observances of the ancient Celts, the ancient Romans, and Christianity.

One of the observances that contributes to the origin of Halloween is the harvest thanksgiving called "Samhain Festival" of the ancient Celts who believed in druidism. According to the ancient Celtic calendar, November 1st was New Year's Day and October 31st, a day before New Year's Day, was New Year's Eve. It was believed that the souls of the dead returned to the family and evil spirits and witches wandered on this night. Therefore, people tried to drive away the evil spirits by making a bonfire.

The second observance is "Fruit Harvest Festival (the festival of Pomona, the goddess of fruit trees)" in the ancient Rome. Since Celtic Britain was invaded and occupied by the Roman Empire around the 1st century, the harvest festival of ancient Rome merged with the above-mentioned Celtic festival. After that, when Christianity spread to Rome, the Celtic festival, the festival of ancient Rome, and All Hallows' Eve

第2節　キリスト教の基礎知識

■ "Trick or Treat" の起源

"Trick or Treat" の起源は、農民が祭り用の食料をもらって村から村へ歩いた様子を真似たものと言われています。

● イースターの基礎知識
■ イースターとは？

イースター（復活祭）とは、キリスト教でイエス・キリストの復活を祝う祭りで、キリスト教で最も古く、最も重要な儀式です。キリスト教では、イエスは十字架に架けられた3日後に復活したとされています。イースターは、春分の日の後の、最初の満月の次の日曜日に行われることになっており、毎年日付が変わる移動祝日です。西方教会では、この方法によってイースターの日付が決まりますが、東方教会では、別の計算方法を用いるため、東西教会でイースターを祝う日が異なることもあります。

■ イースターの起源

イースターという名前の由来は、豊かな恵みと春を象徴するゲルマン神話の春の女神「エオストレ」にあると考えられています（これは、8世紀のキリスト教聖職者ベーダが唱えた説です）。ゲルマン民族の間では、エオストレの祝日である春分の日に春の到来を祝う祭りを行っていました。そして、キリスト教の布教とともに、ゲルマン民族の慣習がキリストの復活祭という慣習の中に取り入れられていったということです。

Section 2

of Christianity (the third observance) were combined and became what Halloween is today.

■ Origin of "Trick or Treat"

The origin of "trick or treat" is said to be mimicry of the farmers who walked from village to village asking for food for a festival.

● Basic knowledge about Easter
■ What is Easter?

Easter is a Christian festival that celebrates the Resurrection of Jesus Christ, which is the oldest and the most important Christian observance. In Christianity, it is believed that Jesus was resurrected three days after he was put on the cross. Easter is always celebrated on the Sunday immediately following the first full moon after the Vernal Equinox and is a moveable feast, meaning that the date varies from year to year. The date of Easter is decided in the Western Church based on this method. However, since the Eastern Church uses another computational method, the day when Easter is celebrated can differ between the East and the West church.

■ Origin of Easter

It is thought that the word Easter is derived from the goddess of spring in Germanic mythology, "Eostre" that symbolizes abundant gifts and spring. (This is a theory that Beda, a Christian clergy of the 8th century, advocated.) The festival that celebrated the coming of spring was conducted on the Vernal Equinox, the feast day of Eostre among Germanic peoples. Germanic custom was incorporated into the custom of celebrating Christ's resurrection with the propagation of Christianity.

第2節　キリスト教の基礎知識

■ イースターエッグとイースター・バニー

イースターのシンボルの1つに、イースターエッグがあります。生命や復活を象徴するものとして卵が使われ、復活祭の典礼中は、信者たちが持ち寄った染め卵が成聖[注]され、信者同士で卵を贈り合う習慣がありました。

もう1つのシンボルにイースター・バニーがあります。子だくさんのうさぎは、古代より、繁栄・多産の象徴とされており、イースターの卵は、イースター・バニーが運んでくるとされていました。

> **関連情報　神聖にすること**
>
> 　本文で「成聖」という語が出てきましたが（注の箇所）、「成聖」は「せいせい」と読み、「聖なるものと成す」ということで、神聖なものに変化することを表します。これは正教会での用語で、カトリックや聖公会では「聖別」（せいべつ）と言います。「成聖」や「聖別」は、具体的には、聖職者の祈りによって、礼拝で使用する器具などを聖なるものとし、他の被造物とは別のものとすることです。聖別解除がなされるまでは、宗教上のものとし、別の目的に使えないとされています。「成聖」や「聖別」の英語は、consecrationが一般的です。動詞では consecrate のほかに、sanctify も使用できます。

Section 2

■ Easter egg and Easter bunny

One of the symbols of Easter is an Easter egg. Eggs were used as a symbol of life and resurrection. During the liturgy of Easter, dyed eggs which believers all brought were consecrated and then customarily presented to one another.

Another symbol is the Easter bunny. The rabbit was a symbol of fertility and prosperity from ancient times, and the egg at Easter was believed to be brought by the Easter bunny.

① キリスト教と仏教
類似点と相違点

■ **キリスト教と仏教の類似点**

キリスト教と仏教は異なる面が多いのですが、共通する点としては、ともに世界宗教で、特定の民族のために存在する民族宗教ではないという点です。だから世界宗教としての特徴が共通しています。例えば、教祖や教典が存在します。キリスト教の場合、教祖はイエス、教典は聖書、仏教の場合は、教祖は釈迦、教典には様々なもの（諸経）があります。

■ **キリスト教と顕教との類似点**

キリスト教では、イエス・キリストを通じて神（＝ゴッド）の御心を知るのですが、仏教の顕教（＝仏教における密教以外のすべての宗派）では、釈迦を通して宇宙仏（＝大ビルシャナ仏）の言葉を知る点が共通していると言えます。

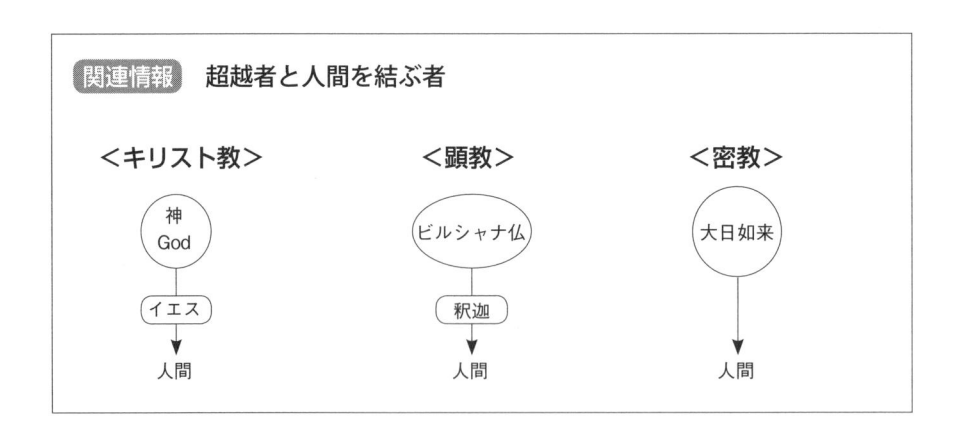

関連情報 超越者と人間を結ぶ者

```
<キリスト教>        <顕教>          <密教>

 (神              (ビルシャナ仏)    (大日如来)
  God)
   ↓                 ↓               ↓
 [イエス]           [釈迦]
   ↓                 ↓               ↓
  人間              人間             人間
```

Section 3

Christianity and Buddhism
Similarities and differences

■ similarities between Christianity and Buddhism

There are many differences between Christianity and Buddhism. A common point is both exist on a global-scale and not for the benefits of a specific ethnic group. In Christianity the founder is Jesus and the religious scripture is the Bible (made up of many books or letters). In Buddhism the founder is Buddha and scripture is comprised of many books.

■ similarities between Christianity and exoteric Buddhist teachings

In Christianity, Christians realize the will of God through Jesus Christ. On the other hand, in exoteric Buddhist teachings (all denominations except Tantric Buddhism), people who believe in exoteric Buddhism realize the word of Buddha of the Universe (Buddha Vairocana) through Gautama Buddha. In view of this, both religions have something in common.

カトリック

仏教

プロテスタント

第3節　キリスト教と他の宗教を比べてみる

注：仏教における密教で代表格と言えば真言宗ですが、こちらは大日如来という宇宙仏の説法を、釈迦を通さず直接聴聞しようとする宗派と言えるでしょう。大日如来のメッセージを受けるために、身口意の三密の修行が必要ということになります（「→」のあとに代表的・象徴的な修行を示す）。

　　身：体の修行　→ 手で印を結ぶこと（印相）
　　口：言葉の修行　→ マントラ（真言）を唱えること
　　意：心の修行　→ マンダラ（曼荼羅）を観想すること

参考：「口」は「体」（肉体・行動）と「心」（思考・感情）を結ぶ器官で、言葉のみならず食べ物や呼吸と関係している。悪い言葉（罵詈雑言［ばりぞうごん］やマイナスの言葉）を発し、悪い食べ物（ジャンクフードなど）を食べ、悪い呼吸（浅い肺呼吸など）をしていたら、身も心も悪化していくのは目に見えているね。

■ キリスト教と仏教の考え方の違い

　キリスト教と仏教の表面上の違いは、p.24を参照していただければ理解できると思うので、ここでは、キリスト教と仏教の考え方の違いについて学びましょう。表にまとめてみます。

・神の概念

キリスト教	仏　教
神は唯一全知全能	仏教を保護する天の存在 ＊仏教では神は仏（＝悟った存在）の下に位置する。

・宇宙のあり方

キリスト教	仏　教
宇宙は神の創造物 ＊もちろん、森羅万象からすべての動物そして人間まであらゆるものの創造は神の手によるものと考える。	宇宙ははじめから存在 ＊天地創造という発想が存在しない。

Section 3

Note : The esoteric Buddhism is represented by the Shingon sect of Buddhism, under which we can say believers are supposed to listen directly to the teaching of the Buddha of the Universe called Dainichi, or Great Sun Buddha, without a help of Gautama. Therefore, three mystic practices are necessary for the reception of the message from Dainichi. (The keyword is shown in the brackets)

- Shin : "body" practice → Symbolic gestures performed with fingers [Mudra]
- Ku : "mouth" practice → Mantra chanting [Mantra]
- I : "mind" practice → Contemplation through Mandalas [Mandala]

■ **Differences in way of thinking between Christianity and Buddhism**

The superficial differences between Christianity and Buddhism are explained on p.25. Below are listed the differences in the ways of thinking between Christianity and Buddhism.

・**Notion of god(s)**

Christianity	Buddhism
There is only one God and He is omniscient and omnipotent.	The celestial existence which protects Buddhism ＊In Buddhism, gods are under Buddha (the one who is spiritually awakened).

注目：「全知」は omniscient（名詞は omniscience）、
　　　「全能」は omnipotent（名詞は omnipotence）。

・**The birth of the universe**

Christianity	Buddhism
The universe was made by God. ＊Of course, it says that everything, creatures and human beings were made by God.	The universe has existed without a beginning. ＊Buddhism has no teaching of the Creation.

第3節　キリスト教と他の宗教を比べてみる

・「愛」について

キリスト教	仏　教
「愛すること」は重要 ＊キリスト教は、ユダヤ教が強調する律法を超えたものとして愛の重要性を訴えた「愛の宗教」とも言えます。	「愛すること」は危険 ＊仏教では「愛」は執着を意味し、否定されます。しかし、「慈悲」(他人を理解し共感する心)を重視します。

・終末観

キリスト教	仏　教
終末論 ＊最後の審判で、人が天国行きか地獄行きが決まる。この発想は仏教にはありません。	末法思想 ＊西洋の発展型歴史観と対局にある「時代はだんだん悪くなる」という下降型歴史観。

・前世

キリスト教	仏　教
存在しない	存在する ＊輪廻転生の教えがあり、魂は流転します。死によって体を失いますが、また体を持って、六道の世界の1つに生まれます。

・「殺」について

キリスト教	仏　教
人を殺してはならない ＊モーセの十戒の1つに「殺すなかれ」とあるが、これは殺人をするな！と戒めています。	全生命体を殺してはならない ＊人に限らず、生けとし生けるものの生命を大切にすることを重視します。

・ひと言で「どんな教え？」

キリスト教	仏　教
救世主であるイエスの教え ＊神やイエスになるための教えではありません。そんな絶対者には到底なれません。	仏の教えであるとともに仏になるための教え ＊仏という超越者になる（＝成仏する＝悟る）ことが重要。

Section 3

• About "love"

Christianity	Buddhism
Loving" is important. ＊It can be considered that Christianity is a "religion of love" because in Christianity, the importance of love is regarded as above the original Jewish teachings of the Torah.	"Loving" is dangerous. ＊In Buddhism, "love" is regarded as attachment and frowned upon. However, "mercy" (feelings which understand others and empathize with them) is regarded as important.

• Notion of the end of the world or final fate of humans

Christianity	Buddhism
eschatology ＊In the Grand Inquest, it is decided that the dead should go to heaven or hell. This idea is not taught in Buddhism.	pessimism due to decadent-age theory ＊This thought is antipodal to the constructive historical standpoint in the West. It is a cyclical historical standpoint that times gradually go wrong.

• Previous life

Christianity	Buddhism
Christianity doesn't espouse transmigration or reincarnation. 注目：transmigration は「輪廻」、reincarnation は「転生」。	Buddhism has this idea. ＊Buddhism has the thought called samsara where souls are in state of flux. After death, human beings lose their bodies but are reborn in a new body.

• About the notion of "killing"

Christianity	Buddhism
Don't murder human beings ＊In one of the Decalogue (＝Decalog), "Do not commit murder" is written.	Don't kill any living creature. ＊Buddhism regards not only human beings' life but also every creature's life as important.

• At a word "what kind of doctrine?"

Christianity	Buddhism
the doctrine of Jesus, who is Messiah. ＊It is not the doctrine to become God or Jesus. It is impossible to become the Creator.	the doctrine of Buddha and to become Buddha ＊It is important to become a Buddha, which is the goal of Buddhists.

宗教の基礎知識 | キリスト教を知る | 聖書を知る | ユダヤ教を知る | イスラム教を知る

第3節　キリスト教と他の宗教を比べてみる

❷ キリスト教とユダヤ教
類似点と相違点

■ キリスト教とユダヤ教の類似点
　どちらも唯一絶対神を信奉する点で一致しています。旧約聖書を聖典の1つとする点も共通しています。さらに、エルサレムも共通した聖地です。

■ キリスト教とユダヤ教の宗教学的分類における違い
　キリスト教は、（仏教やイスラム教と同じく）信者を限定せず、世界に広がる可能性を秘めた世界宗教であるのに対し、ユダヤ教はユダヤ人のみが信仰する民族宗教である点が異なっています。

■ 神の概念における微妙な差
　ユダヤ教が純粋に唯一の存在として神を信奉するのに対し、キリスト教では後世には緩やかな神概念が取り入れられました。その代表と言えるものが「三位一体説」です。神とキリストと聖霊[注1]が微妙なバランスで神として存在するという発想が、三位一体説です。キリストは神の子で救世主、いわば神の化身的存在です。一方、聖霊はいわば神の霊です。

1　日本ハリストス正教会では、「聖霊」に対し、「聖神（せいしん）」という訳語を採用している。

参考：日本ハリストス正教会（Orthodox Church in Japan：OCJ）は、自治独立が認められている正教会に所属する教会。ロシア正教会の聖ニコライによって建てられたニコライ堂（正式名称「東京復活大聖堂」：東京都千代田区神田駿河台）は、日本における代表的なビザンティン建築。1962年6月21日国の重要文化財に指定された。

■ 旧約と新約
　一般にキリスト教における聖書は、「旧約聖書」と「新約聖書」から成っています。そもそも「約」とは、神と人の間に交わされた契約ということです。

Section 3

Christianity and Judaism
Similarities and differences

■ **similarities between Christianity and Judaism**

Christianity and Judaism both teach the existence of a single divine Creator-God. Moreover, they regard the Old Testament as one of the sacred books. In addition, Jerusalem is the holiest place to both Christianity and Judaism.

■ **differences between Christianity and Judaism in the classification of science of religions**

Christianity (like Buddhism or Islam) doesn't limit any race from joining or person from converting and it is a world religion which has expanded around the globe. On the other hand, Judaism is an ethnic religion. In this regard, both are different.

■ **minor differences in the notion of the Creator**

Whereas in Judaism people genuinely believe in God as an infinite divine being, in Christianity a new notion of God evolved over the early years of the religion. This view of God is known as "Trinitarianism." This means that God, Jesus, and the Holy Spirit exist as God as one being made of three. Jesus is the Son of God and also the Messiah; an incarnation of God. On the other hand, the Holy Spirit represents the spirit of God on earth.

■ **the Old and New Testaments**

In general, the Bible is composed of "the Old Testament (kyuyaku)" and "the New Testament (shinyaku)" in Christianity. "Yaku" refers to the original covenant between God and human beings.

第3節　キリスト教と他の宗教を比べてみる

　キリスト教では、旧約聖書を神との旧い契約書として認め、イエスの言行録を含めた新約聖書を神との新しい契約として最重要の聖典としています。一方、ユダヤ教では新約聖書を、聖典として認めません。

■ 偶像崇拝について

　ユダヤ教の発想では、神に形はなく、見ることができない、人知をはるかに超えた存在です。だから、偶像に表すことなどは到底できません。しかも、神以外に超越者は認めないので、偶像崇拝自体を厳しく禁じています。

　これに対しキリスト教では、肉の身を持ったイエスを神の子とすることから、人が神を見て、神の声を聞き、会話したという歴史を持っていると言えます。特にカトリック教会では、絵や像として存在する十字架上のキリスト像や聖母像を崇拝の対象とすることが許されています。つまり、他の宗教の超越者の偶像は禁止であるものの、偶像崇拝自体を厳しく禁じているわけではありません。

....

注１：イエスは、キリスト教では救世主であるが、ユダヤ教では単なる賢者にすぎない。
注２：救世主出現は、ゼパニヤ（ゼファニヤ）書、ミカ書、ダニエル書などに多く預言されているが、キリスト教がきわめて重要な預言として注目しているのが、イザヤ書53章に記された「主の僕［しもべ］の苦難と死」という預言詩です。この中にのちのイエスの言行に一致することが多く見られるので、イエスがキリスト（＝救世主）であると主張するのである。

関連情報　ユダヤ教とキリスト教（イエス）の教えの違い

ユダヤ教	イエスの教え
律法主義を通し形を重視する。	形式的な律法よりも心を重視する。
選民思想（elitism）…ユダヤ人は神に選ばれた。	民族の違いを乗り越え、病人も罪人も全ての人を救済する。
蔑視の対象…病人、罪人、サマリア人、ローマ人、徴税人、売春婦など。	
姦淫は重い罪として認識する。	原罪思想に基づき、姦淫した者にその罪を深く自覚させるとともに、赦しへの道を示す。さらに、姦淫した者を責めるなどの表面的な律法主義や偽善への批判をする。
隣人を愛し、敵を憎め。	敵味方なく、隣人を愛せ。（隣人愛）
復讐の思想：目には目を、歯には歯を。	復讐の禁止：右の頬を打たれたら、左の頬を出せ。

注：有名な「目には目を、歯には歯を」は旧約聖書「出エジプト記」第21章24節にある。

Section 3

In Christianity, it is recognized that the Old Testament is the old covenant with God. Because the New Testament, including its records of Jesus' words and deeds, is the new contract with God, it is regarded as the most important of the sacred books. On the other hand, in Judaism the New Testament is not recognized.

■ about idolatry

Judaism teaches that the Creator is completely transcendental, we can't see it, and it is beyond human's capacity to fully understand. Therefore, it is impossible to put the Creator on a pedestal as a carving or such. Because of this, idolatry is strictly forbidden in Judaism.

On the other hand, because Jesus existed as a real historical figure and because there are past examples of people who claimed to see and hear God, statues and other forms of idolatry have come to exist in Christianity. It is common for statues and artwork of not only Jesus, but also His mother, angels, and saints to be displayed in and around churches, especially Catholic Churches. While this form of idolatry is not prohibited, putting up images of another religion's figures is not allowed.

Note 1 : Jesus is the Messiah in Christianity but he is simply a wise person in Judaism.

Note 2 : The appearance of a Messiah is prophesied in the books such as the books of Zephaniah, Micah, and Daniel. In Christianity, a prophetic poem containing "he surely took up our infirmities and carried our sorrows ...," described in Isaiah 53, is read as the most important prophetical writing. The later New Testament stories of Jesus Christ fulfill many of the prophecies of Isaiah and the mentioning of the coming Messiah.

●Useful Usage● FULFILL
1. She fulfilled her promise. （彼女は約束を果たした）［約束などを果たす］
2. He fulfilled his hopes. （彼は願望を達成した）［願望などを達成する］
3. The plan fulfills the purpose. （その計画は目的にかなう）［目的などにかなう］

第3節　キリスト教と他の宗教を比べてみる

❸ キリスト教とイスラム教
類似点と相違点

■ キリスト教とイスラム教の類似点

唯一全知全能の神を有する点が共通しています。両宗教は、神の名前は異なりますが、1つの神しか認めない一神教であることには違いありません。

■ 預言者と救世主に対する発想の違い

どちらの宗教も預言者の存在を認めていますが、預言者の1人であるイエスやムハンマドをどう見るか？について、2つの宗教は根本的に異なります。

キリスト教では、イエスは神の子であり、救世主です。イスラム教では、イエスは預言者として認めていますが、救世主ではありません。イスラム教では、創始者のムハンマドは、預言者であるが、救世主ではありません。キリスト教では、ムハンマドは預言者と認めていません。

....

参考：イエスはキリスト教では救世主、イスラム教では預言者の1人、ユダヤ教ではラビ（rabbi＝優れた教師）の1人。

■ 聖職者の有無

キリスト教には、他のほとんどの宗教と同じで、聖職者（＝宗教上重要な地位に就いている人間で、宗教を職業にしていると言える人）が存在します。例えば、カトリック教の神父やプロテスタントの牧師が聖職者です。一方、イスラム教には聖職者が存在しません。これは、聖と俗の分離を認めないからで、どの人間も神のもとでは平等であることが強調されています。そして、当然のことながら、イスラム国家は政教分離国家ではなく、祭政一致国家ということになるのです。

Section 3

Christianity and Islam
Similarities and differences

■ Similarities between Christianity and Islam

Christianity and Islam are similar in that both religions worship one almighty supreme being. Therefore, both religions are monotheistic religions which permit only one god, although their gods go by different names.

注目：仏教の阿弥陀信仰では阿弥陀仏のみを拝むよう勧めるが、他の仏も認めるので、一神教（monotheism）ではなく一神崇拝（monolatry）と呼ばれる。

■ Difference in notions of prophets and the Savior

Both religions acknowledge the existence of prophets, but they basically differ on how they interpret the prophecies.

In Christianity, Jesus is the Son of God and the Savior (the Messiah; the Redeemer) of human kind. Islam acknowledges Jesus as a prophet but doesn't regard him as the Savior. In Islam, its founder, Muhammad is a prophet but not the Savior. In Christianity, Muhammad isn't acknowledged as a prophet.

■ Existence or non-existence of clergy

In Christianity, clergy (a devoted person who adopts religion as a profession) exists like in almost all other religions. For example, a Catholic priest and Protestant minister are members of the clergy. On the other hand, the clergy doesn't exist in Islam. This is because it doesn't acknowledge the separation of saints and the secular, and emphasizes everyone should be equal before God. As a matter of course, an Islamic state doesn't acknowledge the separation of religion and politics but instead incorporates both as part of the government.

第3節　キリスト教と他の宗教を比べてみる

■ 共同体の違い

　キリスト教の信者の共同体は「教会」であると考えてよいでしょう。つまり、教会は単なる建物ではなく、「キリストの体」であると同時に「神の民」としての信徒の集団を意味しています。

　一方、イスラム教では共同体はウンマと呼ばれます。これは元来「母」と同義で、「部族」の意味を持ち、部族の強い結束を特色とする遊牧社会を背景に生まれました。現在は、この共同体は、コーランの言葉であるアラビア語を共通語として、世俗の法律や風俗習慣の基礎となるイスラム法によって民族や国家を超えて広がっています。

■ 妻の数の規定

　イスラム教は、妻の数を4人までと定めている唯一の一神教です。これは、同じ一神教のユダヤ教やキリスト教と異なる点です。

....

参考：イスラム教が一夫多妻を認めている点を批判することはできないであろう。歴史を通じ、世界の全地域で裕福な男性は多くの女性と性的関係を結ぶ傾向にあり、そのような現実においては、妾を4人以上持つよりは、正式な妻を4人まで持つというほうが道徳的であるという側面もある。

> **関連情報　女子の早婚**
>
> 　イスラム社会の問題として女子の早婚があげられます。これはイスラム法における女子の最低結婚年齢が9歳であることに起因します。この9歳という年齢は、イスラム教の開祖ムハンマドが結婚したアーイシャという妻との初交渉の年齢です。イランなどイスラム法を遵守する一部のイスラム国では、女子は9歳から結婚できます。さらに、イエメンでは最低結婚年齢を定めない方針をとっています。だから、9歳未満の女子との結婚も可能ということになり、問題視されることもあります。

Section 3

> **●Useful Usage● INCORPORATE**
> 1. He was incorporated a member of the society for the annual fee of $600.
>   (彼は年会費600ドルでその会の会員となった)
> 2. The radical idea eventually incorporated with convention.
>   (結果的に、その急進的な発想が因習と融合した)

■ The difference of community

The community of believers in Christianity is called the church. That is, the church isn't just a building, but means a congregation of People of God as well as the Body of Christ.

On the other hand, an Islamic community is called an Ummah. This word is originally the same as 'Mother' in meaning, which now means 'tribe' and was derived based on a pastoral society where strong bonds among tribes are characteristic. This community, whose common language is the Koranic language, Arabic, is spreading across nations by Islamic law which forms their basis of secular law and manners and customs.

■ The regulation concerning the number of wives

Islam is the only monotheism in which a man is allowed up to four wives. This is where Islam differs from the same monotheistic religion like Christianity or Judaism.

第 3 章

聖書を知る

第1節

聖書の基礎知識

■ 聖書とは?

聖書とは、キリスト教の正典のことで、「旧約聖書」と「新約聖書」の2部から構成されています。

■ 旧約聖書の構成と各書の特徴

旧約聖書はヘブライ語で書かれた39の書物から成り、キリスト教の旧約聖書の場合は、大きく分けて、「律法」(5巻)、「歴史書」(12巻)、「詩歌書」(5巻)、「預言書」(17巻)の4つに分類されます。以下に4つの書物の特徴を述べていきます。

・律法

律法とは、モーセ五書とも呼ばれ、以下の5つの書から成ります。

…創世記、出エジプト記、レビ記、民数［みんすう］記、申命［しんめい］記

「創世記」は、天地創造の物語から始まり、アダムとイブと楽園喪失、カインとアベル、ノアの箱舟、バベルの塔などの物語が記され、最後にヨセフ物語で終わっています。「出エジプト記」から「申命記」までは、モーセを通じて神から与えられたイスラエルの律法が述べられています。

・歴史書

歴史書にはイスラエル民族の歴史的な体験がつづられています。歴史書は以下の12の書から成ります。

…ヨシュア記、士師記、ルツ記、サムエル記（上下）、列王記（上下）、歴代誌（上下）、エズラ記、ネヘミヤ記、エステル記

Section 1

Basic knowledge about the Bible

■ What is the Bible?

The Bible is the Christian biblical canon and is composed of two parts, the "Old Testament" and the "New Testament."

■ Composition of the Old Testament and features of each book

The Old Testament consists of 39 books originally written in Hebrew. In the case of the Christian Old Testament, it is roughly classified into 4 categories: 5 books of "Law," 12 books of "History," 5 books of "Poetry," and 17 books of "Prophecy." The features of the four books are described as follows.

• **Books of Law**

The law is also known as the Five Books of Moses and consists of the following 5 books: Genesis, Exodus, Leviticus, Numbers, and Deuteronomy. "Genesis" starts from the Creation story followed by such stories as the advent of humanity through Adam and Eve, the fall from grace, Cain and Abel, Noah's ark, and the Tower of Babel, and ends with the Story of Joseph. The law of Israel given by God through Moses is described in the books from "Exodus" to "Deuteronomy."

• **Books of History**

The historical experience of Israeli peoples is written in the books of History, which consists of the following 12 books: Book of Joshua, Book of Judges, Book of Ruth, Books of Samuel (two-volume book), Books of Kings (two-volume book), Books of Chronicles (two-volume book), Book of Ezra, Book of Nehemiah, Book of Esther.

第1節　聖書の基礎知識

・詩歌書

詩歌書は、次の5つの書から成ります。

…ヨブ記、詩編、箴言［しんげん］、コヘレトの言葉（伝道の書）、雅歌［がか］

ヨブ記・箴言・コヘレトの言葉は「知恵文学」と呼ばれています。「詩編」は150編から成る神への賛美の詩で、雅歌は愛の歌を集めたものです。

参考：ヘブライ語聖書については208～210ページ参照。ヘブライ語聖書とは、ユダヤ教聖書のことであり、キリスト教の旧約聖書と内容は同じだが、配列が異なる。

・預言書

預言書は、預言者（神から預かった言葉を民に伝えた指導者のこと）の言葉を集めたもので、以下の17の文書から成っています。

イザヤ書、エレミヤ書、哀歌、エゼキエル書、ダニエル書、ホセア書、ヨエル書、アモス書、オバデヤ書、ヨナ書、ミカ書、ナホム書、ハバクク書、ゼファニヤ書、ハガイ書、ゼカリヤ書、マラキ書

参考：イザヤ書からダニエル書までの5巻を大預言書、残りの12巻を小預言書と呼ぶ。またイザヤ書、エレミヤ書、エゼキエル書は三大預言書とされる。

■ 新約聖書の構成と各書の特徴

新約聖書は、ギリシャ語で書かれた27の書から成り立っています。その構成と各書の概要は以下の通りです。

・福音書（4巻）

福音書は、イエスの生涯とその言葉を伝える書物で、以下の4つから構成されています。「マタイによる福音書」「マルコによる福音書」「ルカによる福音書」「ヨハネによる福音書」

・使徒言行録（使徒行伝）（1巻）

使徒言行録は、イエスの使徒たちの働きを、ペトロとパウロを中心に、歴史的視点で述べたものです。使徒言行録は、「ルカによる福音書」とともにルカが著者であるとされています。

Section 1

• Books of Poetry

The books of Poetry consist of the following 5 books: Book of Job, Psalms, Proverbs, Ecclesiastes, Song of Solomon (= Song of Songs), Book of Job, Proverbs and Ecclesiastes are called "Wisdom literature." "Psalms" consists of 150 poems of praise to God, and the Songs of Solomon is a collection of love poems.

• Books of Prophecy

The books of prophecy are a collection of sermons by prophets (leaders who passed on divine prophecy to the people) and consist of the following 17 books: Book of Isaiah, Book of Jeremiah, Book of Lamentations, Book of Ezekiel, Book of Daniel, Book of Hosea, Book of Joel, Book of Amos, Book of Obadiah, Book of Jonah, Book of Micah, Book of Nahum, Book of Habakkuk, Book of Zephaniah, Book of Haggai, Book of Zechariah, Book of Malachi.

■ Composition of the New Testament and features of each book

The New Testament consists of 27 books originally written in Greek. The composition and features of each book are as follows.

• Gospels (4 books)

The Gospels are the books that convey the life of Jesus and his words, and are composed of the following 4 books: "Gospel of Matthew," "Gospel of Mark," "Gospel of Luke," "Gospel of John."

• Acts of the Apostles (1 book)

The Acts of the Apostles is the book in which the activities of the apostles of Jesus, especially Peter and Paul, were described from a historical standpoint. The author of this book is assumed to be Luke who also wrote the "Gospel of Luke."

第1節　聖書の基礎知識

・書簡（21巻）

　書簡は、パウロの書簡13巻と公同書簡7巻を含みます。書簡には、パウロやその他の弟子たちが各地の教会や信者宛てに送った手紙が収められています。

・ヨハネの黙示録（1巻）

　「ヨハネの黙示録」は、ローマ皇帝による厳しい迫害にさらされていた教会と信者たちに対して、帝国（世界）の崩壊が近づいており、キリストの再臨の近いことを告げ、希望を与える目的で記されたとされています。

注：新約聖書唯一の預言書である。

旧約聖書

律法[モーセ五書]（5巻）
| 創世記 | 出エジプト記 | レビ記 | 民数記 | 申命記 |

歴史書（12巻）
| ヨシュア記 | 士師記 | ルツ記 | サムエル記 | … | エステル記 |

詩歌書[知恵文学]（5巻）
| ヨブ記 | 詩編 | 箴言 | コヘレトの言葉 | 雅歌 |

預言書（17巻）
| イザヤ書 | エレミヤ書 | 哀歌 | エゼキエル書 | ダニエル書 | … 12巻 |

大預言書　小預言書

Section 1

- **Epistles (21 books)**

　The Epistles include 13 Pauline epistles and 7 General epistles. They contain the letters that were sent to the churches and the believers of various places by Paul and other church leaders.

- **Book of Revelation (1 book)**

　It is considered that the "Book of Revelation" was a book of hope written to inform churches and believers who were under severe persecution by the Roman Empire that the collapse of the Empire (world) was near and would usher in the second coming of Jesus.

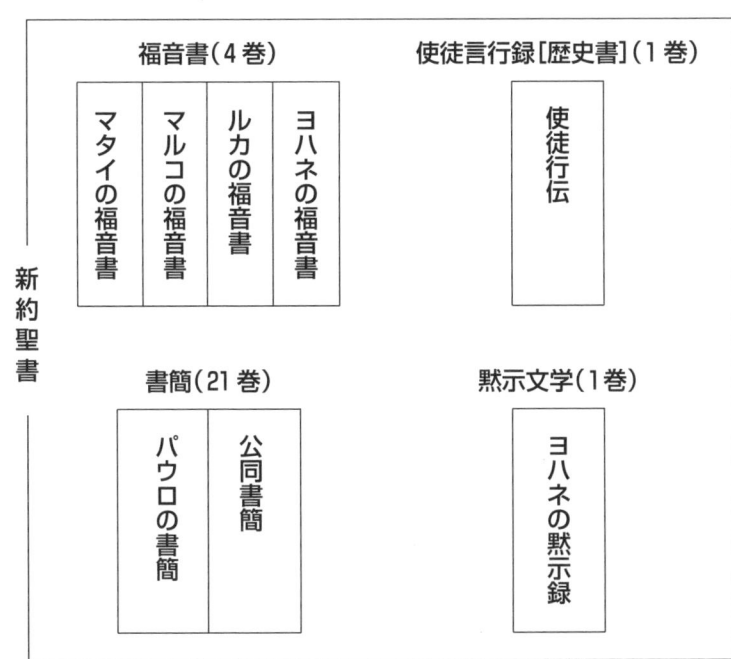

新約聖書	福音書（4巻）				使徒言行録［歴史書］（1巻）
	マタイの福音書	マルコの福音書	ルカの福音書	ヨハネの福音書	使徒行伝
	書簡（21巻）				黙示文学（1巻）
	パウロの書簡	公同書簡			ヨハネの黙示録

第2節

旧約聖書の世界

1 天地創造

■ 7日間の天地創造

　キリスト教の神は、7日間で天地を創造しました。何をどのように創造したのか、順に説明しましょう。

　初日に、神は、「光あれ!」と言って、光を創りました。そして光は闇から分けられたので、光を「昼」、闇を「夜」と名づけました。

　2日目、神は「天空あれ!」と命じ、天空を創りました。そして水を上下に分けました。天空は、「空」と名づけられました。

　3日目、神は下の水に対し、1カ所に集まるように命じ、乾いた土地が現れるようにしました。ここで、下の水は「海」、乾いた土地は「陸地」と名づけられました。陸地には植物が繁茂し、果物が実るよう命じました。

　4日目、神は天空に太陽・月・星を創造し、日や季節や年ができました。太陽は昼を、月は夜を司りました。

　5日目、神は海に魚が泳ぐよう、空には鳥が飛ぶよう命じ、魚や鳥が創造されました。そして、彼らに増えるよう命令しました。

　6日目、神は陸地に生き物がいるよう命じ、野獣・家畜や爬虫類が創造されました。そして、最後に神は、自らに似せて人間を創造しました。

　7日目、神は天地創造を完成したので、休憩しました。

注：「創世記」(Genesis) における天地創造の最後の神の休息の日に由来して、安息日［あんそくび］(the Sabbath) が存在する。この日は、キリスト教では日曜日、ユダヤ教では土曜日、イスラム教では金曜日としている。

Section 2

Old Testament

Creation of the Universe in Genesis

■ The Supernatural Beginning of the Universe through the first seven days

The Christian God spent seven days in creating the universe. Let us explain what God created and how He did it in chronological order.

On the first day, God created light, saying "let there be light!" Since light is divided from the darkness, it was named "day" and the darkness was named "night."

On the second day, God created firmament, ordering it to come into being, and divided the waters into the waters above and the waters below. This firmament was named the "sky."

On the third day, God commanded the waters below to gather in one place so that dry land would appear. The waters below were named "seas" and the dry land was named "earth." He ordered the land to grow plants and fruits in abundance.

On the fourth day, God created the sun, the moon, and the stars in the firmament, so that days, seasons, and years came to be. The sun ruled over the days, while the moon controlled the night.

On the fifth day, God commanded the sea to teem with fish and the skies to abound in birds, and ordered them to multiply.

On the sixth day, God commanded the land to bring forth living things, so that beasts, livestock, and reptiles came into being. Lastly, He created humans in His image.

On the seventh day, since the job of creation was over, He took a divine rest.

第2節　旧約聖書の世界

> **関連情報**　他の世界創造神話との決定的な違いは？
>
> 　日本神話では、最初に高天原が存在し、そこから最初に、造化三神［ぞうかさんしん］が生まれました。ギリシャ神話では、天地の前に混沌のみが存在し、そこから最初に、大地（ガイア［Gaia］）・夜（ニュクス［Nyx］）・闇（エレボス［Erebos］）・愛（エロス［Eros］）と奈落の底（タルタロス［Tartaros］）が生まれました。北欧神話では、氷と炎を除いて他には何もなかったとされています。また、巨大な卵が割れて、底から宇宙が生まれたとされる神話もあります。キリスト教における天地創造物語と、上記の神話との決定的な違いは、キリスト教の物語では、神が「無」からすべて（天地から生物・人間まで）を創造したという点です。他のほとんどの神話では、最初に「何か」がすでに存在しているのです。

＊日本神話については、前著『日本の宗教の知識と英語を身につける』を参照。

2　エデンの園

■ エデンの園とは？

　エデンの園とは、旧約聖書の「創世記」に登場する楽園の名称です。主なる神ヤハウェは、東の方のエデン[注1]に園を設け、そこを管理させるために最初の人間アダムとイブ（エバ）を住まわせました。そして、その地に見るからに好ましく、食べるに良いものをもたらすあらゆる木を植え、園の中央には、生命の木と善悪の知識の木（善悪を知る木）を植えました。

　ヤハウェは、アダムとイブに善悪の知識の木の実を食べることを、食べれば死ぬと警告して禁じていましたが、蛇にそそのかされて、初めにイブが、そしてその次にイブの勧めでアダムが善悪の知識の木の実を食べてしまいました。アダムとイブが神の命令に逆らい、禁じられていた善悪の知識の木の実（禁断の木の実[注2]）を食べたことから、生命の木の実をも食べ、永遠の命を得ることを恐れた神は、2人をエデンの園から追放しました。

Section 2

> ●Useful Usage● **TEEM**
> 1. Fish teems in the river. (＝The river teems with fish.)
>   (その川には魚がいっぱい泳いでいる)
> 2. The Takeshita Street usually teems with teenagers.
>   (竹下通りはいつも10代の人たちでごった返している)

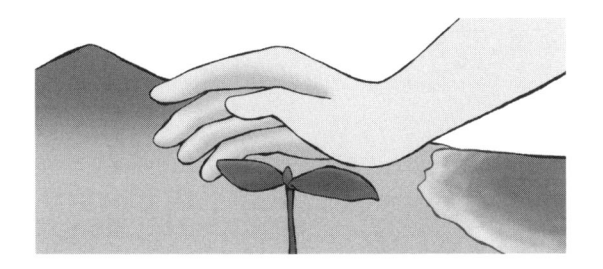

The Garden of Eden

■ The Garden of Eden

The Garden of Eden is the name of the paradise that appears in "Genesis" of the Old Testament. God, or Yahweh in Hebrew, created a garden in Eden in the east and created the first humans, Adam and Eve, to make them control the garden and live there. He planted every tree that is considered beautiful and provided healthy food. In the center of the garden sprouted the Tree of Life and the Tree of the Knowledge of Good and Evil.

Yahweh forbade Adam and Eve to eat the fruit from the tree of the knowledge of good and evil warning them that they would die if they did so. Eve first ate it from the tree after being tempted by a snake. Next, Adam also ate the fruit of the tree on the recommendation of Eve. Since Adam and Eve ate the forbidden fruit of the knowledge of good and evil against God's bidding, God feared Adam and Eve might also eat the fruit of the tree of life and attain eternal life so He banished both of them from the garden of Eden.

第2節　旧約聖書の世界

■ エデンの園があった場所

　「創世記」には、「エデンから1つの川が流れ出ていた。園を潤し、そこから分かれて、4つの川となっていた」という記述があります。この4つの川とは、ピション川、ギホン川、チグリス川、ユーフラテス川のことです。エデンの園がどこにあったかについては諸説ありますが、チグリス川とユーフラテス川の源流は、アルメニアの山地にあるため、エデンの園はアルメニアにあったとする説が多く見受けられます。

1　エデンという言葉はペルシャ語のヘデン（heden）に由来するとされており、もともとは、「周囲を囲まれた」という意味。
2　アダムが食べた禁断の木の実は、アダムの喉に詰まりのどぼとけとなったと言われている。一般に、禁断の木の実はりんごと考えられているため、のどぼとけのことを英語ではAdam's apple（アダムのりんご）と言う。

> **関連情報**　チグリス川とユーフラテス川の間の土地をメソポタミアという理由
> 　英語のMesopotamiaを分析すると、＜Meso（中）+potam（河）+ia（地）＞、すなわち、河と河の間の土地と解釈できます。チグリス川とユーフラテス川の間の土地だから、Mesopotamia（メソポタミア）というわけです。potamは河を表しますが、これは、hippopotamusという単語に表れています。分析すると＜hippo（馬）+potamus（河）＞となり、これは「馬河（バカ）」ならぬ「河馬」ですね。日本語とほぼ発想が同じです。口語でhippoと言えば「河馬」のことです。本当は「馬」を表しているのですが…。

3　原罪と楽園追放

■ アダムとイブの犯した罪

　原罪とは、人類の始祖であるアダムとイブ（エバ）が最初に犯した罪のことです。原罪の思想は聖書の「創世記」に述べられています。「創世記」において、神はアダムとイブにエデンの園にあるどの木の実も食べてよいが、ただ1つ、園の中

Section 2

■ The place where the garden of Eden was located

In "Genesis," there is a description that a river flowed from Eden to water the garden, and from there it divided into four rivers. These four rivers are the Pishon, Gihon, Tigris and Euphrates. There are several theories about the location of the Garden of Eden. However, the theory that the Garden of Eden was in Armenia is especially common since the source of the Tigris and the Euphrates rivers was in a mountainous district of Armenia.

●Useful Usage● **SPROUT**
1. New ideas always sprouted out in her mind.
 (彼女の心には、新しい考えが常にわいてきました)
2. Sprout and boil the potatoes.
 (ジャガイモは芽を取ってゆでてください)
 ＊sproutの「(…の) 芽を取る」の意味がある。

Original Sin and Expulsion from Paradise

■ The sin committed by Adam and Eve

Original sin is the sin that Adam and Eve, the progenitors of the human race, committed first. The concept of the original sin is described in "Genesis" of the Bible. In "Genesis," God told Adam and Eve that they

第2節　旧約聖書の世界

央にある善悪の知識の木の実だけは食べてはならないと言いました。しかし、神に創られた生き物のうち一番狡猾であった蛇が、イブをそそのかしてその禁断の木の実を食べさせ、そしてイブはアダムにも勧めて食べさせました。これが、アダムとイブが最初に犯した罪、原罪です。

■ アダムとイブの受けた罰

善悪の知識の木の実を食べたことによって、知恵を持ったアダムとイブは、自分たちが裸であることを恥ずかしいと思うようになり、イチジクの葉をつづり合わせて、腰に巻きました。そして事の次第を知った神は、神の命令に背いたアダムとイブに試練を与えました。アダムに対しては労働の苦しみを、イブに対しては出産の苦しみでした[注1]。神は、彼らがさらに手を伸ばし、生命の木の実をも取って食べ永遠に生きないように、両者をエデンの園から永遠に追放しました。これが、アダムとイブの楽園追放の物語です。

...

1　イブをそそのかした蛇への罰として、神は蛇をあらゆる家畜、あらゆる野の獣の中で呪われるものとし、生涯這いまわり、塵［ちり］を食らうものとした。

■ 原罪説

原罪説とは、アダムとイブの犯した罪が、彼ら2人の罪であるに止まらず、子孫であるすべての人間に引き継がれるという思想のことです。この思想は、キリスト教の最も重要な教義の1つとなっています。

Section 2

were allowed to eat any fruits in the garden of Eden except for the fruit of the tree of the knowledge of good and evil at the center of the garden. However, the snake which was the most cunning creature that God had made instigated Eve to eat the forbidden fruit, and Eve then urged Adam to eat it, too. This is what is known as the original sin or crime against God.

■ The punishment Adam and Eve suffered

Adam and Eve gained wisdom from eating the fruit from the tree of the knowledge of good and evil and came to feel shame for the first time at being naked, so they wove together fig leaves and wrapped them around their waists. Then, God realized what had happened and put a curse on Adam and Eve because they disobeyed his command: God subjected Adam and all men through him to toil as they were forced to work the earth for their own food. To Eve, and all women through her, God made it so childbirth would be a most painful event. God banished both of them from the garden of Eden forever so that they would not partake of the fruit of the tree of life as well, and live for eternity. This is a story of the Expulsion of Adam and Eve from Paradise.

■ Theory of Original Sin

The Theory of Original Sin is a concept that the sin committed by Adam and Eve does not remain only Adam and Eve's but is inherited by all humans, descendants of Adam and Eve. This concept is one of the major elements of Christianity.

第2節　旧約聖書の世界

> **関連情報　アダムとイブの楽園追放の意味**
>
> 　アダムとイブは神の掟を破ったこと（＝罪）で、楽園を追放されること（＝罰）になります。
>
> 　楽園では存分に食べ物が用意されていたのですが、追放後は、アダムは労働の苦しみをイブは生みの苦しみ、すなわち、陣痛を背負うことになります。だから英語の「労働」と「陣痛」は同じ単語なのです。どちらもlaborと言いますが、特に陣痛もlaborと言うので注意です。労働が罰だから、西洋人はworkを「働くこと→苦しむこと」のようなマイナスイメージで捉え、eat（食べること→楽しむこと）が重要だと発想します。つまり、work to eat（＝workはeatのための手段にすぎない）と考える傾向があるのです。

4　ノアの箱舟

■ 神が起こした大洪水

　ノアの箱舟とは、ノアとその一族が、巨大な箱舟に乗って大洪水から救われたという、「創世記」に登場する物語のことです（ノアは、アダムより数えて10代目の子孫です）。

　アダムとイブの子孫は増えていきましたが、地上には人の悪が増大するようになっていました。そして、神は地上に人を創ったことを悔やみ、洪水を起こして彼らを全滅させることにしました。

　しかし、ノアだけはその時代にあっても正しい人であったため、神は、彼とその家族は救済することにしました。神はノアに箱舟を作るよう命じ、それにノアの家族と、すべての動物のつがいを乗せることを命じました。その後、洪水が始まり、地上のすべての生き物は滅びました。

■ 生き残ったノアの一家

　ノアと箱舟の中にいたものだけが生き残りました。洪水の水が引くまでに150日間かかった末に、箱舟はアララト山（現在のトルコ東部の山）の上に止まりました。

Section 2

Noah's Ark

■ The Great Flood

Noah's ark is the story in "Genesis" of Noah and his family being saved from a great flood due to having built an ark to escape the deluge. The Bible lists Noah as the tenth descendant of Adam.

As the descendants of Adam and Eve increased, the evil of man also increased on earth. God came to regret that he had made mankind and decided to destroy all of humanity with a flood.

However, since Noah was a righteous man in his generation, God decided to save Noah and his family. God ordered Noah to build a huge ark and to put his family and pairs of every kind of animals in the ark. Then, the flood occurred, and all creatures living on land were destroyed.

■ Surviving Noah's family

Only Noah and those in the Ark survived. After 150 days, the floodwaters receded and the ark finally landed on peak of Mount Ararat which was still slightly underwater (a mountain in the eastern part of

第2節　旧約聖書の世界

　40日後、ノアは箱舟の窓からカラスと鳩を飛ばしましたが、休む場所を見つけられず、すぐに戻ってきました。1週間後、今度は鳩を飛ばしてみましたが、鳩はくちばしにオリーヴの葉をくわえて戻ってきました。これは、土地が乾いた証拠でした。翌週、もう一度鳩を飛ばすと、鳩はもう戻ってきませんでした。

　水が引いたことを知ったノアは、家族と動物たちとともに箱舟を出ると、祭壇を築き、神にいけにえとして、動物を捧げました。神はそれを喜び、地上のすべての生き物を打ち滅ぼすような大洪水は二度と起こさないことを契約しました。そして、その契約のしるしとして、神は空に虹を架けました。生き残ったノアの3人の息子、セム、ハム、ヤフェト（ヤペテ）とそれぞれの妻たちから、大洪水後のすべての民族が生まれました。

参考：ノアは500歳で3人の息子をもうけたと言われる。

> **関連情報**　スバールバル諸島の「ノアの箱舟」
> 　北極の大地にあるノルウェー領スバールバル諸島のスピッツベルゲン島に＜現代の植物版「ノアの箱舟」＞があります。これは、地球温暖化や戦争などにより植物が絶滅するのを防ぐため、さらには人類滅亡の危機に備えて、およそ約450万種の植物の種を保存する予定の施設です。この施設内の種子庫は、2008年2月にオープンしましたが、これまで約52万種以上の種子が集まっています。

5　バベルの塔

■ バベルの塔の物語

　バベルの塔とは、旧約聖書の「創世記」中に登場する煉瓦造りの巨大な塔です。創世記には、神が人々の言葉を乱したのでその町の名はバベルと呼ばれたと記されています。このバベルという言葉の由来は、「混乱」を意味するヘブライ語の「バラル」にあるという説があります。また、「神の門」を意味するアッカド語のバビイルが語源で、のちにこれがギリシャ語読みされたのがバベルであるという説もあります。

　創世記に記されている物語によれば、人類はもともと1つの同じ言葉を話して

Section 2

present day Turkey).

Forty days later, Noah released a crow and a dove from the window of the ark, but they soon flew back to him because they found no place to rest. A week later, he released the dove this time. Then, it flew back to him with an olive leaf in its beak, which proved that the earth had dried. The next week, he released the dove again, and this time it did not come back.

Noah, who knew water had receded, came out of the ark with his family and animals, and promptly built an altar and sacrificed some animals to God. God was pleased with Noah's offering and promised that he would never again send another great flood to destroy all living creatures on earth. And, as a sign of this covenant, God displayed a rainbow in the sky. All the peoples who were born after the great flood were the descendants of Noah's three sons, Shem, Ham, Japheth and their respective wives who survived.

Tower of Babel

■ The story of the Tower of Babel

The Tower of Babel is a huge brick tower that appears in "Genesis" of the Old Testament. It is described in Genesis that the name of the city was called Babel because God confused the languages of the people. One idea suggests that the word Babel is derived from the Hebrew word "balal" which means "Confusion." There is another theory that the origin of the word Babel is the Akkadian word, Babili (Babiru) that means "God's gate" and later it was read as Babel in Greek.

第2節　旧約聖書の世界

いました。しかし、ノアの大洪水のあと、東の方から移動してきた人々はシンアル（バビロニア）の平地に煉瓦とアスファルトを用いて町と塔を建て、その頂を天にまで届かせようとしました。この塔を見た神は、人々がこのようなことをしたのは、みんなが同じ言葉を話していることが原因であると考えました。そして、人々の言葉を混乱させ、互いの言葉を理解できないようにしました。そのため、バベルの塔の建設は途中で中断し、町の建設も取りやめとなりました。

■ バベルの塔の原型

バベルの塔の原型とされているのは、古代メソポタミアの中心都市であったバビロンに実在したエ・テメン・アン・キ（天と地の礎石となる建物という意味）という名のジッグラト（聖塔）です。古代メソポタミアにおいて、各大都市はこのジッグラトと呼ばれる階段状の聖塔を建造し、そこでは様々な祭儀が行われていました。

■ バベルの塔の象徴するもの

バベルの塔の物語は、人間の傲慢を戒める物語として解釈されてきました。また、実現不可能な計画のたとえとしても用いられています。

関連情報　バベルの塔の物語の意味

人々が神に近づこうとすること（＝罪）に対する罰として、神が言葉を分けたと解釈することが可能です。また、現在、世界中に言語がたくさん存在する理由を、バベルの塔の話が説明しています。このバベルの塔の話における罪は、アダムとイブが犯した罪と似た側面があります。アダムとイブは、神の掟を破り、善悪を知ることにより、神に近づいたと考えることもできるからです。神に近づくことを試みることは、唯一絶対全知全能の神にとっては大問題ということになるのでしょう。なお、アダムとイブの楽園追放の話が労働が大変な理由を説明していることは言うまでもありません。

Section 2

According to the story written in Genesis, human beings originally spoke one and the same language. However, after the great flood of Noah, people who had moved from the east built the town and the tower with bricks and asphalts on the plain of Shinar (Babylonia) with the goal of making the top of the tower reach heaven. God saw what mankind was capable of when having a shared language and sought to put a limit on mankind's progress. God changed the languages of the builders and prevented them from understanding one another. Therefore, the construction of the Tower of Babel stopped and the construction of the city also came to a halt.

■ The prototype of the Tower of Babel

The prototype of the Tower of Babel is assumed to be the ziggurat named Etemenanki (meaning the building of the foundation of heaven and earth) that existed in Babylon, a central city of ancient Mesopotamia. In ancient Mesopotamia, each big city built a stepped temple tower called a ziggurat, where various rituals were performed.

■ What the Tower of Babel symbolizes

The story of the Tower of Babel has been interpreted as a story that admonishes human beings for their arrogance. In addition, it is used as a metaphor of a plan that cannot be achieved.

第2節　旧約聖書の世界

6　民族の祖となった族長たち

■ イスラエルの先祖

　天地創造からバベルの塔までの物語は、特定の民族というよりは、人類全体の話でしたが、聖書が特に力を込めて語るのが、その後の古代イスラエルの民の物語です。
　最初にアブラハムという名前が出てきます。アブラハムはイスラエルの先祖である族長の名前です。アブラハムは神の命令で、現在のパレスチナの辺りにあるカナンの地に移り住みます。アブラハムは神と契約を結び、国民の父となります。妻のサラは子をもうけ、イサクと名づけます。

参考：アブラハムとサラの子、イサクはユダヤ人の祖とされている。アブラハムは別の妻ハガル（Hagar）との間にもうけた子にイシュマエル（Ishmael）がいるが、このイシュマエルはアラブ人の祖とユダヤ人は考えている。

■ モリヤ山の試練

　あるとき、神はアブラハムの信仰心を試されました。神は、モリヤの山でイサク（アブラハムの独り子）を捧げるように命じました。アブラハムがイサクを殺そうとしたとき、アブラハムの信仰が厚いのを知り、命令を撤回したのです。この一件で、アブラハムはユダヤ教徒やキリスト教徒の模範とされるようになりました。

■ イサクの子、エサウとヤコブ

　イサクはアブラハムが出発した地であるハランからリベカという名の妻を迎えました。やがて双子の男の子が生まれ、エサウ（兄）とヤコブ（弟）と名づけられました。
　父のイサクは年老いて目が見えなくなったとき、自分が寵愛するエサウを呼んで、好きな狩りで獲物を獲ってくるように命じました。死ぬ前にその肉を食べて、エサウを祝福*しようとしたのです。そのとき、ヤコブを愛する母のリベカは、彼女が用意した子やぎの料理をエサウのふりをして父のもとに持って行き、祝福を受けるように言いました。イサクは間違ってヤコブを祝福しました。

Section 2

Patriarchs who became ethnic ancestors

■ Israel's ancestor

Though the stories from the Creation to the Tower of Babel were about the entire human race rather than a specific race, it is the subsequent story about the people in ancient Israel that the Bible especially emphasizes.

In terms of patriarchs connected with the eventual creation of the kingdom of Israel itself, Abraham is the first to appear. Abraham migrated to Canaan near modern day Palestine by God's command. By making contact with God, Abraham becomes the father of the Israeli people. His wife Sarah gives birth to a child and names him Isaac.

■ The trial on Mount Moriah

On one occasion, God tested the faith of Abraham. God ordered Abraham to sacrifice Isaac (Abraham's only son) as an offering to God on mount Moriah. God found out that Abraham was a deeply religious man when he was about to kill Isaac, and he revoked his original order. Abraham's devotion to God has made him a model for Jews and Christians.

■ Isaac's children, Esau and Jacob

Isaac married a woman named Rebecca from Haran, the place where Abraham stopped on his journey. Before long, twin boys were born named Esau (the older brother) and Jacob (the younger brother).

When Isaac grew old and blind, he called Esau, whom he loved tenderly, and ordered him to hunt venison and present it to him so he could bless his son before he died. Then, Rebecca, who loved Jacob, told him to bring the dish of kid goats which she had prepared to his father, pretending to be Esau so he could receive his father's blessing. Isaac

第2節　旧約聖書の世界

*祝福には財産の相続も含まれていたと思われる。
注：ヤコブはイスラエルの民（12部族）の先祖、エサウはイスラエル近郊に住むエドム人の先祖とされており、この話は選民思想の1つの表れであると考えられる。

■ ヤコブの物語

　父に祝福されそこなったエサウはヤコブを殺そうと企てますが、ヤコブは母リベカの故郷のハランへと逃れていきます。ヤコブはハランの地で、リベカの兄ラバン（つまり、伯父）と会います。この伯父にだまされてこき使われるなどし、長い間苦労しますが、その娘たち2人と結婚し、ヤコブはついにカナンの地に帰ることになります。

　カナンの地に向かうある夜、何者かが現れ、夜が白むまでヤコブと格闘することになります。その人は「夜が明けてしまうから、もう帰らせてくれ」と言うと、ヤコブは「いいえ、祝福してくださるまで離しません」と言いました。「お前の名前は何だ？」とその人が尋ねると、「ヤコブです」と答えました。すると「お前はもうヤコブではない。イスラエルと名乗りなさい。神と戦って勝ったからだ」と。

　ヤコブは、カナンの地で生活を始めたころには、息子が12人になり、これがイスラエルの12部族の発祥とされています。

参考：アブラハム　→ イスラエルの先祖
　　　イサク　　　→ ユダヤ人の祖
　　　ヤコブ　　　→ イスラエル12部族の長

■ ヨセフの物語

　ヤコブの12人の息子たちの中で、下から2番目のヨセフは、父イスラエル（＝ヤコブ）に特にかわいがられていたので、他の兄弟たちから妬まれていました。ある日、兄弟たちはヨセフを空の井戸に投げ捨てます。ヨセフは通りがかりの商人に拾われ、エジプトのファラオの高官に売り飛ばされます。やがて高官の信頼を得たヨセフでしたが、高官の妻の誘惑を断ったことで、逆恨みされ投獄されます。

　しかし、ヨセフの特殊な能力である夢占いのおかげで、エジプトを飢饉などから救うことに貢献し、ファラオはヨセフを宰相に任命します。つまり、エジプトで異例の出世を遂げることになるのです。

Section 2

blessed Jacob by mistake and gave him his inheritance.

> ●Useful Usage● **PRETEND**
> 1. Let's pretend we're pirates. （海賊ごっこをしよう）
> 2. I cannot pretend to advise you. （あなたに忠告しようという気になれない）
> 3. I don't pretend to scholarship. （私は自分に学識があるとは言いません）

■ The story about Jacob

Esau wasn't able to receive his father's blessing so he attempted to kill Jacob but failed. He escaped to Haran, the hometown of Rebecca, the mother of Jacob. Jacob met Rebecca's older brother, his uncle, Laban in Haran. Jacob experiences hardships for a long time as he is used and taken advantage of by his uncle. However, he marries the uncle's two daughters and ends up returning to the land of Canaan.

One night when he heads to the land of Canaan, someone appears and wrestles with Jacob until the dawn breaks. When the man said, "Let me go home since the day breaks," Jacob said, "No, I won't let you go until you bless me." When the man asked, "What's your name?," Jacob replied, "I am Jacob." Then, the man said, "Your name will no longer be Jacob. You shall be known as Israel since you fought with God and beat him."

When Jacob started his life in the land of Canaan, he had 12 sons, which is believed to be the origin of the 12 Tribes of Israel.

■ The story about Joseph

Since Joseph, who was the second youngest of Jacob's 12 sons, was especially cherished by his father Israel (Jacob), he was begrudged by his brothers. One day, the brothers throw Joseph into an empty well. Joseph is picked up by a merchant who is passing by and is sold as a slave to a high official of the pharaoh in Egypt. In due course, Joseph gains the trust of the high official. However, since he resists the temptations of the high official's wife, he earns her resentment and is thrown in jail.

However, thanks to Joseph's ability to interpret dreams which foretell the future, he helps save Egypt from famines and the pharaoh appoints

第2節　旧約聖書の世界

関連情報　ヨセフの夢占い

　ヨセフがどんな夢占いをしていたか、その一部を紹介しましょう。（創世記第37章、41章）

太陽と月と11の星がヨセフにひれ伏した。	⇒	父母兄弟がヨセフに従う。
ぶどうの木の3本の枝に花が咲き、房がなった。給仕長がその果汁を絞り、ファラオに捧げた。	⇒	3日後には、ファラオによって無罪とされて、元の役職に戻る。
ナイル川の畔で7頭の肥えた雌牛が、7頭のやせた雌牛に食べられた。	⇒	7年間豊作のあと、7年間の凶作が続く（豊作時に穀物を備蓄せよ）。

Section 2

Joseph as the vizier. This positioned him as the second highest authority in Egypt.

関連情報 アダムとイブの時代からダビデやソロモンの時代まで

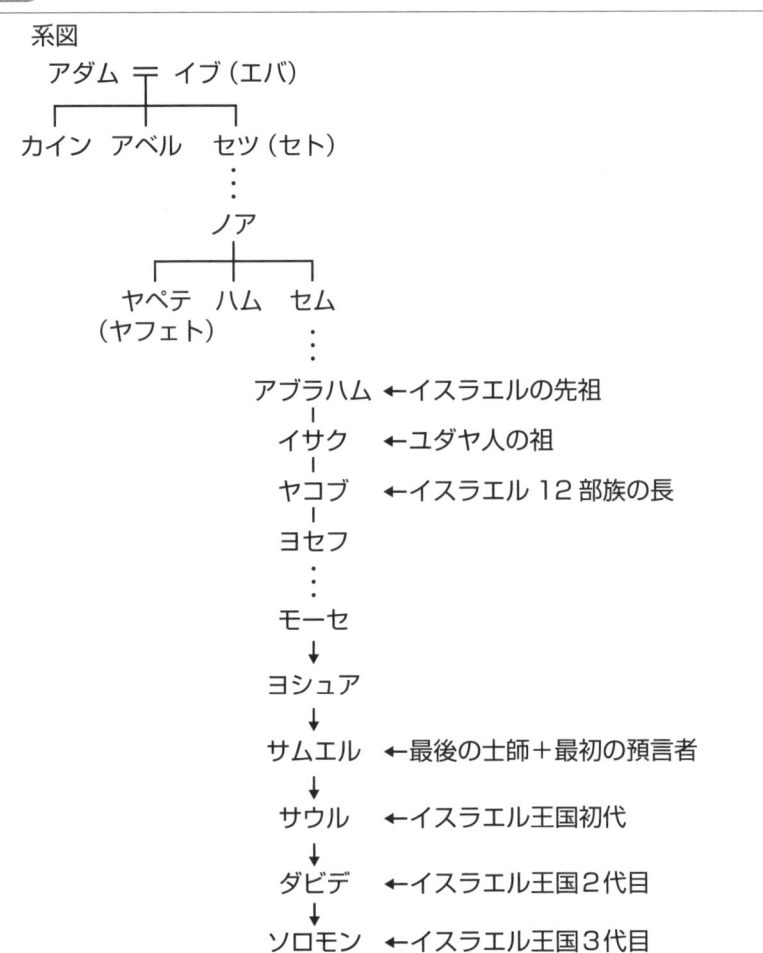

系図
```
アダム ─┬─ イブ（エバ）
    ┌───┼───┐
  カイン アベル セツ（セト）
              ⋮
              ノア
         ┌────┼────┐
       ヤペテ  ハム  セム
      （ヤフェト）
                    ⋮
                アブラハム ←イスラエルの先祖
                    │
                  イサク  ←ユダヤ人の祖
                    │
                  ヤコブ  ←イスラエル12部族の長
                    │
                  ヨセフ
                    ⋮
                  モーセ
                    ↓
                  ヨシュア
                    ↓
                  サムエル ←最後の士師＋最初の預言者
                    ↓
                  サウル  ←イスラエル王国初代
                    ↓
                  ダビデ  ←イスラエル王国2代目
                    ↓
                  ソロモン ←イスラエル王国3代目
```

第2節　旧約聖書の世界

7　出エジプト

■ 出エジプト記

　出エジプト記は、旧約聖書の2番目の書で、指導者モーセ[注1]が、神の命を受けて、イスラエルの民を連れ、エジプトを脱出した様子が描かれています。

■ エジプト脱出

　飢饉に悩むイスラエル一族[注2]は、エジプトに移住しました。やがて、イスラエル人の数が増えるにつれ、彼らが勢力を増すことを恐れたエジプト王（ファラオ）は、イスラエル人に奴隷として過酷な労働を強いるようになりました。そこにモーセという指導者が登場し、正確な数字は確認できていないものの、一説には数十万人とも言われるイスラエル人をエジプトから連れ出し、約束の地カナンへと向かいました。

■ 紅海の奇跡

　モーセ一行を追ってきたエジプト軍が彼らに追いついたとき、「紅海の奇跡」が起きました。モーセが海に向かって手を差し伸べると、水が引き、海の中に1本の道が現れ、イスラエル人たちはそこを渡ることができました。しかし、イスラエル人たちが渡りきると、海の道が閉じてしまい、エジプト軍は海に呑み込まれてしまったのです。

■ 十戒

　「十戒」とは、モーセがシナイ山の頂で神から授けられた10カ条の戒律のことで、モーセは、この神から授かった掟をイスラエルの民に読み聞かせ、それを厳守させました。

Section 2

Exodus

■ Book of Exodus

The Book of Exodus is the second book of the Old Testament. The Book describes how the leader Moses led the people of Israel out of Egypt under the order from God.

■ Escape from Egypt

After suffering from famine, the people of Israel migrated to Egypt. As the people of Israel grew in number, the supreme leader of Egypt, the pharaoh, feared that they would gain strength so decided to impose hard slave labor on the people of Israel. After some time passed, Moses took charge of the plight of the Jews and led, according to one theory though not known the exact number, hundreds of thousands of Israelis out from Egypt and headed for the Promised Land, Canaan.

■ Red Sea Miracle

"The miracle of the Red Sea" took place when the pursuing forces of the Egyptian army had cornered Moses and his people with their backs to the Red Sea. Upon God's command, when Moses raised his holy staff and held out his hand over the sea, the water parted to the sides in order to allow the Israelites through. The Israelites were able to safely cross to the other side. However, as soon as they all reached the other side, the path in the sea closed with the waters of the sea swallowed up the Egyptian army.

■ Decalogue

The "Decalogue" is the ten commandments, which were given to Moses by God on the top of Mount Sinai. Moses read the commandments given by God to the people of Israel and made them obey the commandments.

第2節　旧約聖書の世界

1. モーセはエジプトでイスラエル人の子として生まれたが、男児殺害の命令がファラオにより下され、それを逃れるために母親によりナイル川の葦の茂みに置かれた。このときエジプト王女に拾われて育てられたと言われている。
2. 「イスラエル」とは、ヤコブが後に神から与えられた新しい名前で、このイスラエルという名は、彼の子孫である民族の名ともされた。

参考：エジプトを飢饉の脅威から救ったのはヤコブの子ヨセフであったため、ヤコブの子孫は繁栄し、エジプトに満ち溢れた。やがて、ヨセフの威光を知らない世代になると、イスラエルの民が邪魔となってくる。ファラオは、イスラエルの民に強制労働を強いるだけでなく、「イスラエル人の間に生まれた男の子はすべて殺せ」という命令を下す。あるとき、イスラエルのレビ族の男の子供を、見つからないようにと葦の籠に入れてナイルに浮かべる。それを偶然見つけたのがファラオの娘で、その子をモーセと名付けた。

8　約束の地

■ 約束の地カナン

カナンとは、聖書で「乳と蜜の流れる場所」と表現される、神がアブラハムの子孫に与えると約束した土地で、地中海とヨルダン川、死海に挟まれた地域一帯の古代の地名です。

モーセ率いるイスラエルの民は、その約束の地カナンの手前までやってきました。約束の地にはすでに人が住んでいるので、イスラエル12部族から1人ずつ選んで、モーセは偵察に行かせます。12人のうち、10人は、この地征服のために戦っても勝ち目がないと報告したのに対し、エフライム族のヨシュアとユダ族のカレブの2人は「神が自分たちを導いてくれるのだから、きっと勝てる」と主張しました。

■ エリコの攻略

モーセがカナンの地を見下ろす山の頂で死を迎えたのち、神はヨシュアを後継者に選びました。ヨシュアたちは、神の助けでヨルダン川を渡ることに成功し、ヨルダン川西岸のエリコを目指し、この地を征服します。

Section 2

> **●Useful Usage●　OBEY**
> 1. She obeys common sense.（彼女は常識に従って行動している）
> 2. He obeys his instincts.（彼は本能のままに行動する人だ）
> 3. My boss told me to keep my word, and I obeyed.
>   （上司が約束は守れと言ったので、私は従った）

The Promised Land

■ The Promised Land Canaan

Canaan is the land that God promised to give to the descendants of Abraham and is expressed as "a land flowing with milk and honey" in the Bible. It is the ancient name of the land between the Mediterranean sea, the Jordan River and the Dead Sea.

Over a long period of time, Moses led the Semites out of Egypt to the borders of Canaan. Since the Promised Land was already being occupied by potential enemies, Moses chooses one man from each of the 12 tribes of Israel and makes him go scout out the situation. Ten out of the twelve reported that they had no chance of winning if they fought for the land. On the other hand, both Joshua of Ephraim and Caleb of Judah insisted, "As God leads us, we will be sure to win."

■ The attack on Jericho

After Moses died on the top of a mountain above the land of Canaan, God chose Joshua as Moses' successor. Joshua and his people succeed in

第2節　旧約聖書の世界

参考：現在のパレスチナ自治区は、ガザ地区（東京23区の約半分の大きさ）（全5県）とヨルダン川西岸地区（三重県と同じくらい）（全11県）に分かれ、エリコはヨルダン川西岸地区の中のエリコ県に当たる。

その後、概ね順調にカナンの地を征服していくことになります。こうしてイスラエルの民はカナンに定住します。イスラエルの民がカナン定住を開始したのは、紀元前1250年ぐらいのことで、諸都市を征服したのが紀元前1150年ごろであると考えられています。

....

注：カナンの地の位置と特徴
　ヨシュアによって征服された約束の地カナンは、現在のイスラエル、レバノンとシリアを指します。この地には、各地に城壁で囲まれた都市国家は成立しましたが、大河がなかったため、メソポタミアやエジプトとは異なり統一国家はできませんでした。

Note：The promised land Canaan conquered by Joshua made up the whole area of modern day Israel, Lebanon, and Syria. City-states enclosed by castle walls were established in various places. However, as there was no huge river, a unified state was not created unlike Mesopotamia and Egypt.

9 ｜ 士師記

■ カナンの地で異教に傾倒するイスラエルの民

　ヨシュアによってカナンを征服したといっても、すべての土地と民族を制圧したわけではありませんでした。イスラエルの民は土着のカナン人の影響を受け、異教に傾倒してしまいます。怒った神は、周囲の国々にイスラエルを攻撃させ、悔い改めた民が助けを求めると、士師［しし］と呼ばれる指導者を遣わして民を救います。しかし、士師が死ぬと、また異教に傾倒してしまいます。このサイク

Section 2

crossing the Jordan River with the help of God and head to Jericho along the West Bank of the River Jordan. They attack the mighty city and are able to take it.

Following their victory, they go on to conquer the land of Canaan relatively smoothly. Thus, the people of Israel settle down in Canaan. It is considered that they started to settle down in Canaan about 1250 B.C. and spread out by overpowering other neighboring cities by about 1150 B.C.

関連情報　モーセの十戒（日本聖書協会、口語訳聖書、「出エジプト記」第20章）

第1戒　あなたは私のほかに何者をも神としてはならない。
第2戒　あなたは自分のために刻んだ像を造ってはならない。
第3戒　あなたは、あなたの神、主の名前をみだりに唱えてはならない。
第4戒　安息日を覚えて、これを聖とせよ。
第5戒　あなたの父と母を敬え。
第6戒　あなたは殺してはならない。
第7戒　あなたは姦淫してはならない。
第8戒　あなたは盗んではならない。
第9戒　あなたは隣人について偽証してはならない。
第10戒　あなたは隣人の家をむさぼってはならない。

Book of Judges

■ The Pagan Israelites in Canaan

Even though Joshua conquered Canaan, he wasn't able to control all lands and ethnic groups. The people of Israel became influenced by the native Canaanites and devoted themselves to a pagan religion. God became furious and caused the surrounding countries to attack Israel. He creates the position of a tribal leader called a Judge and saves those who

第2節　旧約聖書の世界

ルを何回も繰り返すことになりました。

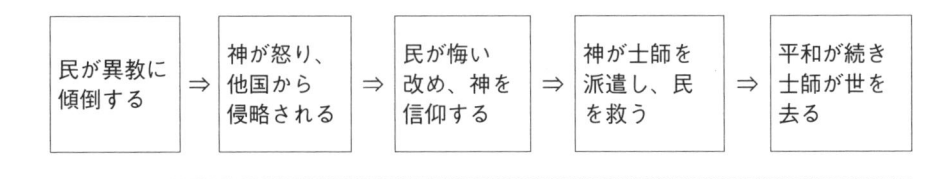

| 民が異教に傾倒する | ⇒ | 神が怒り、他国から侵略される | ⇒ | 民が悔い改め、神を信仰する | ⇒ | 神が士師を派遣し、民を救う | ⇒ | 平和が続き士師が世を去る |

注：神は、ヨシュアのあとの後継者を選ぶことはなく、上記のように、必要に応じて士師を派遣する形をとった（12人の士師が登場する）。

■ 士師サムソン

　紀元前1200年ごろにペリシテ人がカナン沿岸部に定住を開始し、次第に内陸部への侵攻を始め、イスラエルの民を圧迫していました。ペリシテ人は、優れた武器を用い、戦闘にも長けていたので、神は勇者サムソンを送り込み、ペリシテ人制圧に能力を発揮します。

　しかし、このサムソンは2人の女性に振り回され、悲劇的な最期を迎えます。1人目は妻となったペリシテ人です。妻の実家ともめたとき、300匹のジャッカルの尾を2匹ずつにしてつなぎ、たいまつをつけて畑に放ち、ペリシテ人の畑を焼け野原にするという無茶な行動に出ました。よほど異邦の女に惹かれるのか、2人目もペリシテ人でした。彼女にサムソンの力の秘密を聞き出され、ついに「髪を切られると力がなくなる」と本当のことを言ってしまい、彼は、髪を切り落とされ、ただの人になってしまいました。

　そして、捕えられたサムソンは、目をくりぬかれ、足かせにつながれて、石臼で粉を挽くという重労働をさせられます。ある日、ガザの祭りで見世物にされたサムソンは、伸びつつあった髪のおかげで、渾身の力で、建物を引き倒し、そのとき集まった何千人ものペリシテ人を道連れに命を落としたのでした。

Section 2

repent and ask for God's help. However, when the Judge dies, the people devote themselves to the pagan religion once again. This cycle was repeated many times.

■ The Judge Samson

Philistines began settling down on the coast of Canaan around 1200 B.C. They gradually launched an invasion into the inland area against the people of Israel. Since Philistines used excellent weapons and were good at fighting, God dispatched a brave man of extraordinary physical strength named Samson in order to prove His power to the Philistines.

However, Samson gives in to two women and faces a tragic end. The first is a Philistine who became his wife. After having a fight with his wife's family, he tied torches to the tails of 300 jackals by dividing them into groups of two and set them loose in the fields which turned the Philistine's fields into a burnt wasteland. Samson was attracted to the women of the foreign country, so his second wife was also a Philistine. She extracted the secret of Samson's strength when he finally told the truth, "If my hair is cut, I lose my power." So, she cut his hair and rendered him as weak as any common man.

Samson was caught and, after having his eyes gouged out, was forced to do heavy work such as grinding grain in a stone mill. Later on, Samson was put on show in a Gaza temple to be gawked at by the proud Philistines and their rulers. By then his hair was growing back, so he summoned all his strength and pulled the pillars of the temple until the whole structure came crashing down taking his own life as well as the thousands of Philistines who were gathered there.

第2節　旧約聖書の世界

10 | サムエル記

■ 最後の士師で最初の預言者サムエル

　指導者ヨシュアの後、士師の時代がきたということを述べてきましたが、その後、古代イスラエルは王政の時代を歩み始めます。この王政の起こりに関係する重要人物がサムエルです。サムエルは、最後の士師であり、最初の預言者と言われています。

　紀元前1100年ごろのこと、生まれて3歳になったサムエルは祭司エリの内弟子になります。ある夜、サムエルは自分を呼ぶ声に気づき、エリのところに行きましたが、エリはサムエルを呼んでいないと答え、彼は神がサムエルに話しかけているのだと教えました。このときから、サムエルは神と対話する力を得たのです。サムエルは、神と人の仲介者的存在である預言者となったのです。

■ イスラエルに誕生した初めての王サウル

　混迷のイスラエルに神は、誰よりも背が高く美しいベニヤミン族[注1]のサウルを選び、サムエルはサウルに「油注ぎ」[注2]の儀式を行い、王に任命します。イスラエルの民が王政を望んだ真の理由は、ペリシテ人[注3]の脅威だと言われています。イスラエルは中央集権的な統治体制と軍人組織を持つ王政へと変貌せざるを得なかったのです。

1　ヤコブの子とされる12部族は、宿営する位置が決まっており、その位置で分類すると、次のようになる。
　　東側：ユダ（Judah）族、イッサカル（Issachar）族、ゼブルン（Zebulun）族
　　西側：エフライム（＝ヨセフの子）族、マナセ（Manasseh）（＝ヨセフの子）族、ベニヤミン族
　　南側：ルベン（Reuben）族、シメオン（Simeon）族、ガド（Gad）族
　　北側：ダン（Dan）族、アシェル（Asher）族、ナフタリ（Naphtali）族
2　「メシア」（Messiah）という単語は「油を注がれし者」という意味のヘブライ語が語源である。この語は元来、神から特別な権利を与えられた王や司祭、預言者を指していた。これらの人は、油注ぎの儀式を経て聖職にかかわっていたからである。ソロモン王の絶頂期以降、悲運な状況から自分たちを解放する救世主の意味で使われるようになった。

Section 2

Books of Samuel

■ The last judge and the first prophet Samuel

As stated previously, the time of Judges came after the time of the leader Joshua. After that, ancient Israel enters a period of monarchal rule. The most important facilitator of this nascent monarchy was a man named Samuel. It is said that Samuel was the last Judge and the first prophet.

About 1100 B.C., the 3 year old Samuel became the apprentice of the high priest Eli. One night, Samuel heard a voice calling his name and went to Eli. However, Eli answered that he had not called Samuel and informed him that God had talked to Samuel. From this moment, Samuel obtained the power to converse with God and henceforth became a prophet who served as a mediator between God and man.

■ The first king, Saul of Israel

God chooses Saul of the tribe of Benjamin who is taller and more beautiful than anyone in chaotic Israel. Samuel presides over the ceremony of "anointing" for Saul and appoints him to be king. It is said that the people of Israel wanted to live under a united monarchy because of the threat from Philistine. Israel could not help changing its system of government to a more centralized and organized structure of governance.

油注ぎ

第2節　旧約聖書の世界

3　イスラエルの民にとってペリシテ人は常に脅威であった。実は、カナン周辺の地を指すパレスチナという地名は、このペリシテ人の土地という意味が語源である。しかし、現在のパレスチナ人と古代のペリシテ人には直接の関係はない。

11 ダビデとソロモン

■ 2代目の王ダビデ（紀元前1000年ころ）

　謙虚な王であった初代王のサウルは、戦勝を重ねるに連れて、次第に傲慢になっていきます。神の命令を無視するようになったサウルのもとを預言者サムエルは去ります。神は、新たな後継者にダビデを選びます。

　神にも見捨てられたサウルは心身のバランスを崩し、その状況を心配した側近が竪琴の名手を呼び、サウルは癒されます。その名手こそダビデだったのです。ある日、ダビデは、どう見ても勝ち目がないペリシテ人の大男ゴリアテと戦って勝ちます。一躍英雄となって人望を集めるダビデにサウルは嫉妬し、ついにダビデ殺害の計画を立てます。サウルの娘でダビデの妻となったミカルがダビデを逃がしてくれたおかげでダビデは命拾いしたのです。

　ダビデは、サウルの死後、紀元前1000年にヘブロン（Hebron）においてユダ（Judas）の王に、そして紀元前994年にイスラエル全土の王になりました。

参考：身長3メートルの大男ゴリアテに対し、ダビデは杖と石投げ、川で拾った5つの石だけを持って戦いを挑んだ。石投げを使って、石を1つだけ放つと、ゴリアトの額に命中し、ダビデは簡単に勝利を収める。有名なミケランジェロ（Michelangelo）のダビデ像は、このときの姿を表したものと言われている。

■ 3代目の王ソロモン（紀元前965-926に統治）

　ダビデはその後、南北イスラエルを統一し、エルサレムを征服するなど数々の実績を残しますが、試練も多く、最後には王位を狙う反乱も起きます。年老いたダビデは、後継者に自分の子、ソロモンを選びます。

Section 2

> ●Useful Usage●　PRESIDE
> 1. The conference was presided over by Mr. Johnson.
>   （会議はジョンソン氏が司会を務めた）
> 2. The acting manager presides over the business of this shop.
>   （部長代理がこの店の業務を統括している）

David and Solomon

■ The second king David (about 1000 B.C.)

　The first king Saul who was a modest king at first gradually become arrogant as he racks up victories. The prophet Samuel leaves Saul after he disregarded God's orders. God chooses David as the successor.

　Saul was abandoned by God and suffered a physical and mental breakdown. An aide who worried about Saul's condition invited an expert of the harp whose sound soothed the soul of Saul. This musician was David. He gained further fame when one day, David fights against the Philistine giant Goliath whom David has no chance of beating in every respect. With the odds stacked against him, David comes out on top and slays Goliath. Saul envies David who suddenly becomes a hero so he finally hatches a plan to kill David. Michal, who is Saul's daughter and becomes David's wife, helps him avoid this fate, thus saving his life.

　After the death of Saul, David became the king of Judas in Hebron in 1000 B.C., and the king of the whole Israel in 994 B.C.

■ The third king Solomon (reigning from 965-926 B.C.)

　Afterwards, David has a long list of accomplishments such as the unification of North and South Israel and the conquest of Jerusalem. However, he goes through numerous hardships and eventually a revolt against his throne. The aged David chooses his son Solomon as his successor.

第2節　旧約聖書の世界

　ダビデの後を継いだソロモンは、神が望むものを与えると夢枕で聞いて、知恵を求め、賢王となります。彼の口から出た格言は3,000、歌は1,500を超えたと言われています。こうした知恵に基づく政治的手腕で、イスラエルはかつてない繁栄の道をたどります。

　外交政策の一環として、ソロモンは近隣諸国から700人もの妻と300人もの側室（そばめ）を迎えていました。妻たちから故郷の神に祈りたいとねだられたソロモンは、神殿の中に異国の神々の宮を建てることを許し、自らも異教の神を拝み出しました。これが神の怒りを買い、イスラエル王国は崩壊の兆しが徐々に表れてきます。

12　王国の分裂と北王国滅亡

■ 内乱勃発と王国の分裂

　ソロモンの死後、イスラエル王国内で内乱が勃発します。紀元前922年ごろに、ユダ族とベニヤミン族から成るユダ王国（首都エルサレム）と、ユダ族・ベニヤミン族以外の10部族から成る北イスラエル王国（首都サマリア）に分裂してしまいます。

　その後2世紀にわたり、両国間で頻繁に衝突が起こります。北イスラエル王国では内乱が絶えず、さらに外国からも攻撃を頻繁に受け、紀元前8世紀後半、アッシリア（首都アッシュール、ニネヴェ）に滅ぼされてしまいます。

　一方、ユダ王国は、ソロモンの子孫らによって約350年間続いたのち、新バビロニア（首都バビロン）に滅ぼされます。

Section 2

Solomon, who succeeded David, hears in his sleep that God will give him whatever he wants. He asks for wisdom and becomes a wise king. It is said that he spoke 3000 proverbs and wrote over 1500 songs. Israel was suddenly on the path to unprecedented prosperity with his political skill based on his God-given wisdom.

Solomon invited 700 wives and 300 concubines from neighboring countries as part of a foreign policy. Solomon, who was told by his wives that they wanted to worship the gods of their hometown, permitted them to build shrines for the gods of foreign countries in the temple and he himself began to worship the pagan gods. This angered God and the Kingdom of Israel gradually began to show signs of collapse.

> ●Useful Usage● **REIGN**
> The king reigned only three years. [= was on the throne]
> （王の在位はわずか3年だった）

The Partition of the Kingdom and the Destruction of the Northern Kingdom

■ **The eruption of civil war and the partition of the Kingdom**

After the death of Solomon, a civil war erupted in the Kingdom of Israel. In 922 B.C., the Kingdom of Israel divided into the Kingdom of Judah (with the capital Jerusalem) which consisted of the Tribe of Judah and the Tribe of Benjamin, and the Northern Kingdom of Israel (with the capital Samaria) which consisted of 10 tribes other than the Tribe of Judah and Benjamin.

Conflicts frequently occurred between both countries for two centuries afterward. There were endless civil wars in the Northern Kingdom of Israel. In addition, it was frequently attacked by foreign countries. In the latter half of the 8th century B.C., it was destroyed by Assyria (with the capitals Assur and then Nineve).

第2節　旧約聖書の世界

■ 北イスラエル王国の崩壊と民族の消滅

　北イスラエル王国がアッシリアに滅ぼされたのは、紀元前722年で、南北分裂から約200年後でした。アッシリアは、首都サマリアに住む27,290人のイスラエルの民を他の地域へ強制移住させました。また、他の地域から他の民族を移住させてくるなどして、イスラエルの民と他民族との混交を図りました。

　この結果、イスラエルの民は、民族としてのまとまりを失い、新しい民族として溶解していきました。このようにして出現してきた民族の代表がサマリア人（＝イスラエルの民とアッシリアから来た移民との間に生まれた人々とその子孫）です。こうして、イスラエル王国を構成していた北部10部族は消滅していきました。

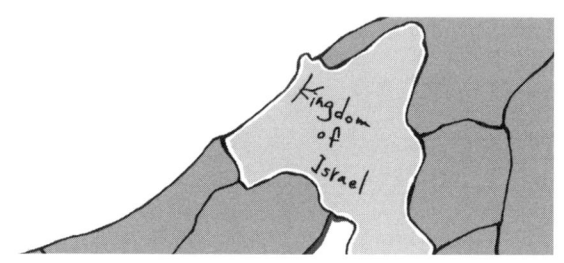

参考：民族が滅びるとは、他民族との混交であることがほとんどである。民族がすべて死に絶えるというわけでもなく、ミステリーのごとく忽然と姿を消すというわけでもない。

関連情報　アッシリア

　アッシリアは、紀元前1950年ごろにメソポタミア（現在のイラク）北部に興った国で、南側にバビロニアと隣接します。チグリス川とユーフラテス川の上流地域を中心に栄え、最盛期にはイラン西部からエジプト本土全域に及ぶ世界帝国を築きました。紀元前625年にはアッシリアからバビロンを奪取し、新バビロニアが建国されました。そこでエジプト王ネコ2世と組んで、新バビロニアと抗戦しましたが、これも空しく、紀元前612年にはアッシリアはついに滅亡しました。アッシリアのあとに続く、新バビロニアやアケメネス朝ペルシャは、アッシリアの行政機構を多く取り入れました。

Section 2

On the other hand, the Kingdom of Judah was able to hold out for about 350 years through Solomon's descendants, until it was destroyed by the Neo-Babylonian Empire (with the capital Babylon).

■ **The collapse of the Northern Kingdom of Israel and the eradication of a race**

It was 722 B.C. when the Northern Kingdom of Israel was destroyed by Assyria. This was about 200 years after the partition of North and South Israel. Assyria forced 27,290 people of Israel who lived in its capital Samaria to migrate to other regions. Moreover, it intended to mix the people of Israel and other races by making other races immigrate from other regions.

As a result, the people of Israel lost race cohesiveness and were bred into becoming a new race. The descendants of the people who were born between the people of Israel and the immigrants from Assyria came to be called Samaritans. Thus, the northern 10 tribes which made up the Kingdom of Israel disappeared.

●Useful Usage● **ERUPT**
1. The volcano erupted suddenly. (その火山は突然噴火した)
2. He erupted into laughter. (彼は急に笑い出した)
3. A rash erupted on her back. (発疹が急に彼女の背中に吹き出てきた)

第2節　旧約聖書の世界

13　ユダの興亡とバビロン捕囚

■ ユダの興亡

　南のユダ王国は北イスラエル王国に比べ、比較的安定した政権でした。アハズの時代になんと同胞のイスラエル王国を圧迫するアッシリアに助けを求め、アッシリアに隷属することになりました。

　北イスラエル王国がアッシリアに滅ぼされたことが伝わったヒゼキヤの時代には、表面的にはアッシリアに忠誠を誓いつつ、独立する機会を窺っていました。ヒゼキヤは、エルサレムの防備を固め、ついに反乱を企てますが、ユダの諸都市は次々に陥落します。しかし、エルサレムだけは陥落せずに済んだため、エルサレムには神の加護があるという考えが強まり、難攻不落の神の都であるという信仰が広まっていくことになります。

　ヨシヤの時代になり、ユダ王国はアッシリアの圧力から逃れ、経済的復興を成し遂げました。ヨシヤが活躍した時代は、アッシリアの衰退期でした。アッシリアから独立した新バビロニアが、アッシリアを圧迫していたのです。ヨシヤの死後は、ユダ王国も衰退し始め、紀元前586年に、アッシリアに代わり、中東オリエント世界の覇者になっていた新バビロニアに滅ぼされました。

■ バビロン捕囚

　ユダ王国の衰退期、新バビロニア王のネブカドネザル2世により、ユダ王国の民が無理やり新バビロニアの首都バビロンに連行されました。これが、いわゆるバビロン捕囚です。紀元前597年の第1回バビロン捕囚で連行された民は10,832人（政府高官、兵士、職人などを含む）に上ったと言われています。エレミア書

Section 2

The rise and fall of the Kingdom of Judah and the Babylonian Captivity

■ The rise and fall of the Kingdom of Judah

The Southern Kingdom of Judah maintained a relatively stable government compared to the Northern Kingdom of Israel. In the time of Ahaz, it asked for and received help from Assyria which oppressed the Kingdom of Israel and therefore Judah became a vassal to Assyria.

In the days of Hezekiah when it was learned that the Northern Kingdom of Israel had been destroyed by Assyria, the kingdom of Judah superficially pledged its fidelity to Assyria but waited for the opportunity to become independent. Though Hezekiah built up the defense of Jerusalem and finally planned a revolt, various cities in Judah surrendered themselves to Assyria one after another. Only Jerusalem avoided capitulation so the idea that Jerusalem was divinely protected by an invincible God grew.

When the time of Josiah came, the Kingdom of Judah gained a measure of independence from Assyria and accomplished an economical revival. This was possible due to Assyria being in a state of decline at the time of Josiah's rule. The Neo-Babylonian Empire broke free from the clutches of the Assyrian Empire and worked towards destroying Assyria. After the death of Josiah, the Kingdom of Judah also began to decline and was destroyed by the rising Neo-Babylonian Empire which became the dominating force of the Middle Eastern Orient world in place of Assyria in 586 B.C.

■ The Babylonian Captivity

When the Kingdom of Judah was at its ebb, its people were taken to Babylon, the capital of the Neo-Babylonian Empire by its king, Nebuchadnezzar II. This is what is called the Babylonian Captivity. It is said that the number of people who were taken at the 1st Babylonian

第2節　旧約聖書の世界

によると、捕虜としてバビロンに拉致された有力者の数は3,023人とされています。

　第2回バビロン捕囚は紀元前586年に行われ、その後も何度かバビロン捕囚は起こりますが、新バビロニアがアケメネス朝ペルシャに滅ぼされた紀元前537年、ペルシャ王キュロスによりユダヤ人たちは解放されました。最初に故郷エルサレムに帰還したユダヤ人の数は42,462人と言われています。

参考：北のイスラエル王国（北王国）の滅亡とともにイスラエル10部族は消滅したが、南のユダ王国（南王国）のイスラエルの民は、ユダ王国滅亡後も、そのアイデンティティを保持できた。これは、移民政策の違いによる。北王国を滅ぼしたアッシリアは、イスラエルの民を各地に移住させたのであるが、南王国を滅ぼした新バビロニアは、民をバビロンに集中させた。バビロンに連行した形のバビロン捕囚は、イスラエルの民の民族的結束を強化し、ユダヤ人という民族的概念が生まれたのも、この捕囚の結果と言える。

14　現代に通じる人生の教訓書

■ ヨブ記

　ヨブ記は、旧約聖書の中の代表的な知恵文学の一書で、人生の不条理と悪の問題について論じています。この書物の主人公であるヨブは、無垢な正しい人で、神を畏れ、悪を避けて生きていました。しかし、ヨブの信仰を試すために、天上で神とサタンが賭けをした結果、ヨブを次々と災難が襲うようになりました。ヨブは自分の苦しみの原因を神に問い、神を責めましたが、神への忠誠を保っていたことを神は褒め称えました。その後まもなく、神はヨブの健康を回復させ、さらに財産を2倍にしました。

参考：このヨブ記は万人の書と呼ばれ、人間の心身の苦悩の問題の正しい理解のためには、しばしば人の視野が不十分であることを強調している。

■ 詩　編

　詩編は、ヘブライ語では「テヒリーム」と呼ばれ、賛美を意味します。詩編は5部に分かれており、神への賛美の詩が150作品収録されています。全体の約半

Section 2

Captivity in 597 B.C. came to 10,832 (including high government officials, soldiers, and craftsmen). According to Jeremiah, the number of the influential people who were abducted to Babylon as captives is assumed to be 3,023.

The 2nd Babylonian Captivity occurred in 586 B.C., and after that, it occurred several times. However, Jews were liberated by the Persian king Cyrus in 537 B.C. when the Neo-Babylonian Empire was destroyed by the Achaemenid Empire of Persia. The first group of Jews who returned to their home of Jerusalem is said to number 42,462.

Timeless moral books for life

■ The Book of Job

The Book of Job is a work of Wisdom Literature in the Old Testament that discusses the absurdity of life and the problem of evil. Job, who is the lead character of this book, is described as an innocent and upright man, fearing God and turning away from evil. However, as a result of a bet made between God and Satan to test the belief of Job, misfortunes are visited upon him one after another. Though Job finally asks God about the cause of his suffering and blamed Him, God applauds Job for maintaining his loyalty to Him. Immediately thereafter, God restores Job to normal health. In addition, God doubles his property.

■ The Book of Psalms

The Book of Psalms is called "Tehillim" in Hebrew, meaning praise. It is divided into 5 parts and contains 150 poems of praise to God. About half of the books are assumed to be attributed to King David

第2節　旧約聖書の世界

分はダビデ王の作で、他にアサフ、コラの子たち、ソロモンなどによって作られたとされる詩が含まれています。詩編の中には、楽器による伴奏がつけられるものもありました。詩編は様々な用いられ方をしました。イエスは説教のときに詩編を引用し、初代教会では礼拝に用いられ、また、新約聖書の著者たちも、詩編から多くを引用していました。

■ 雅　歌

雅歌は、ヘブライ語では「歌の中の歌」と言われ、歌の中でも最も優れた歌を意味しています。第1章1節の表題として「ソロモンの雅歌」とあるように、著者は伝統的にイスラエル王ソロモンとされています。雅歌は、男女の恋愛を歌ったものですが、その解釈をめぐっては、古代から大いに議論されてきました。ユダヤ教においては、「神とイスラエル民族との愛の関係」を描写している歌であると解釈されてきました。一方、キリスト教においては、「キリストと教会の関係」に関する歌であるという解釈がされてきました。

■ ダニエル書

ダニエル書は、シリア王アンティオコス4世の迫害に苦しむユダヤ人たちを励ますために書かれたと考えられています。2つの部分で構成されており、第1〜6章ではバビロンに捕虜として連れて行かれた少年ダニエルと他の3人の友人たちの出来事が記され、第7〜12章では黙示文学の形式をとり、ダニエルが見た幻について語られています。ダニエル書の中で有名な箇所は、第6章の獅子の穴のエピソードです。これは、ダニエルがライオンの穴に投げ込まれても、まるで奇跡のごとく無傷で生還するという物語で、どのような状況下でも神に忠実な者は救われるというメッセージがこの書には込められています。

Section 2

with additional poetries which are assumed to be attributed to Asaph, the sons of Korah, and Solomon. Some of the Psalms were meant to be accompanied by musical instruments. The Book of Psalms was used in various ways: Jesus quoted it in his preaching, the early church used it for worship, and the authors of the New Testament also quoted directly from it a number of times.

■ The Song of Solomon

The Song of Solomon is known as the "Song of Songs" in Hebrew, meaning the most excellent of all songs. As the title of verse 1, chapter 1, is stated as the "Song of Solomon," the author is traditionally believed to be the King of Israel, Solomon. Though the Song of Solomon is a song of love between men and women, there has been lots of discussions on its interpretation since ancient times. In Judaism, it has been understood as the song which describes the love between God and the people of Israel. On the other hand, it has been interpreted as the song concerning the relationship between Christ and the church, in Christianity.

■ The Book of Daniel

The Book of Daniel is considered to be written to encourage the Jews who suffered oppression under the Syrian king Antiochus IV. It is composed of two parts: Chapters 1 to 6 describe what happened to a young Daniel and three friends taken as captives into Babylon. Chapters 7-12 are written in the form of Apocalyptic Literature and these chapters describe the prophetic phantom that Daniel saw. A famous part in the Book of Daniel is the lion's den episode of Chapter 6. In this story Daniel is thrown into a den of lions but is able to return home unscathed as if by miracle. This book presents the following message: No matter what the situation is, if a person stays faithful to God, he will be saved.

第2節　旧約聖書の世界

■ 箴言

　箴言は、古代イスラエルの人たちに、いかに正しく生きていくかを教えた教訓や格言を集めたものです。箴言は31章から成り、その多くが、ソロモンの言葉として伝えられていますが、その他アグルやレムエルといった賢人の言葉として伝えられている章もあります。箴言では、「知恵の重要さ」「神への畏敬の重要さ」が主題となっています。この書の中には、「主を畏れることは知識の初めである」という有名な文があります。主を畏れるとは、恐怖ではなく神への畏敬の念を持って従うことで、全体としては、全能の神の尊さを知ることが知識の始まりであるということを表しています。

■ コヘレトの言葉

　コヘレトの言葉は12章から成り、その著者はソロモンであると考えられています。この書は「空の空、空の空、いっさいは空」（口語訳聖書より）という有名な文で始まります。伝道者は、人の世におけるあらゆることを経験した結果、財産や名声、知恵などを求めても、すべてはむなしく風を追うようなものだと語ります。そして最後に、「神を畏れ、その戒めを守れ。これこそ人間のすべて」と語り、真の幸福は、ただ神を畏れ神に仕えることにあることを示しています。

関連情報　ソロモンの知恵の話

　2人の遊女がある子を自分の子だと訴えました。ソロモンは刀を持ってきて子供を2つに切り分けるよう命じました。1人の女は「相手の人にあげてください」、もう1人の女は「公平に分けてください」と言いました。ソロモンは最初の女が本当の母親と見抜き、その女にその子を与えるように言いました（神の知恵と言うほどの知恵ではない？）。

Section 2

■ The Book of Proverbs

The Book of Proverbs is a collection of lessons and maxims which show the people in ancient Israel how to live well. It's comprised of 31 chapters, most of which are conveyed as the words of Solomon. However, there are other chapters which are attributed to the words of wise men such as Agur and Lemuel. The themes in the Book of Proverbs are the "importance of wisdom" and the "importance of reverence for God." In this book, there is a famous sentence: "The fear of the Lord is the beginning of knowledge." The word, "the fear of the Lord" does not mean being afraid of God but means obeying God with reverence for Him. As a whole, it means that it is the beginning of knowledge to know the dignity of the Almighty God.

■ Ecclesiastes

Ecclesiastes is comprised of 12 chapters and its author is considered to be Solomon. This book begins with a famous sentence: "Meaningless! Meaningless! Utterly meaningless! Everything is meaningless." The preacher tells that everything is meaningless. A person chases who yearns for and makes every effort to gain property, fame, and wisdom is like a person chasing the wind. He says in the end of Ecclesiastes: "Fear God, and keep his commandments; for this is the whole duty of man." It teaches believers that true happiness lies in reverence for God and service to God.

●Useful Usage● CHASE
1. Joy chased all fear from her mind. （喜びが彼女の恐怖心を完全に追い払った）
2. The child chased up something to eat. （子供は何か食べたいとせがんだ）

第3節

新約聖書の世界

1 聖誕前夜

■ 新約聖書の位置づけ
　（本書の）第3章第2節では旧約聖書の中の物語を扱ってきましたが、ここから新約聖書の物語を扱います。旧約聖書は、古代イスラエルの民の宗教がユダヤ人の宗教となるまでの話ですが、新約聖書は、救世主であるイエス・キリストについての話を中心とします。

■ イエス・キリストの意味
　イエス・キリストという名称は、イエスが名前でキリストが苗字というわけではありません。つまり、キリスト家のイエスではないのです。実際のところ、イエスは名前ですが、キリストは救世主を意味します。だから、キリストとは一種の称号なのです。
　また、イエスという名前は、旧約聖書に表れるヨシュアと同じで「救いは神にあり」という意味からきているとされています。
　だから、イエス・キリストとは「神の使命を帯びて、民を導くために遣わされた救世主」（つまり、簡単に言えば、イエスは救世主である）という意味になります。

注：キリスト教とは、イエスの教えというよりも、イエスについての教えで、イエスが始めたのではなく、イエスをキリストと信じた人が始めた宗教であるという点に注意。

Section 3

The New Testament

The Night Before Christmas

■ The position of the New Testament

3-2 dealt with the stories in the Old Testament. This section is however dedicated to the stories of the New Testament. The New Testament focuses on the story of the Messiah, Jesus Christ, while the Old Testament is the story on how the religion of the people of ancient Israel became the religion of Jews.

■ The meaning of the name Jesus Christ

The name of Jesus Christ does not mean that Jesus is a first name and Christ is a family name. That is, it does not mean Jesus of the Christ family. Actually, Jesus is a first name, but Christ means Messiah. Therefore, Christ is a kind of a title.

Moreover, the name of Jesus is assumed to come from the meaning "God is my salvation," and is derived from the same name as Joshua, who appears in the Old Testament.

Therefore, Jesus Christ means "the Messiah who was sent on a mission from God to lead the people," simply declaring that Jesus is the Messiah.

Note : It is necessary to pay attention to the point that Christianity is the teachings about Jesus rather than the teachings of Jesus as it was a religion that was not started by Jesus but was started by the people who believed in Jesus as the Christ.

第3節　新約聖書の世界

■ イエス生誕前後のユダヤ教の状況

このころのユダヤ教は、大きく分けて、サドカイ派、ファリサイ派（パリサイ派）、エッセネ派、熱心党（ゼロテ派）の4つに分かれていました。表にして比べてみましょう。

宗派	一言説明
サドカイ派	貴族層・地主層が主要な構成員。モーセ五書のみを拘束力のある律法とみなし、ユダヤ社会の支配権を掌握していた。
ファリサイ派*	一般大衆や一部の祭司に支持された。モーセ五書に加え、律法学者の口伝律法も重視し、律法を厳格に守ることを求めた。
エッセネ派	ファリサイ派よりもさらに、厳格に律法を遵守し、閉鎖的な社会空間を作り、徹底的な禁欲主義を貫いた。
熱心党	ローマへの不服従を唱え、ローマへの納税を拒否し、ローマ皇帝の像を刻んだ貨幣も偶像として拒絶した、政治的で急進的な宗派。

*注：福音書の中では、イエスの論敵として登場し、イエスに厳しく批判される。

2 受胎告知

■ マリアへの受胎告知

ガリラヤ地方のナザレに住んでいたマリアは、同じ町に住むヨセフという大工と婚約していました。ある日、彼女のもとに、天使ガブリエルが現れて「おめでとう、恵まれた方、主があなたとともにおられる」と告げたのです。そして、彼女がすでに妊娠しており、男の子を生み、その子をイエスと名づけるよう告知しました。

しかし、彼女は処女でした。驚くと同時に謙虚になった彼女に向かってガブリエルは「神にできないことは何ひとつない」と告げました。マリアの妊娠は聖霊の力によるものだとされています。

注：この受胎告知は「ルカによる福音書」第1章28節に出てくる。

Section 3

■ **The situation of Judaism before and after the birth of Jesus**

Judaism of this period was largely divided into four groups: Sadducees, Pharisees, Essenes, and Zealots. Let's compare them in tabular form. (See on the left page.)

●Useful Usage● **COMPARE**
1. She compared the translation with the original.
   (彼女は翻訳を原書と比べてみました)
2. He impolitely compared my homemade bread to a rock.
   (彼は失礼にも私の自家製のパンを石みたいだと言った)

The Annunciation

■ **The Annunciation to Mary**

Mary, who lived in Nazareth in Galilee, was engaged to the carpenter named Joseph, who lived in the same town. One day, the angel Gabriel appeared to her and said, "Congratulations, favored lady! The Lord is with you!" He then announced to her that she had already become pregnant and would give birth to a boy to be named Jesus.

However, she was a virgin. Gabriel's words astonished and humbled her, "There is nothing God cannot do." It is assumed that Mary got pregnant by the power of the Holy Spirit.

Note : This Annunciation appears in "the Gospel according to Luke," chapter 1, verse 28.

第3節　新約聖書の世界

■ ヨセフにも下されたお告げ

　マリアと婚約していたヨセフはダビデの子孫で、敬虔なユダヤ教徒でした。当時は、婚約中はお互いに性交渉をしてはならないとされていたのですが、現実にマリアが妊娠したということでヨセフは悩みます。そんな中、彼の夢に天使が現れ「恐れず妻マリアを迎え入れなさい」と告げられたので、ヨセフは結婚を決意します。

注：この受胎告知は「マタイによる福音書」第1章20節・21節にある。

> **関連情報**　**福音書**
>
> 　福音書はマタイ、マルコ、ルカ、ヨハネによる福音書、つまり、4書あります。これらのうち、最初の3書は、あらすじは大体共通しています。この3書は「共観福音書」と呼ばれ、照らし合わせながら読む福音書ということです。最初のマタイによる福音書が一番インパクトがあるように編集されていますが、年代的にはマルコによる福音書が最も古く、この福音書を基本にして、マタイ、ルカの記述を併せ読むことで、それぞれの特徴や意義を見てとることができます。
>
> 　ちなみに、福音書の「福音（エヴァンゲリオン）」とは、ギリシャ語で「良い（エウ）知らせ（アンゲリオン）」のことで、この言葉は、主に2つの具体的な意味で使用されます。1つは、「神が直接司る世の中が始まりつつある」という知らせで、イエスが言ったことになっています。もう1つは、「イエスの死により人々の罪が許された」という知らせです。

3　イエス誕生と少年時代

■ ベツレヘムで誕生したイエス

　マリアがイエスを身ごもっている間、ローマ皇帝アウグストゥスが、人口調査をするため、領土内の全住民に自分の祖先の地で住民登録することを命じました。
　マリアの夫のヨセフは、ダビデの子孫で、ダビデが生活した地はベツレヘムであったため、身重のマリアを連れて、ナザレからベツレヘムへ向かいました。そ

Section 3

■ The prophecy announced to Joseph

Joseph, who was engaged to Mary, was a descendant of David and a pious Jew. It is thought that engaged couples were not permitted to engage in sexual intercourse at that time. However, Mary was somehow pregnant, which troubled Joseph. Afterwards an angel appeared to him in a dream and said: "Don't be afraid to take Mary." Therefore, Joseph chose to go through with the marriage.

Note：This Annunciation appears in "the Gospel according to Matthew," chapter 1, verses 20-21.

●Useful Usage● ENGAGE
1. He engaged to complete the task within three days.
   （彼は3日以内にその仕事を完成すると約束した）
2. The unique fashion engaged young women's interest for some years.
   （そのユニークなファッションが数年間、若い女性の興味を引いた）
3. The four cogwheels engage firmly.
   （その4つの歯車がしっかりとかみ合っている）

The birth and boyhood of Jesus

■ Jesus born in Bethlehem

While Mary was carrying Jesus, the Roman Emperor Augustus ordered all residents in his territory to register their residences in the land of their ancestors in order to take a census.

Mary's husband Joseph was a descendant of David and the place

第3節　新約聖書の世界

の旅の途中、ベツレヘムの宿で、マリアはイエスを出産します。

参考：ナザレは、現在、イスラエル北部地区ナザレ市に相当し、人口は65,500人（2007年）で、一方、ベツレヘムは、現在、パレスチナのヨルダン川西岸地区のベツレヘム県ベツレヘム市に相当し、人口は25,266人（2007年）。

■ イエス生誕の一部始終

「ルカによる福音書」（第2章1節～40節）によると、羊飼いたちの前に天使が現れ、救世主が誕生したことと、その子が飼い葉桶の中にいることを告げました。さらに無数の天使が現れ「天の神に栄光を、地の民に平和を」と歌ったと言います。そこで羊飼いたちがベツレヘムに向かい、その地で、ヨセフとマリア、そして、飼い葉桶の中のイエスに会いました。

注：イエスは馬小屋で生まれたと、福音書に書いてあるわけではないが、飼い葉桶で生まれたなら、そこは馬小屋だろうとの推測で、生誕は馬小屋という説が広まった。

■ イエスの少年時代

その後、ヨセフ一家はナザレに戻って生活をしていましたが、イエスが12歳のころ、神殿に詣でるため、エルサレムを訪れます。ところが、突然、イエスが行方不明になってしまいます。両親は懸命に探しますが、見つかりません。3日後、エルサレムの神殿で高名な学者たちに囲まれているところを発見します。幼いイエスは、学者たちを前に堂々と議論をしていたのです。聖書によれば、イエスの智恵はますます進み、神と人々から愛されたと書かれています。

Section 3

where David lived was Bethlehem. Therefore, he went from Nazareth to Bethlehem with a pregnant Mary. During their journey, Mary gave birth to Jesus outside an inn in Bethlehem.

■ All the details of the birth of Jesus

According to the Gospel of Luke (chapter 2, verses 1-40), an angel showed up in front of shepherds and announced that the Messiah was born and the child was in a manger. Moreover, it is said that myriads of angels appeared and sang, "Glory to God in the highest, and peace on earth." Then, the shepherds headed for Bethlehem, where they met Joseph, Mary, and Jesus in the manger.

Note : It is not written in the gospel that Jesus was born in a stable. However, the theory that Jesus was born in a stable spread based on the speculation that the place of his birth would be a stable if he were born in a manger.

■ The boyhood of Jesus

After that, the family returned to Nazareth and lived there. When Jesus was 12 years old, they went to Jerusalem to visit a shrine. However, Jesus suddenly went missing. He could not be found even though his parents made great efforts to find him. Three days later, they found Jesus surrounded by famous scholars in a shrine in Jerusalem. Young Jesus was confidently having discussions with the scholars. It is written in the Bible that Jesus advanced in wisdom and was loved both by God and by people.

第3節　新約聖書の世界

4 ｜ 洗礼者ヨハネ

■ 洗礼者のヨハネの登場

　イエスの幼年期・少年期については、「ルカによる福音書」のみが、その神童めいた様子を伝えていますが、イエスが本格的な活動を開始するのは、30歳になったころからです。そのイエスの前に、イエスの先駆者的な人がいました。その人こそ、バプテスマのヨハネ（洗礼者ヨハネ）と呼ばれる人物です。

参考：キリスト教関連でヨハネという人物は3人まで想定される。

区別するための呼び名	どういう人物か？
①洗礼者ヨハネ	新約聖書に登場する預言者、イエスに洗礼を授けた人
②使徒ヨハネ	イエスの12人の弟子の一人
③福音記者ヨハネ	ヨハネによる福音書、ヨハネの第1〜第3の手紙、黙示録の著者とされる人（これらも同一著者でないという学者も多い）

　＊②と③は伝統的には同一人物であるとされるが、これを否定する学者もいる。

注1：バプテスマとは洗礼のことで、身を水に沈め、罪を消滅させ、生まれ変わる儀式のこと。ヨハネの洗礼は、流れる川に沈めるもの、すなわち、川に全身をつけて生まれ変わらせるといった形であった。現在でも、多くの教会ではこれを行うが、大きく分けて浸礼［しんれい（全身を水に浸す方式）］と滴礼［てきれい（水滴を頭にふりかける方式）］の2つの方法がある。

注2：カトリック教会では、滴礼の形や小さな浴槽に赤ん坊を入れて洗礼をするが、プロテスタントの中には、成人してから、川や湖で体を沈めて儀式的な洗礼をする教会もある。

■ イエスに洗礼を授けるヨハネ

　ヨルダン川で洗礼を授けるヨハネの前に、ある男がやってきます。その男こそ、イエスだったのです。当時約30歳であると思われるイエスは、ヨハネに洗礼を頼みます。ヨハネは「私こそ、あなたから洗礼を受けるべきなのに」と言って、これを拒みます。

　しかし、神の御心にかなう正しい行為であると、イエスに促され、ヨハネはイエスに洗礼を授けます。すると、聖霊がハトのように降りてきて、「これは私の愛する子、私の心にかなう者」という声が響いたと言います。

Section 3

John the Baptist

■ The appearance of John the Baptist

Jesus was 30 years old when he officially started preaching, with only the Gospel of Luke making a smattering of references to his childhood and life before then. The most important moment of Jesus' adult life was when he came face to face with his precursor, a man called John the Baptist.

Note 1 : Baptism means the ceremony of washing away sin and realizing spiritual rebirth by water. John was practicing a form a baptism where the whole body of a person is immersed in a river to become reborn in spirit. Today, churches hold this ceremony roughly in two ways: immersion baptism and baptism by affusion or aspersion.

Note 2 : Catholic Church baptize by sprinkling drops of water or putting a baby in a small bath, while some Protestant churches ceremonially immerse their members in rivers or lakes when they are adults.

■ John baptizes Jesus

Jesus appears before John wishing to be baptized in the Jordan River. Jesus, who was assumed to be about 30 years old at the time, asked John to baptize him. John refuses to do this, saying, "I need to be baptized by you ..."

However, as Jesus persuaded John by saying that the baptism was the will of God, he could be baptized by the relenting John. It is said that the Holy Spirit descended on him like a dove and a voice resounded : "This is my Son, whom I love; with him I am well pleased."

第3節　新約聖書の世界

注：イエスには罪がないので、実際には洗礼を受けるのはおかしいことになる。しかし、罪深い人々を救うため、あえて洗礼を受けたと解釈される。

5 │ 荒野の誘惑

■ サタンの妨害

ヨハネから洗礼を受けたイエスは、ユダの荒野［あらの］へ向かい、40日間断食をします。そのさなか、悪魔（サタン）がイエスの前に現れます。サタンが「あなたが神の子なら、この石をパンになるように命じたらどうだ」と言うと、イエスは「人はパンだけで生きるのではない。神の口から出る1つひとつの言葉で生きる」と旧約聖書の言葉を引用して、サタンを退けました。この話は、「マタイによる福音書」第4章3節・4節にあります。

注：40という数字は、かつてイスラエルの民がエジプト脱出後に、40年間荒野をさまよったことにちなんだとも言われている。

■ サタンを撃退

続いて、サタンはエルサレム神殿の上にイエスを立たせ、「神の子なら飛び降りたらどうだ」とささやきます。神の子なら天使に守ってもらえるというわけです。「あなたは神である主を試してはならない」と、またも、旧約聖書の言葉を引用して、サタンを退けます。

それでも、サタンは諦めません。サタンはイエスにこの世の栄華を見せ、「ひれ伏して私を拝むなら、これをみな与えよう」と誘惑します。イエスは「退け。サタン！」と厳しく言い放ち、「あなたの神である主を拝み、ただ主に仕えよ」という旧約聖書の言葉を引用して、サタンを跳ね除けます。ついに、サタンは誘惑を断念し、退いていきました[注]。

イエスはその後、洗礼者ヨハネが、ガリラヤの領主ヘロデ・アンティパスによって逮捕されたと聞き、ガリラヤに向かいました。

Section 3

Note : As Jesus has no sin, it is actually strange that he was baptized. However, this is interpreted as follows : Jesus dared to be baptized to save sinners.

The temptation in the wilderness

■ Satan tests Jesus

After being baptized by John, Jesus heads for the wilderness in Judea and fasts for forty days. During his fast, the devil (Satan) appears in front of Jesus. Satan said to him, "If you are the Son of God, order this stone to turn into bread." Jesus defeated Satan by quoting from the Old Testament: "Man does not live on bread alone, but on every word that comes from the mouth of God." This story is described in "the Gospel according to Matthew," chapter 4, verses 3, 4.

Note: The number 40 is said to come from the fact that the people of Israel once wandered in the wilderness for 40 years after their escape from Egypt.

■ Repelling Satan

Satan next has Jesus stand on the Jerusalem Temple and whispers, "If you're the Son of God, throw yourself down." If he is the Son of God, he can be protected by an angel. He again triumphs over Satan by quoting once again from the Old Testament: "You must not try the Lord God."

Satan doesn't give up though. Satan takes Jesus to a mountain overlooking all of civilization and tempts him by saying, "All this I will give you if you bow down and worship me." Jesus says sharply to Satan, "Away from me, Satan!", and opposes him by quoting one more time from the Old Testament: "You shall worship the Lord your God, and serve only Him." Finally, Satan gave up the temptation of Jesus and left him.

Then, Jesus heard that John the Baptist was arrested by Herod

●●●補足情報●●●

このサタンによるいわゆる荒野の誘惑の箇所が、ロシアの文学者ドストエフスキーの『カラマーゾフの兄弟』という小説の中の「大審問官（The Grand Inquisitor）」の話に引用されていることは有名である。この3つの誘惑の中には、"世界と人類の全未来史が完全なる箇として凝縮して"おり、"この地上における人間性の歴史的矛盾をことごとく包含した3つの形態が現れている"といった意味内容が記されている。

その内容とは、「パン」と、「聖なる権威」と「国家権力」、言い換えると、「経済」「精神的（宗教的）拠り所」「政治的権威」の問題になる。すなわち、第1は、経済・生活問題、第2は宗教・心の問題、第3は政治・社会問題である。この3つは、普通の人が不安を覚えず、自由で幸福に日常の生活を営むために不可欠な必須の条件ということになる。ただ、ここでの悪魔の誘惑の真意が、"現実"としてのキリストの神的性質と神における自由の意味を忘却させ、現世的なレベルでこの3つを牛耳る（最終的に悪魔を拝む）ことを勧告する点にあったために、キリストはこれを退けたのである。

ドストエフスキーのストーリーでは、他の無神論者の登場人物に対して、大審問官は、人類救済の事業を成し遂げるために悪魔の3つの誘惑を受け入れ、神とキリストの名のもとに、一種の社会主義的専制主義の思想を展開している。

6 十二弟子

■ 大漁をきっかけに弟子となった漁師たち

ガリラヤにやってきたイエスは、各地のシナゴーグ（ユダヤ教会堂）で、説教をして伝道活動を展開します。

イエスはある日、船のそばで網を洗っていた漁師シモンに、ガリラヤの海（＝実際はガリラヤ湖）で自分を乗せて船を漕ぎ、岸から少し離れたところにとめるよう指示しました。イエスはそこで教えを説いたあと、イエスはシモンからなかなか魚が獲れないと聞いたのでシモンに網を入れるよう命令しました。イエスの言う通りにすると、引き上げた網には大量の魚がかかっていました。これを見ていたシモン（のちのペトロ）と彼の弟アンデレ、ゼベダイの子ヤコブとその弟ヨ

Section 3

Antipas, the tetrarch of Galilee, and headed for Galilee.

> ●Useful Usage●　ARREST
> 1. The fallen trees arrested the current of a brook.
> （倒れた木々が小川の流れをさえぎっていた）［(運動や進行などを)止める］
> 2. The grandeur of the remains arrested me.
> （その遺跡の壮大さに私は圧倒した）［(人目や注意を)引く］

The twelve disciples

■ The fishermen who became disciples in the wake of a good catch

Jesus, who came to Galilee, expanded. his mission by preaching in synagogues (Jewish houses of worship) in various places.

One day, Jesus instructed Simon and other fishermen, who were washing their nets near a boat, to carry him out on the Sea of Galilee and anchor a little away from the shore so that he could preach to them on the boat. While on the boat, Jesus heard from Simon that he was having difficulty catching fish so he ordered Simon to row out deeper and drop his nets. The fishermen did as they were told and hauled in the largest catch they had ever seen. Simon (later known as Peter) and his brother Andrew, as well as James, son of Zebedee and his younger brother John became disciples of Jesus this day.

第3節　新約聖書の世界

ハネが弟子となりました。

■ 各地の伝道を担う十二弟子

イエスは、最初の弟子の漁師4人に加え、トマス、熱心党（→p.162）のシモン、徴税人のマタイ、アルファイの子ヤコブ、イスカリオテ出身のユダ、フィリポとその友人バルトロマイ、タダイの12人が、イエスに選ばれ、各地への伝道を担当することになりました。

この12人の弟子は、十二使徒と呼ばれ、常にイエスに忠誠を誓い、イエスとともに行動しました。イエスが一声かけると、いかに各地に散らばっていても、すぐにイエスのもとに集まってきたと言われています。

注：12の意味
弟子の数の12という数は、イスラエル民族を構成していた12部族の数を象徴し、ユダヤでは神聖で、完全な数とみなされていた。この「12」は、イエスの死後も守られ、のちにイスカリオテのユダがイエスを裏切り、自殺すると、マティアという人物が代わりに加えられている。

7 イエスの奇跡と救い

■ イエスの奇跡

聖書には、イエスの教えとともに、数々の奇跡が語られています。イエスの奇跡の一部を表にして紹介しましょう。

どんな奇跡？	さらなる説明
水をぶどう酒に変える	ナザレ近くのカナという町で行われた婚礼の宴で、ぶどう酒がたりなくなり、急遽［きゅうきょ］イエスが水を大変味の良いぶどう酒に変えた。
空腹の5,000人を満腹にした	イエスに5,000人もの人たちがつき従っているとき、1人の少年が持っていた2匹の魚とパン5つで、全員を満腹にさせた。
病気を癒す	イエスが、ある中風の人に「あなたの罪は許された」と言ったら、自分が担がれてきた担架を担いで帰っていった。
死者をよみがえらせる	死後4日過ぎたラザロに対し、「ラザロ、出てきなさい」と大声で叫んだら、ラザロは墓から立ち上がって外に出てきた。

Section 3

■ The twelve disciples who oversaw Jesus' mission

The 12 people were Thomas, Simon the Zealot, Matthew the tax gatherer, James the son of Alphaeus, Judas Iscariot, Philip, his friends Bartholomew and Jude, in addition to 4 fishermen. These first disciples were chosen by Jesus and oversaw aspects of his mission in various places.

These 12 disciples were called the Twelve Apostles, who pledged their fidelity to Jesus and acted in accordance with his will. It is said that they quickly gathered around Jesus no matter where they were when Jesus summoned them by uttering a word.

Note : The meaning of twelve
Twelve, the number of the disciples represents the number of the twelve tribes which made up the people of Israel and was regarded as the divine and perfect number in Judea. This number "twelve" was observed even after the death of Jesus. When Judas Iscariot betrayed Jesus and killed himself, a person named Matthias took his place as the twelfth disciple.

The miracles and salvation of Jesus

■ The miracles of Jesus

The Bible tells of many miracles that Jesus performed as well as the teachings of Jesus. Below are some of the miracles of Jesus in tabular form.

Miracle	Further explanation
Changed water into wine	At a wedding in Cana near Nazareth, Jesus quickly changed water into wine because of a shortage of it.
Fed 5000 hungry people	When 5000 people in tow, Jesus was able to feed them all by dividing 2 fishes and 5 loaves of bread which a boy had.
Cured human ailments	When Jesus said to the paralytic, "Your sins are forgiven," he went home carrying the stretcher on which he was carried.

第3節　新約聖書の世界

■ イエスの救い

　イエスの時代のユダヤは男性優位の社会でしたが、イエスは女性に対しても平等に救いの手を差し伸べています。また、当時のユダヤ人はサマリアに住む人たちを蔑んでいたのです。だから、サマリア人の女性などに、話しかけることは皆無に等しいことでした。しかし、イエスがサマリアを通ったとき、井戸に水を汲みに来た女性に、福音を説きました。その結果、わずか2日間のサマリア滞在の折に、多くのサマリア人が信者となりました。

　イエスに救われたその他の女性を表で紹介しましょう。

女性の名	さらなる説明
マグダラのマリア	7つの悪霊に憑かれた病をイエスによって癒された。磔[はりつけ]にされたイエスを遠くから見守り、イエスの復活に最初に立ち会った。
姦通の女	エルサレムの長老たちに捕らえられ、イエスのもとに連れて来られ、人々が石打ちの刑を主張したが、イエスは「罪を犯したことがない者が、まず、石を投げよ」と言って、この言葉に女が救われた。

注：イエスは、ユダヤ人が嫌う以下の人たちにも、救いの手を差し伸べた。
　①病人・罪人　②サマリア人　③ローマ人　④徴税人　⑤姦通の女
　ユダヤ人の価値観では、①は律法を守れない人、②はイスラエルの純血を汚した人、③はユダヤ人を支配する人、④はローマ人の手先になり同胞から重税を取り立て、私服を肥やす人、⑤はユダヤの律法で最も憎むべき罪である姦通の罪を犯した人である。

8　山上の説教

■ 幸いの教え

　イエスは、ガリラヤ湖畔の丘の上で、集まってきた人たちに「山上の説教」（または「山上の垂訓[すいくん]」）と呼ばれる教えを説きます。イエスがここで説教したのは、山は神聖なところだと考えられていたし、何より、モーセが十戒を授けられたのがシナイ山であったことと関係があるという説があります。

　山上の説教の中には、有名な説教が多いのですが、幸いの教えを紹介します（「マタイによる福音書」第5章）。

Section 3

| Brought the dead back to life | When Jesus cried out with a loud voice in front of the grave of Lazarus (Lazaros), who had been dead for four days, "Lazarus, come forth," Lazarus got up and came out of his grave. |

■ The salvation of Jesus

Jesus equally offered a helping hand to women though Judea in the time of Jesus was a male-oriented society. Moreover, Jews at that time despised the people who lived in Samaria. Therefore, there was little opportunity to talk with Samaritan women. However, when Jesus passed through Samaria, he preached the gospel to a woman who came to a well to draw some water. As a result, a lot of Samaritans became believers during his two day stay in Samaria.

Below are other women saved by Jesus.

Name of woman	Further explanation
Mary Magdalene	Jesus healed her of possession by seven evil spirits. She witnessed Jesus' crucifixion from a distance and was the first witness of the Resurrection of Jesus.
The adulterous woman	She was captured by presbyters in Jerusalem and brought to Jesus. Jesus said, "Whichever one of you has committed no sin may throw a stone at her." Though people demanded she be stoned, they could not go through with it. As a result, the woman was saved by his interjection.

The Sermon on the Mount

■ The teaching on happiness

Jesus preaches a sermon known as "the Sermon on the Mount" to people who gathered on the hill by the lake in Galilee. The reason why Jesus preached in this place is that a mountain was thought to be a sacred place. Also, there is a theory that it relates to the fact that the place where Moses received the Ten Commandments was Mount Sinai.

Let me introduce the teachings on happiness though there are many

第3節　新約聖書の世界

- 心の貧しい人々は、幸いである、天の国はその人たちのものである。
- 悲しむ人々は、幸いである、その人たちは慰められる。
- 柔和な人々は、幸いである、その人たちは地を受け継ぐ。
- 義に飢え渇く人々は、幸いである、その人たちは満たされる。
- 憐れみ深い人々は、幸いである、その人たちは憐れみを受ける。
- 心の清い人々は幸いである、その人たちは神を見る。
- 平和を実現する人々は、幸いである、その人たちは神の子と呼ばれる。
- 義のために迫害される人々は幸いである、天の国はその人たちのものである。

注：逆に不幸な者の例として、満腹の者、今笑っている者、周囲から褒められている者などがあげられていて、これらはすべて一時的幸せで、本当の幸福者ではないとされている。

■ 有名な言葉

この山上の説教の中に、キリスト教に詳しくない人でも、聞いたことがある教えがいくつかあります。これらはすべて、「マタイによる福音書」第5章～7章にあります。表にして示しましょう（口語訳聖書より）。

マタイ福音書	そこにある教え
第5章39節	誰かがあなたの右の頬を打つなら、左の頬をも向けてやりなさい。
第7章7節	求めよ、そうすれば与えられるであろう。捜せ、そうすれば見出すであろう。門を叩け、そうすれば開けてもらえるであろう。

＊「ルカによる福音書」には「敵を愛し、憎む者に親切にせよ」というのが出てくる。

参考：イエスは、律法を廃するためではなく完成するために来たと言い、「殺すな」を「腹を立ててはいけない」「馬鹿にしてもいけない」、「姦淫するな」を「みだらな気持ちで女を見たら、心の中で犯している」などというように基準を厳しくしている。

Section 3

famous teachings in the Sermon on the Mount.
- Blessed are the poor in spirit, for theirs is the kingdom of heaven.
- Blessed are those who mourn, for they will be comforted.
- Blessed are the meek, for they shall inherit the earth.
- Blessed are those who hunger and thirst for justice, for they shall be satisfied.
- Blessed are the merciful, for they shall obtain mercy.
- Blessed are the pure in heart, for they shall see God.
- Blessed are the peacemakers, for they shall be called sons of God.
- Blessed are those who are persecuted for righteousness' sake, for theirs is the kingdom of heaven.

Note : In contrast, Jesus points out that the people who are prosperous, carefree, and popular amongst people are in truth unhappy. It is considered that these people are temporarily happy but not truly happy.

■ Famous sayings

In the Sermon on the Mount, there are some teachings which even the person who is unfamiliar with Christianity has probably heard. All of these teachings are described in "the Gospel according to Matthew," chapters 5-7. They are below in tabular form.

Gospel of Matthew	Quoted from the gospel
Chapter 5, verse 39	If someone strikes you on the right cheek, turn to him the other cheek.
Chapter 7, verse 7	Ask, and it shall be given you; seek, and you shall find; knock, and it shall be opened for you.

第3節　新約聖書の世界

9　たとえ話

■「良きサマリア人のたとえ」

　イエスは、教えの内容をわかりやすくするため、頻繁にたとえ話をしました。有名なものの中に、「良きサマリア人のたとえ」というのがあります。

　あるユダヤ人男性がエルサレムからエリコに向かう途中、盗賊に襲われ、着物を剥ぎ取られ、半殺しにされ、道端に放置されました。そこを何人かの人たちが通り過ぎて行きます。最初に通りかかったのはユダヤの祭司、次に通りかかったのは、神殿に仕えるレビ人でした。この2人は、かかわるのを恐れ、道端に倒れている男性を無視して、道の反対側を通って行きました。3人目に通りかかった人はサマリア人でした。サマリア人は、ユダヤ人とは敵対関係にあったのですが、負傷した男性を介抱し、宿屋まで連れて行ったのです。彼は、銀貨2枚を宿屋の主人に渡して、費用がもっとかかったら帰りに払うとまで言ったのでした。

　このたとえ話のあと、イエスは律法学者に、「あなたはこの3人の中で、誰が、盗賊に襲われた人の隣人になったと思うか？」と質問します。答えはもちろん、サマリア人。イエスにとって隣人とは、民族や距離の遠近に関係なく、憐れみの心を持って自ら行動する人のことなのです*。

----

*さらに言えば、イエスにとって隣人とは、自分にとっての隣人ではなく、相手にとっての隣人となる人のことである。

■「放蕩［ほうとう］息子のたとえ」

　ある金持ちに2人の息子がいました。長男は真面目な性格でしたが、次男は放蕩息子でした。財産分与のときになり、父親は周囲の心配をよそに、次男にも財産を分けました。その財産を手に旅に出た次男は、予想通り、放蕩の限りを尽くして無一文になって帰ってきました。長男は厳しく次男を責めますが、父親は温かく次男を迎え入れます。これは、子供の自由を尊重し、かつ、改心を待つ親の姿を描いています。

　この話は、父が神で、次男が人間を表しています。人間は幾度となく神を忘れるが、神は人間を許し続けるということを表します。ここで大切なのは、「改心」つまり、「悔い改め」が存在することです。神の愛とともに悔い改めの重要性を

Section 3

The parables

■ "The parable of the good Samaritan"

Jesus frequently used parables to make his teachings understandable. "The parable of the good Samaritan" is one of his famous parables.

On the way from Jerusalem to Jericho, a Jewish man was attacked by robbers, who stripped his clothes off, nearly killed him, and left him by the roadside. Some folks walked past the scene. The first man who happened to pass by was a Jewish priest, and the second man was a Levite who served in the temple. These two people were afraid to get involved so they ignored the man who was lying by the roadside and crossed to the other side of the road. The third man who happened to pass by was a Samaritan. The Samaritan cared for the injured man and took him to an inn even though Samaritans had hostile relations with Jews. He handed two silver coins to the boniface and went so far as to say that he would pay more if the total cost came to more than that.

After this parable, Jesus asked the rabbi, "Of these three men, who do you think became a neighbor to the man who was attacked by the robbers?" The answer is of course the Samaritan. For Jesus, a neighbor is a person who acts voluntarily with a heart of compassion regardless of race or boundaries.

■ "The parable of the prodigal son"

A rich man had 2 sons. The second son was a prodigal son while the elder son was a serious-minded man. At the time of determining inheritance of property, their father gave the second son his share of the inheritance despite the worries of the people around him. The second son set out on a journey with his newly gotten wealth and came back without a shirt to his back after running the whole gamut of dissipation as expected. The father receives the repentant younger son warmly though the elder son severely chastises him. This story depicts the parents who

第3節　新約聖書の世界

も教える話となっています。

参考：次男は異邦人・取税人・遊女たち、長男はパリサイ派ユダヤ人を指しているとも言われている。

■ その他のたとえ話

他にイエスが好んだたとえ話を、表にして4つ紹介します。

タイトル	どんな話?
羊と銀貨のたとえ	100匹の羊のうち1匹が迷子になったとき、1匹を必死に探し、見つかったとき、また、貧しい女性がやっと貯めた10枚の銀貨のうち1枚がなくなって、必死に探した結果、見つかったとき、喜びは相当なもの。これは1人の罪人が悔い改めることが、多数の善人よりも、神にとってはうれしいことを示す。
金持ちに関するたとえ	生きている間は裕福で乞食を蔑む人が天国では立場が逆転する話と、自分の畑が豊作で、新たな蔵を建てて収穫物をしまいこむ金持ちに神が「今命を取り上げられたら、どうするのか？」と問い質す話。この2つの話は、現在富めるものであっても、神の国では現世の財産は空しいものという教え。
種をまく人のたとえ	悪い土地に落ちた種は、芽を出さなかったり、芽が出ても枯れてしまったが、良い土地に落ちた種は、実を結び、大いに成長したという話。これは、「いくら神の言葉を伝えようとしても相手に聞く気がなければ難しい」という戒めで、＜教えを説く者の心構え＞を説いたものと考えられている。
10人の乙女のたとえ	結婚の宴で花婿を迎える10人のうち、5人は予備の油を持っていたが、5人は持っていなかった。花婿が遅れて到着し、火が消えたとき、油を持っていた乙女のみ花婿を迎え入れることができた。「これは神の国に入りたいなら、準備を怠るな」という戒めで、＜教えを受ける側の心構え＞を説いたもの。

参考：仏教の法華経にもある「放蕩息子のたとえ」
　聖書の「放蕩息子のたとえ」は「ルカによる福音書」第15章11節〜32節に出ているが、仏教の代表的経典である「妙法蓮華経」の第4章信解品［しんげほん］にも、これに似た話がある。

Section 3

respect the freedom of their child and wait for him to reform.

In this story, the father represents God, while the second son represents humans. It shows that God continues to permit humans though they forget God many times. It is important that "reformation," or "repentance," exists in the mind of each person. This is a story to teach the importance of repentance as well as the love of God.

■ **Other parables**

Let me introduce you to four other parables which Jesus liked in tabular form.

Title	What story?
Parables of sheep and silver coins	The person feels great joy in the following situations: When one of 100 sheep went missing and a man searched desperately for the one lost sheep, which finally was found. When one of 10 silver coins which a poor woman saved up with effort was lost and she found it as a result of searching for it frantically. These stories show that there will be more rejoicing in God over one sinner who repents than a lot of righteous persons.
Parables of rich men	The first story is about a person who is rich and despises the beggar in his lifetime has his tables turned in heaven. In the second story, God asked a rich man who put up a new warehouse where he stored his yield because of the good harvest: "What will happen if you are deprived of your life now?" These 2 stories teach that the property in this world is meaningless in the kingdom of God.
Parable of the sower	This is a story about seeds planted in fertile land bearing robust fruit while seeds planted in infertile land did not sprout or died after budding. This teaches us that it is hard to convey the word of God to the people no matter how hard we try it if they have no mind to hear it. This story is thought to tell of the mental attitude of people who preach sermons.
Parable of the ten maidens	Five among ten maidens who waited for their grooms at a wedding had extra oil but the remaining 5 maidens had no extra oil. When the grooms arrived late and the fire went out, only the maidens who had extra oil were able to welcome their grooms. This teaches us that we should not neglect preparation if we want to enter the kingdom of God and tells of the mental attitude of the people who receive sermons.

第3節　新約聖書の世界

　50年間失踪した息子を探し求めていた父親が、ついに息子を見つけた。そのとき、父親は大金持ち、息子は貧乏。父親は息子をさらに20年見守った。父親は親戚の前で、きれいな心になった息子に、全財産を譲ることを宣言する。

　この話のポイントは、父親は仏陀で、息子は我々衆生ということになる。仏陀の慈悲が、我々の罪（＝息子の放蕩）を許し、仏陀は、自らの知恵（＝父親の全財産）を授けるという話であると読めるのである。

10　受　難

■ イエスのエルサレム入城

　ある日、イエスはロバに乗ってエルサレムに入城します[注1]。ユダヤの王がロバに乗ってエルサレムに入城する場面は旧約聖書に預言されていた[注2]ことで、これを踏襲することにより、イエスは自らが救世主であると世に主張しました。

1　聖地エルサレムへは地方から多くの人が訪れていたが、同時に多くの預言者が殺されるなど、危険な地域でもあった。実際、イエスを殺害しようとするユダヤ教指導者層もいたようである。
2　これは、旧約聖書「ゼカリア書」第9章9節にある。

■ ユダヤ教の指導者たちとの論戦

　ユダヤ教の指導者たちは、イエスを陥れるため、数々の論争を仕掛けましたが、イエスはことごとく、それをかわしたと言われています。そのうちの1つに、税金に関する論争があります。

　ある指導者が「ユダヤ人である我々がローマの皇帝に税金を納めるのは、律法に適ったことか？」と質問をしました。もし「税を支払うべき」と答えるとローマ支配を嫌うユダヤ人から反感を買い、「税を支払うべきでない」と答えるとローマ人を怒らせ逮捕されてしまうので、どちらの答えもイエスを窮地に陥れることができるのです。

　イエスは、質問に答える前に、「税金はどんなもので納められるのか？」と逆に質問し、相手が銀貨を見せると、そこに彫られているローマ皇帝の肖像を指して、「ローマ皇帝のものは皇帝に、神のものは神に返しなさい」と言い放ったのです。

Section 3

The Passion

■ Jesus' entry into Jerusalem

Jesus dramatically enters Jerusalem riding on a donkey. The scene of a Jewish king entering Jerusalem riding on a donkey was foretold in the Old Testament. By following this prophecy, Jesus announces that he himself is a Messiah.

Note1 : A lot of people visited the Holy City of Jerusalem from the provinces. At the same time, it was a dangerous area since a lot of prophets were killed for their views. Jewish rulers, along with Roman authorities, were keen to squash any religious demonstrations by killing the cult leaders. Jesus was no exception to this rule.

Note2 : You will see this in "The Book of Zechariah" chapter 9, verse 9 in the Old Testament.

■ The argument with the Jewish rulers

It is said that Jesus fended off every provocation the Jewish Rulers could come up with in order to get him arrested. One of them is the controversy regarding the tax.

One ruler asked, "Does it conform to the law that we Jews pay the tax to the Roman Emperor?" If Jesus replies, "You should pay the tax," he will antagonize Jews who hate Roman rule. If he replies, "You should not pay the tax," it makes Romans upset and he will be arrested by them. Therefore, both answers are detrimental to Jesus.

第3節　新約聖書の世界

　この答えは、肖像は偶像の一種とみなされるので、偶像崇拝を嫌うユダヤ人も納得し、皇帝のものが皇帝に戻る（税金を支払うことになる）ので、ローマ人も納得します。結局、イエスは、この狡猾な質問を退けたのです。

参考　イエスの教えを弟子が理解しなかったときもあった!
　イエスの12人の弟子たちが、自分たちの中で誰が一番偉いのかという序列について論争したことがある。そんな弟子たちに対し、イエスは「子供のように素直にならないと神の国に入れない」と諭す。また、ベタニア（Bethany）の女性がイエスの頭に高価な香油をかけて歓迎した際、ユダが無駄遣いだと憤慨したのに対しイエスは、「彼女は私によいことをしてくれた。…中略…私の体に香油を注いで、私を葬る準備をしてくれた」と女性を擁護した。
＊ベタニアは、イエスがエルサレムに入る前に滞在した土地。

11 最後の晩餐と十字架磔刑

■ 弟子たちの足を洗うイエス

　イエスが十字架に架けられる前日、夕食（最後の晩餐）前に、弟子たち全員の足を洗おうとします。恐縮したペトロは「やめてください」と言いましたが、「もし私が洗わなければ、あなたと私とは何の関係もないことになる」と言われ、手も頭も洗ってもらおうとしました。当時のユダヤで足を洗うのは奴隷の仕事で、弟子が師匠の足を洗うことはありましたが、イエスはその習慣を逆転させ、謙遜とはどういう行為であるかを、身を持って示したわけです。

■ 最後の晩餐

　晩餐が始まると、イエスは「あなた方のうちの1人が私を裏切ろうとしている」と衝撃的なことを述べます。一同が騒然とする中、イエスはパンを取り、「取って食べなさい。これは私の体である」と言って、そしてぶどう酒を取り、「飲みなさい。これは私の契約の血である」と言って、弟子たちに分け与えます。その後、ユダは部屋を出て行きます。他の弟子たちは、イエスの命令で出て行ったのだと思いましたが、実は、そうではなかったのです。このユダこそが裏切り者であったのです。

Section 3

Jesus answered the question with a question of his own: "By what do you pay tax?"

When the ruler showed silver coins, Jesus pointed to the portrait of the Roman emperor which was inscribed on the coins and said strictly: "Give to Caesar what is Caesar's and give to God what is God's".

As the portrait is considered to be a kind of idol, Jews who disliked idol worship were convinced by this answer. Since that which belonged to the emperor's is returned to the emperor (the tax will be paid), Romans were also convinced. In this way, Jesus dismissed this insidious question.

注目：キリスト教用語で「受難」のことをthe Passionと言う。そもそも、このpassionという単語は、ラテン語で「苦難をこうむる」の意味の動詞からきている。the Passionは「（福音書の）キリスト受難の物語」や「キリスト受難曲」「キリスト受難絵画」をも指す。

The Last Supper and the Crucifixion on the cross

■ Jesus washes his disciples' feet

Jesus tries to wash the feet of all his disciples before the supper (the Last Supper) of the day before his Crucifixion. Peter who couldn't bear to see his master do such a lowly thing, said to Jesus, "Please stop it." However, Jesus said, "If I do not wash your feet, you will have no relation to me." Therefore, he had his hands and head as well washed by Jesus. The washing feet was a slave's work in ancient Judea and a disciple sometimes washed his master's feet. However, Jesus reversed the custom and demonstrated extreme modesty.

■ The Last Supper

At the start of the supper, Jesus says something shocking: "One of you will betray me." While all of them are seething from what Jesus

第3節　新約聖書の世界

■ イエスの逮捕と裁判そして処刑

　イエスを支持する群衆の目の届かないところで、イエスは逮捕されます。捕えられ、縛られたイエスはユダヤ教指導者たちのもとへ連行されます。彼らは、エルサレム神殿と律法に関する冒涜［ぼうとく］の罪で、イエスを死刑にすることに決めていました。しかし裁判では死刑にすべき有力な証拠は出てきません。だから彼らの計画は危険にさらされます。そこで彼らはローマ当局にイエスを苦しめてもらおうということになります。

　ユダヤ総督のピラトは、イエスの無罪を見抜き、イエスを釈放しようとしますが、不満げなユダヤの支配者たちは「イエスは死刑だ」と訴えます。ユダヤ人からのさらなる説得もあり、また暴動を避ける意味でも、ピラトは自らの主張を弱めます。処刑を言い渡されたイエスは、十字架を背負い、ゴルゴダの丘へと連れて行かれます。ゴルゴダの丘に着けば、十字架上で両手両足を釘で打ちつけられます。釘を打つ前に痛みを麻痺させる薬入りのぶどう酒が与えられたのですが、イエスは拒否したと言われています。

　イエスは十字架に架けられながらも「父よ、彼らをお救しください。自分が何をしているのか知らないのです」と、人々のために祈りを捧げました。

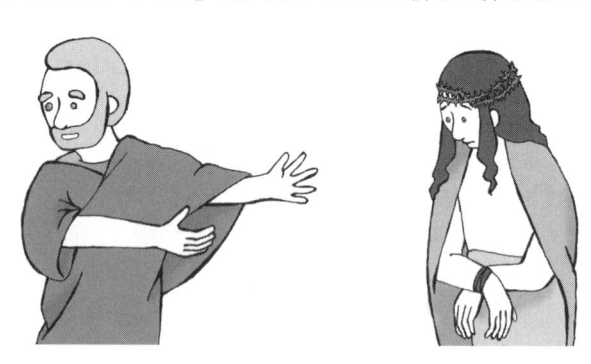

■ 十字架の意味

　この十字架によるイエスの処刑は、イエスが人類に代わって、人類の罪（＝原罪）を負い、処刑されることで、人類の罪を許すという「イエス＝キリスト（救世主）＝神」の愛を表しているのです。

....

注1：この十字架での処刑をもって人類の罪が完全に許されたかどうかは、宗派や学者によって異なるが、少なくとも、キリストの再臨や最後の審判が預言されている以上、完全に人類が救われたわけではないと言えそうである。

Section 3

said, Jesus takes bread and says, "Take this and eat; this is my body." And he takes a cup of wine and says, "Drink from it. This is my blood of the covenant." Then, he divides them among his disciples. After that, Judas goes out of the room. The disciples thought that Jesus asked Judas to leave for some reason, but actually he went out on his own accord for Judas was on his way to betray Jesus to the authorities.

■ The Arrest, Trials, and Execution of Jesus

Jesus is arrested at night in a place beyond the reach of the eye of the people who support him. Jesus was bound and taken to the Jewish religious rulers. They had decided to execute Jesus on the charge of blasphemy against Jewish law and the Temple. However, during the trial there is insufficient evidence against Jesus so the rulers' plan is in jeopardy. They have Jesus tortured by Roman authorities.

The discontented Jewish rulers complain that "Jesus should be executed" though the Roman governor of Judea, Pontius Pilate, sees no reason to execute Jesus, who appears innocent of any wrongdoing, and pilate tries to release him. After further convincing from the Jews and in order to quell any uprising, Pilate relents. Jesus carries his cross to the hill of Golgotha (Calvary), where he is suspended on the cross with nails which are hammered into both hands and feet. It is said that Jesus refused anesthetic wine to lessen the pain.

Even though Jesus was crucified on the cross, he prayed for the people; "Father, forgive them, for they don't know what they are doing."

■ The meaning of a cross

Jesus' execution on the cross shows the love of "Jesus＝Christ (Messiah)＝God" in that the sins of the human race are forgiven by Jesus bearing the sins of the human race (＝original sin) and being executed in place of the human race.

Note 1：The understanding of whether the sins of the human race were completely forgiven by the execution on the cross depends on sects and scholars.

第3節　新約聖書の世界

注2：十字架が象徴するもの
- 神の愛の象徴
- イエス・キリストの死と復活の象徴
- キリスト教自体のシンボル

注3：「十」の形が意味すること
　「十」の形のうちの「｜」は上に上るイメージから「火」（か）を表し、「一」は水平に流れるイメージから「水」（み）を表す。だから、これを組み合わせた「十」は「神」を象徴することになる。これがキリスト教のシンボルになったと言える。ちなみに、仏教のシンボルである「卍」は、「十」が右方向に回転している姿を暗示する。仏教では「右」が神聖な仏を表すので、右回りが重視される（それゆえ、仏教寺院の拝観順序は右回りである）が、「卍」にもそれが表れている。

TIPS　ユダはなぜ裏切ったのか？

　なぜユダがイエスを裏切ったかについては、様々な説があります。箇条書きであげてみましょう。
- 荒野でイエスに退けられたサタンが、晩餐のときにユダに入ったという説。
- 人々を率いてローマを撃退することをイエスに期待していたユダは、それがかなわないと知って裏切ったという説。
- ユダは会計係であったが、イエスの金を着服したことがきっかけで、背信行為に走ってしまったという説。
- イエスが死をもって人類の罪を償おうとしていると知り、憎まれ役を買って出たという説。

Section 3

However, we can possibly say that human beings are not completely saved if we take into account prophecies regarding the Second Advent of Christ and the Last Judgment.

Note 2： What a cross represents
- A symbol of the love of God
- A symbol of the death and resurrection of Jesus Christ
- A symbol of Christianity itself

Note 3： What the shape of a "cross (+)" means

"The vertical line (｜)" of the shape of a "cross (+)" represents "fire" (in Japanese "ka") out of the image of going up and "the horizontal line (―)" represents "water" (in Japanese "mi") out of the image of flowing horizontally. Therefore, the combination of these, the cross (+), symbolizes God (in Japanese "kami"). We can say that this shape became a symbol of Christianity. By the way, the left-facing swastika (卍), which is a symbol of Buddhism, implies a cross (+) rotating to the right. A clockwise rotation is valued because "right" represents a sacred Buddhist image in Buddhism (therefore, the order of walking through a Buddhist temple is clockwise), which is also expressed in a left-facing swastika (卍).

TIPS　Why did Judas betray Jesus?

There are several theories about the reason why Judas betrayed Jesus. They are examined in itemized form.
- The theory that Satan, repelled by Jesus in the wilderness, entered into Judas at the supper.
- The theory that Judas, who expected Jesus to lead the people against Rome, betrayed Jesus because Jesus did not meet his expectations.
- The theory that Judas embezzled money from Jesus though he was an accountant, therefore betraying Jesus' trust and damaging their relationship irreparably.
- The theory that Judas played the bad guy to force prophecy and set into motion the expiation of the sins of the human race through Jesus' sacrifice.

第3節 新約聖書の世界

12 | 復活と昇天

■ イエスの復活

イエスは十字架で命を落とし、墓に埋葬されました。3日後、マグダラのマリアが、墓の扉が開いているのを発見し、そこにはイエスの遺体はありませんでした。その後、イエスは弟子たちの前にも現れました。例えば、トマスの前に現れ、十字架の傷に触ってみるよう促したと言います。

■ 復活の意味

イエスは復活したということですが、復活の意味を述べておきましょう。人間は神との契約を破り、本来あるべき神と人間の関係を否定しました。イエスはこれによって生じた罪をすべて背負い十字架に架けられました。そして、イエスが復活することにより、イエスのとりなしが神によって聞き入れられ、救いの保証が与えられました。だから、復活は神と人間の新たな契約を意味するのです。

■ イエスの昇天

復活から40日後、イエスは食事をしている弟子たちの前に現れて「あなたたちはまもなく聖霊によって洗礼を受けられる」と述べ、弟子たちが福音を伝える使徒になることを告げました。

この告知の後、弟子たちとともにオリーブ山近くのベタニアまで行ったイエスは、手をあげて彼らを祝福しつつ、彼らの目の前で昇天していきました。

■ 昇天の意味

イエスの昇天は、次の2つの意味を持つと考えてよいでしょう。
　(1) 天へのアクセスを人間に対して保証すること
　(2) 人間に対して聖霊が与えられていること、その聖霊によって人間が神とともに存在できるということを教えること

Section 3

The resurrection and the ascension

■ The resurrection of Jesus

Jesus died on the cross and was laid to rest in a tomb. Three days later, Mary Magdalene noticed that the door of the tomb was left open and the body of Jesus wasn't there. Later, Jesus appeared to his disciples. For instance, it is said that Jesus appeared before Thomas and urged the disbelieving man to touch the wounds that he had received on the cross.

■ The meaning of the resurrection

The story of the resurrection holds deep significance in Christianity. In Eden, man broke the covenant with God and was denied the ideal relationship between God and man. Jesus bore this original sin as well as all subsequent sins and took them with him to the cross. Through the resurrection of Jesus, God accepted what Jesus did as reasonable and guaranteed salvation to people. Therefore, the resurrection signifies the new covenant between God and man.

■ The ascension of Jesus

Forty days after the resurrection of Jesus, he appeared in front of his disciples who were eating and said to them, "You will soon be baptized with the Holy Spirit." Then, he told them that they would become the apostles who preached the gospel.

After the announcement, Jesus, who went to Bethany near the Mount of Olives with his disciples, ascended into heaven in their presence, raising his hands and blessing them.

■ The meaning of the ascension

The ascension of Jesus has the following 2 meanings:
(1) Guaranteeing man has access to heaven
(2) Teaching that the Holy Spirit is given to man and man can exist with

第3節　新約聖書の世界

> **関連情報**　復活日と昇天日
> イエス・キリストの復活を祝う復活祭（イースター）はキリスト教最大の祭りですが、復活祭から40日後（正確には、復活祭を第1日目とするので39日後）には、昇天を祝う昇天祭（昇天日とも言う）があります。

13　聖霊降臨と弟子の伝道

■ 聖霊の降臨
　イエスの復活後、最初の五旬節の日、十二弟子たちと信徒たちは、エルサレムのある家に集まっていました。すると、天から激しい風が吹き、家を震わせて鳴り響きました。そして、炎の舌のようなものが現れ、十二弟子一人ひとりの上にとどまったのです。これが、イエスが告げた聖霊降臨です。

参考：五旬節とは、元来は収穫の鎌納めの祭りである。ユダヤ教では、十戒が与えられた律法記念日、キリスト教ではキリスト教会の誕生記念日として祝われる。

■ 弟子たちが各国の言葉で話し始める
　聖霊に満たされた弟子たちは、そのころユダヤで話されていたアラム語ではなく、いろいろな国の言葉で話し始めました。当時のエルサレムには、バビロン捕囚後、各国に散っていった民の子孫が戻ってきたりしていたので、様々な言葉を話す人たちがエルサレムにいたのです。彼らは、自分たちの故郷の言葉が話されているのを聞いて驚きました。

参考：アラム語は、シリア、メソポタミアで紀元前500〜600年ころ話された言語で、アッシリア、新バビロニア、アケメネス朝ペルシャでも使用された。

■ キリスト教会の始まり
　ペトロは、他の11人の弟子たちとともに、説教を始め、イエスの教えとその復活について語りました。すると、大勢の人がイエスを信じるようになりました。

Section 3

God by the power of the Holy Spirit

The Descent of the Holy Spirit and the preaching of the disciples

■ The Descent of the Holy Spirit

The twelve disciples and believers gathered together in a certain house in Jerusalem on the first Pentecost after the resurrection of Jesus. A violent wind suddenly blew from heaven and shook the house. After that, what looked like tongues of flame appeared and settled on each of the twelve disciples. Thus the Descent of the Holy Spirit which Jesus announced came to pass.

■ The disciples start to speak in the languages of each country

The disciples, filled with the Holy Spirit, began to speak in the languages of various countries instead of Aramaic, which was spoken in Judea at the time. There were people who spoke various languages in Jerusalem as the descendants of the people who returned to Jerusalem after having been forced to live in other regions during the Babylonian Captivity. They were surprised to hear the languages of their native countries spoken.

■ The origin of the Christian Church

On this day, Peter began preaching with the 11 other disciples and talked about the teachings of Jesus and his resurrection. Many people came to believe in Jesus. It is said that the number of people who were

第3節　新約聖書の世界

この日、ペトロによって洗礼を受けた者の数は、3,000人に上ったと言われています。3,000人の人々が洗礼を受けたこの日が、キリスト教会の始まりだとされています。

■ ペトロの伝道

ペトロは、他の11人のイエスの弟子たちの先頭に立って伝道を始めます。ペトロがヨハネとともに、エルサレム神殿に行ったとき、足の不自由な物乞いの男を癒す奇跡を起こします。そして集まった人たちに説法し、5,000人の信者を得たと言われています。

注：この段階では、イエスの信者は、まだユダヤ教の一派に過ぎなかった。イエスの教えはユダヤ教指導者から反発を受けていたので、ペトロは逮捕されるが、堂々と彼らを論破し難を逃れた。

■ コルネリウスの洗礼の意義

ペトロは、十二弟子の中で唯一、エルサレム以外で伝道したと伝えられています。ローマの百人隊長コルネリウスもペトロによって洗礼を受けました。これが異邦人に対する初めての洗礼と言われています。この出来事は、イエスの教えが、幅広く異邦人にも伝わるきっかけとなりました。

■ 原始キリスト教会の対立

原始キリスト教は、ヘブライ語を話すユダヤ人（ヘブライスト）とギリシャ語を話すユダヤ人（ヘレニスト）の2つに分かれていました。この両者の間で、キリストや教義に関して発想が異なるため、摩擦が生まれつつありました。以下に、2つの派の違いをまとめてみましょう。

ヘブライスト	ヘレニスト
ヘブライ語を話す。	ギリシャ語を話す。
以前からユダヤに住んでいた。	離散した後、ユダヤに帰ってきた。
イエスは律法の完成者と考えた。	イエスはメシアであると考えた。
イエスに従うと同時に、ユダヤ教の律法を重視した。	イエスの福音を信じることが重要で、ユダヤ教の律法を守る必要はない。
キリスト教は、ユダヤ教の中のイエス派として存在した。	キリスト教とユダヤ教は別物と発想する。
エルサレム神殿参りを欠かさず実行する。	エルサレム神殿に価値を認めない。

Section 3

baptized by Peter during this Pentecost numbered 3000. This day, when so many were baptized, is assumed to be the beginning of the Christian Church.

■ The preaching of Peter

Peter took the lead amongst the disciples and began preaching the teachings of Jesus. When Peter went to the Jerusalem Temple with John, he performed his first miracle by healing a lame beggar. There, he preached to the people who gathered around him and is said to have obtained 5000 believers.

■ The meaning of the baptism of Cornelius

It is said that among the 12 disciples, only Peter preached the gospel outside of Jerusalem. It is said the first baptism of a foreigner was performed by Peter on Cornelius the Centurion. The teachings of Jesus widely spread to foreigners through this incident.

■ The conflict within the Primitive Church

The Primitive Church was divided into two groups: Jews who spoke Hebrew (Hebraists) and Jews who spoke Greek (Hellenists). Friction was rising between the two groups because of different views of who Jesus was and how his doctrine was to be interpreted. The differences between the two sects are as follows:

Hebraists	Hellenists
Speak Hebrew	Speak Greek
Had lived in Judea for a long time.	Came back to Judea after the break up.
Considered Jesus to be the end of law.	Considered Jesus to be a Messiah.
Not only followed Jesus but also valued the laws of Judaism.	Thought it important to believe the gospel of Jesus and thought it needless to observe the laws of Judaism.
Christianity existed as the Jesus faction within the sphere of Judaism.	Think that Christianity is one thing and Judaism is another.
Regularly visit the Jerusalem Temple.	Do not acknowledge the value of the Jerusalem Temple.

第3節　新約聖書の世界

■ ステファノの殉教

　神殿批判を繰り広げるヘレニストの代表的人物にステファノがいました。彼はついに、ユダヤ人たちに捕えられましたが、彼は群衆を前に堂々と大演説を行いました。人々は怒り狂って、ステファノを殺しました。ステファノはキリスト教における最初の殉教者となったのです。

　この事件と同時に、キリスト教徒に対する迫害が始まり、その多くがエルサレムから逃亡しました。彼らは逃亡先で、福音を伝えたので、迫害がかえってキリスト教を広めるきっかけとなったのは間違いないでしょう。

注：ステファノの最期の言葉は「主よ、この罪を彼らに負わせないでください」というイエスの最期の言葉と同じであった。

■ サウロからパウロへ

　ステファノを殺した人々の中にサウロという熱心なユダヤ教徒がいました。あるとき、サウロはダマスコにいるキリスト教徒を逮捕しようと、エルサレムを発ったのですが、途中で天からの光に照らされ、落馬し、目が見えなくなってしまいました。

　3日後、キリスト教徒のアナニアの夢にイエスが現れ、サウロを尋ねるように告げました。アナニアがサウロに会って、盲いたサウロの上に手をかざすと、目から鱗のようなものが落ちて、サウロの目が回復しました。

　この出来事により、回心したサウロは、一転して熱心なキリスト教徒であるパウロになったのです。パウロは今日ではキリスト教最大の伝道者として知られています。

Section 3

■ The martyrdom of Stephen

Stephen was an exponent of Hellenists who criticized the Temple. He made a controversial speech in a dignified manner in front of a crowd and was finally apprehended by Jews who stoned him to death. Therefore, Stephen became the first Christian martyr.

Concurrently with this incident, the persecution of Christians started and most of them escaped from Jerusalem. As they preached the gospel in the places where they escaped to, there is no doubt that the persecution facilitated the spread of Christianity.

■ From Saul to Paul

Amongst the people who killed Stephen was an ardent Jew named Saul. Saul, who as a Roman citizen made it his mission to hunt down and persecute Christians, left Jerusalem to arrest a Christian in Damascus. However, he was bathed in light from heaven on the road to the city, fell from his horse and lost his sight.

Three days later, Jesus showed up in the dream of a Christian called Ananias and told him to visit the bed-ridden Saul. When Ananias met Saul and held his hand above the blind man, something like scales fell from Saul's eyes and his eyesight was restored.

Saul was converted by this event and made a complete about-face to become a highly devoted Christian, Paul, who is now known as the greatest preacher of Christianity.

第3節　新約聖書の世界

■ パウロの3度の伝道旅行

パウロは熱心にキリスト教の伝道を始めます。有名な伝道旅行は合計3回あります。これを表にまとめてみましょう。

第1回 伝道旅行	パウロとその相棒バルナバは、キプロスから小アジアに赴く。パウロの説教がユダヤ人の反感を買い、パウロは石打ちに遭う。
第2回 伝道旅行	パウロはバルナバと別れ、のちに福音書を書くルカをはじめ、テモテとシラス、計4人でマケドニアに赴く。ヨーロッパ伝道が始まる。
第3回 伝道旅行	大地の女神であるアルテミス信仰の盛んなトルコのエフェソスで伝道に成功したため、これを快く思わない人たちがパウロを拘留した。そこはまさに、パウロがいくつかの有名な書簡を書いた場所であった。

＊アルテミスはローマ神話の狩の女神ディアーナ（Diana）に相当。

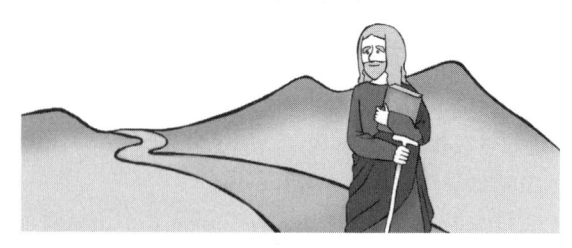

■ 使徒たちの殉教

イエスの直弟子である十二使徒（十二弟子をこう呼ぶ）たちは、イエスが十字架に架けられたとき、保身のために身を隠していました。しかし、イエスの復活と聖霊の降臨を経て、彼らは熱心な伝道活動を開始しました。迫害は激しさを増し、死を恐れず各地で伝道していた使徒たちは、それぞれ壮絶な殉教を遂げていくことになります。

十二弟子（使徒）たちのうち、首を吊って自殺したとされるユダも除けば、天寿を全うしたのは、ヨハネただ一人でした。トルコやローマで何度も迫害に遭いましたが、その都度切り抜け94歳まで生きたと言われています。

14　黙示録

■「ヨハネの黙示録」とは?

新約聖書を締めくくり、歴史の終点を記述するという重要な役割を演じている

Section 3

■ Paul's three missionary trips

Paul ardently starts his Christian mission. He spreads the Gospel in three well-known trips as a missionary. These trips are as follows:

The first missionary trip	Paul and his partner Barnabas travel from Cyprus to Asia Minor. Paul's preaching antagonizes Jews, who stone Paul.
The second missionary trip	Paul parts from Barnabas and travels to Macedonia with Timothy and Silas, including Luke, who is to write his gospel later. Paul begins his missionary journey into Europe.
The third missionary trip	Paul succeeded in his mission to Ephesus in Turkey (Anatolia) where the worship of Artemis, goddess of the earth, flourished. Those who were offended at his preaching had him detained there. It was there that he wrote some of his famous letters which would make up a large portion of the New Testament.

■ The martyrdom of the apostles

When Jesus was put on the cross, the twelve apostles, who were direct disciples of Jesus, hid themselves from authorities for the purpose of defending their own interests. However, they passionately began their missionary work after the resurrection of Jesus and the descent of the Holy Spirit. The persecution grew intense and many of the apostles who were bravely engaged in their missionary work in various places were to become martyrs.

Among the twelve disciples (apostles), the only disciple who died a natural death was John, except for Judas, who is said to have hanged himself. He was persecuted and beaten in Turkey (then, Anatolia) and Rome. However, he persevered and is said to have lived to 94 years old.

The Book of Revelation

■ What is the "Revelation of St. John the Divine?"

It is "the Revelation of St. John the Divine" that finalizes the New

第3節　新約聖書の世界

のが「ヨハネの黙示録」です。

■ ヨハネの見た幻想

　ヨハネはあるとき、7つの角と7つの目をした子羊が神と思われる存在から7つの巻物を渡されるという幻を見ました。この巻物の封印を解くたびに、地上に災いが降り注ぎます。第7の封印を解いたとき、7人の天使にラッパが与えられます。天使たちが順番に合計7回ラッパを吹き鳴らし、そのたびに、また災いが降りかかります。さらに、7人の天使が7つの鉢を神から受け取り、その鉢から神の怒りが地上に注がれます。

注1：子羊はキリストと同一視される。
注2：具体的にどんなことが書かれているかを少し紹介する。
　　第6の巻物の封印を解いたとき → 大地震が起き、太陽は暗くなり、星が地上に落ちる。
　　第5のラッパを天使が吹いたとき →蝗（いなご）が額に神の刻印がない人を5カ月間苦しめる。
　　第7の鉢を注いだとき → 大地震が起き、島も山も消える。

■「黙示録」執筆の目的

　「ヨハネの黙示録」が書かれたのは、1世紀の終わりごろと考えられます。この当時のキリスト教は、ローマ皇帝ドミティアヌスによる迫害に苦しんでいました。それまでも迫害はあったのですが、この迫害は、ローマ帝国全体に及ぶ大規模なものでした。

　キリスト教徒は、迫害に対しても無抵抗を貫いたのですが、「黙示録」は、そんなキリスト教徒を励ます目的で書かれたものだと考えられています。だからこそ、内容が激しいものになっています。

注：ローマ皇帝がキリスト教徒を迫害したのは、彼らが皇帝崇拝や兵役を拒否したためだと考えられている。

> **関連情報　キリスト教を迫害したローマ皇帝**
> 　ネロ、ドミティアヌス、マルクス・アウレリウス、デキウス、ディオクレティアヌスが有名です。ディオクレティアヌスの迫害のあと、コンスタンティヌスにより

Section 3

Testament and plays an important role in describing the end of history.

■ What John saw in his vision

John had a prophetic vision: A lamb with 7 horns and 7 eyes received 7 scrolls from what appeared to be God. A disaster will befall the earth each time the lamb opened the seal of a scroll. When the lamb opens the 7th seal, trumpets are given to 7 angels. Angels play the trumpet 7 times in total by rotation. Each time, another disaster occurs. In addition, the 7 angels receive 7 bowls from God. From the bowls, the wrath of God will be poured upon the earth.

Note 1：A lamb and Christ are viewed as one.
Note 2：Detailed descriptions from the Book of Revelation.
　When the lamb opens the seal of the 6th scroll → A big earthquake occurs, the sun becomes black and the stars fall to earth.
　When the angel plays the 5th trumpet → For 5 months, locusts torment men who did not receive the seal of God on their foreheads.
　When the 7th bowl is poured out → A tremendous earthquake occurs and islands and mountains disappear.

■ The purpose of writing the Book of Revelation

It is assumed that the Revelation of St. John the Divine was written about the end of the 1st century. Christians at that time suffered from persecution under Domitian, the Roman emperor. While there had been persecutions against early Christians for some time, under Domitian, these persecutions spread far and wide to encompass most of the Roman Empire's lands.

Christians had a policy of non-resistance towards the persecutions. It is considered that the Book of Revelation was written to encourage such Christians. For this reason, its content is bitter.

Note：The reason why Roman emperors persecuted Christians is assumed that they refused emperor worship and military service.

第3節　新約聖書の世界

> キリスト教が公認されることになり、長かった迫害の歴史にピリオドが打たれます。

■ 千年王国

　神の怒りが地上に注がれて、終末を迎えたあと、千年王国の時代がやってきます。キリストが再臨し、サタン(悪魔)を幽閉し、活動できないようにします。その後、主に殉教者たちが復活し、逆に、悪人たちは滅ぼされているので、不安のない幸せな生活を送ることができる時代が到来し、キリストのもと、1000年続くのです。

　しかし、千年王国は永遠に続くものではありません。1000年後、サタンが再度現れます。ところが、炎が天から降り注ぎ、サタンは滅ぶことになります。これが、この世の終末ということになります。

注：この世の終末は、神の怒りを買って、人類が全滅するというよりも、殉教者がよみ
　　がえり、逆に、サタンが滅びるという現象なのである。

■ 最後の審判

　千年王国が終わり、サタンが滅ぶと、今度は、限られた人たち（殉教者など）ではなく、すべての死者を復活させることになります。復活させるのは、最後の審判を受けさせるためです。ここで、天国に行く者と地獄に落ちる者との振り分けが行われるのです。

　ところが、死者たちの生前の行いを記載した「命の書」というものを神が持っており、そこに名前がない者は、悪魔と同じ火の池に投げ込まれてしまいます。これが永遠の死ということになります。

　天国の住人として選ばれた者の前には、新しい天と地が姿を現します。そして、聖なる都エルサレムが降臨し、人々はこの神の王国で永遠に幸せに暮らすことになると黙示録は語っています。

参考：新しいエルサレムの風景
　エルサレムは12の門を持った高い城壁で囲まれ、その土台石はあらゆる宝石で飾られている。大通りは純金でできており、都は光り輝き、夜はこないとされ、水晶のごとく輝く川が大通りの中央を流れている。その川の両岸に命の木が並び、1年に12回実を結んでいる。

Section 3

■ The millennium

After the wrath of God spread across the globe, the world will come to an end, and a new millennium will come. Jesus will return to battle and imprison Satan, the personification of Evil. Peace will reign on earth with martyrs being raised from the dead while those who sinned, doomed to eternal damnation. This will continue for 1000 years under Christ.

However, the millennium doesn't last forever. After the thousand years are up, Satan makes his return. This time, fire will come down from heaven and Satan will perish. This signifies the end of the world.

Note：The end of the world refers to the phenomenon of martyrs being resurrected and Satan perishing rather than the notion that the entire human race is completely destroyed as a result of the wrath of God.

注目：終末論の１つとしての「千年王国説」はmillenarianismまたはmillennialismと言う。

■ The Last Judgment

When the millennium ends and Satan ceases to be, then all the remaining dead (besides the already revived martyrs) will be raised. The newly resurrected will be subject to a process known as the Last Judgment. At the Last Judgment, people will be divided into those who go to heaven and those who go to hell.

God has what is called "the Book of life" which describes the behavior of the dead in their lifetime. The people whose names are not listed in the book will be thrown into a lake of fire as Satan was beforehand. This means an eternal death.

A new heaven and a new earth appear for the people chosen as residents of heaven. The Book of Revelation tells that the holy capital known as New Jerusalem will descend to earth and people will live happily in the kingdom of God forever.

第4章

ユダヤ教を知る

第1節　ユダヤ教の基礎知識

❶ ユダヤ教とは？

■ ユダヤ教とは？

「唯一神」（＝全知全能の絶対神）との契約に基づく古代イスラエルの宗教を継承する民族宗教です。前20世紀ごろを起源とする宗教です。

ユダヤ教には、布教の概念はないのですが、人種・国籍にかかわらず、ユダヤ教への改宗者は等しくユダヤ人とみなされます。つまり、「ユダヤ教徒＝ユダヤ人」です。

注1：旧約聖書や新約聖書における「約」は「契約」の意味で、「旧約」とは「古い契約」ということになる。ユダヤ教は古い契約を重視する。その契約の意味は、神に対する絶対的帰依と引き換えに、最終的に永遠の魂が与えられるという、いわばギブアンドテイクの契約である。
注2：教団の公式の発足は前5世紀後半。
注3：例えば、日本人がユダヤ教徒になれば、国籍的には日本人であっても、宗教的にはユダヤ人ということになる。

■ ユダヤ教の聖典

ユダヤ教の聖典は、2つに分類できます。1つは、『TNK』（タナハ）と呼ばれるもので、「律法（＝トーラー）」(T)、「預言者（＝ネイビーム）」(N)、および「諸書（＝ケトゥビーム）」(K) をまとめたものです。これはキリスト教の旧約聖書に当たり、特に、ヘブライ語聖書と言われています。なお、律法は、モーセ五書（創世記、出エジプト記、レビ記、民数記、申命記）に相当します。

2つ目は『タルムード』です。『タルムード』とは、紀元後200年ごろに成文化された口伝律法（ミシュナ）に、律法の教師であるラビの解釈（ゲマラ）を付け加え、400年から500年ごろに成立した聖典です。日常生活における心構えと知恵などが記されています。

Section 1

What is Judaism?

■ What is Judaism?

Judaism is an ethnic religion which inherits the ancient Israeli faith based on the covenant with the Absolute God, or the Omniscient and Omnipotent One. This religion originated around the 20th century B.C.

Judaism has no concept of propagation; however, any person who has converted to Judaism is equally considered Jewish. This means anyone who believes in Judaism is Jewish.

Note 1 : "Yaku" in Kyuyaku or Shinyaku means contract; therefore, "Kyuyaku" means the old contract, or covenant, which Judaism centers on. Behind the contract is the principle of give and take in which God will grant eternal life to anyone if he or she has absolute faith in Him.
Note 2 : The religious society was officially established in late 5th century B. C.
Note 3 : For example, immediately after a Japanese person becomes a believer in Judaism, he or she is religiously Jewish though officially Japanese.

■ Holy Books in Judaism

The holy books are roughly divided into two : One is called TNK, which represents the Torah, or teachings, the Nevim, or prophets, and the Ketubim, or writings. This TNK corresponds to the Old Testament, which is called the Hebrew Bible. The Torah is equal to the Five Books of Moses, containing Genesis, Exodus, Leviticus, Numbers, and Deuteronomy.

The other is the Talmud, which was a holy scripture established around 400 to 500 A.D. by adding the Gemara, or comments of rabbis, Torah's preachers, to the Mishnah, or oral Torah documents codified around 200 A.D. The Talmud contains instructions and guidelines for every day life of Jews.

第1節　ユダヤ教の基礎知識

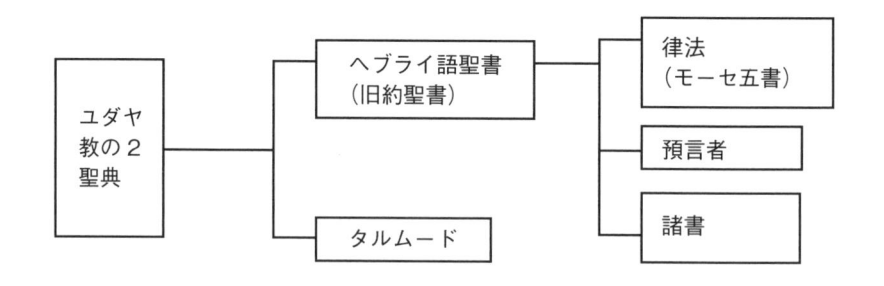

```
                            ┌─ 律法
               ┌─ ヘブライ語聖書 ─┤  （モーセ五書）
ユダヤ         │  （旧約聖書）   ├─ 預言者
教の２ ────────┤                 └─ 諸書
聖典           │
               └─ タルムード
```

　ヘブライ語聖書は神との契約書で、タルムードはその注釈書であると言えるでしょう。

■ ラビ

　ラビとはユダヤ人社会を運営する指導者のことで、律法の教師とみなされています。シナゴーグという礼拝施設での律法（トーラー）の読誦をはじめとする儀式の執行をも兼務しています。

■ 選民思想

　神が契約する相手として唯一選んだ民族が古代イスラエル人（現在のユダヤ民族）であると言われています。このような経緯から「自分たちは神に選ばれた民」という宗教観がユダヤ人の意識の根底に生まれましたが、この発想は選民思想と呼ばれています。のちに、キリスト教の開祖イエスが、この思想を痛烈に批判しました。

■ 安息日

　今日世界的に使用されている１週間７日の制度を発明したのはユダヤ人であると言えます。その典拠となるのは、もちろん旧約聖書の「創世記」の天地創造（p.116参照）です。
　ところで、文化史的（宗教史的）に、１週間は日曜日に始まり土曜日に終わります[注1]。ユダヤ教では、金曜日の日没から、土曜日の日没までが安息日（シャバット）となり、実質的な休日です。安息日は、神聖な日だから一切仕事をしてはならないとされています[注2]。

Section 1

We can safely say that the Hebrew Bible is the so-called contract with God, while the Talmud is its commentary.

■ Rabbi

A rabbi is a leader who manages Jewish society and is regarded as a teacher of the Torah. He also engages in performing ceremonies like chanting from the Torah at a sacred place called a synagogue.

■ The idea of "A Chosen People"

It is said that God chose the ancient Israeli people (present Jews) as the people He would form a covenant with. This way of thinking contributed to the occurrence of the idea in the depth of Jews' mind that they are part of a chosen people by God. This idea can be called Jewish elitism, or Judaistic ethnocentrism. Later, Jesus, founder of Christianity, criticized this idea severely.

■ The Sabbath

We can say it were Jews that invented a system of seven days a week, which is used around the world now. This system is based on the Creation of the Universe stated in Genesis.

Incidentally, from the viewpoint of cultural history, or religious history, one week begins on Sunday and ends on Saturday. In the case of Judaism, the Sabbath is from the sunset of Friday to that of Saturday, which period of time is practically a holiday. Since the Sabbath is a sacred day, it is regarded as the day when you must not work at all.

第1節　ユダヤ教の基礎知識

注1：キリスト教徒は、イエスが日曜日の朝に復活したことから、日曜日を聖なる日（安息日）としている。神が天地創造を終えて休んだ日が日曜日だから、それを安息日としたという、俗に考えられている発想は誤っている。

注2：安息日には、外出せず、神に祈りと感謝を捧げる。そのため、例えば、銀行は金曜日の午前中だけ開いており、金曜の午後から土曜日にかけては休みとなる。また、バスも全路線が土曜日には運休する。

> **関連情報**　「安息日」は3つの読み方があります。
> (1)「あんそくにち」…『文語訳聖書』『口語訳聖書』『新改訳聖書』
> (2)「あんそくじつ」…『フランシスコ会訳聖書』
> (3)「あんそくび」…『新共同訳聖書』
> ＊NHKでは（3）の読み方をします。

Section 1

Note 1：Christianity regards Sunday as the Sabbath, a sacred day, because Jesus was resurrected on Sunday morning. The popularly held belief that since the day when God rested after the Creation was Sunday, Sunday eventually became the Sabbath of Christianity is wrong.

Note 2：On the Sabbath, people are supposed to offer prayer and gratitude to God without going out; therefore, banks, for example, are closed from Friday afternoon to Saturday though they are open on Friday morning. Moreover, all the bus routes of the week days are not available in the least on Saturday.

第1節　ユダヤ教の基礎知識

❷ ユダヤ教の教義：戒律とタルムード

■戒　律

　ユダヤ教においては、日常の宗教的規範はすべて戒律に基づいています。その戒律の基本となるものは、モーセがシナイ山で神より与えられた「十戒」(p.141)です。

　他にも、ノアの七戒（創世記に記された人間が生きる上で必要な基本的な戒律）などもあり、旧約聖書全体に記された戒律は、全部で613にも及びます。これらの戒律は、出エジプト記から申命記にまとめられています。その内訳は、義務事項（しなければならない）が248個、禁忌事項（してはならない）が365個です。

注：「食べてはならない動物」がレビ記第11章や申命記第14章に出てくる。例えば、ラクダ、野うさぎ、狸、地を這う爬虫類、羽を持つ昆虫、死んだ動物などは食べてはならないが、ひづめが割れて反芻する動物、すなわち、牛、羊、ヤギ、鹿の肉は食べてよい。さらに、鱗のない水生動物、すなわち、蛸、烏賊、海老、蟹、鰻、鯨などは食べてはいけないのに対し、鱗のある水生動物は全般に食べてよい。

食べてはいけない動物

Section 1

The Judaic doctrine: Religious precepts and the Talmud

■ Religious Precepts

In Judaism, all the religious rules in everyday life are based on religious precepts. The fundamental parts of the precepts were given to Moses on Mt. Sinai by God in the form of the Ten Commandments.

Other precepts include Noah's seven commandments, which are basic teachings needed for life that are mentioned in Genesis. The total number of commandments depicted in the Old Testament amounts to 613. These are explained in the Old Testament from Exodus to Deuteronomy. They are divided into two categories: "do's," or something you have to do, and "don't's," or something you must not do, the former numbering 248, the latter 365.

Note: "Animals you must not eat" are mentioned in Chapter 11 of Leviticus and Chapter 14 of Deuteronomy. For example, we must not eat camels, hares, raccoon dogs, the reptiles crawling on the ground, insects with wings, and dead animals, while we are allowed to eat ruminants with cloven hoofs like oxen, sheep, goats and deer. Moreover, water creatures without scales like octopi, squid, shrimp, crab, and whales cannot be eaten, whereas, any water creatures with scales are generally permitted.

第1節　ユダヤ教の基礎知識

■ タルムードとは?

　タルムードとは、ヘブライ語で「教訓・教義」の意味です。タルムードは神との契約（ヘブライ語聖書）をさらに具体的に生活全般の規範として成文化したものです。その項目はユダヤ教徒の生活上で必要な事項のすべてにわたっています。新たな命題が生じて、これまでの文書の中に解答が発見されない場合は、ラビからの回答（レスポンス）として審議され、増補されることがあります。

注：タルムードの構成（＝生活規定の分類）
　（1）種子（ゼライーム）：農業全般に関する規定
　（2）季節（モエード）：安息日と諸祝祭に関する規定
　（3）女（ナシーム）：婚姻・離婚に関する規定
　（4）損害（ネズィキーン）：市民の商売に関する規定や民法・刑法
　（5）聖物（コダシーム）：儀礼、犠牲、神殿と食事に関する規定
　（6）清浄（トホロート）：宗教的な浄・不浄の規定
　　　＊ページの中央にミシュナを、周囲にゲマラを配置する形式になっている。

Section 1

■ **What is the Talmud?**

The word "Talmud" means "precepts and doctrines" in Hebrew. The Talmud is a codified document containing specified standards of life in general, which is based on the contract with God, or the Hebrew Bible. Articles in the Talmud cover all the aspects and phases needed for Jews' life. In cases where no answers can be found in the Talmud after some new proposition arises, new deliberation takes place among rabbis and official answers from them can be added.

Note : Structure of the Talmud (=Classification of Regulations in Life)
   (1) Zeraim ⋯ regulations regarding agriculture in general
   (2) Moed ⋯ regulations regarding the Sabbath and festivals in general
   (3) Nashim ⋯ regulations mainly regarding marriages and divorces
   (4) Nezikin ⋯ regulations regarding citizens' business, civil codes and the criminal law
   (5) Kodshim ⋯ regulations regarding courtesy, sacrifice, sanctuary and foods
   (6) Tohorot ⋯ regulations regarding religious purity and impurity
      ＊In the center of a page is the Mishnah, and the Gemara is added around the Mishnah.

第1節　ユダヤ教の基礎知識

❸ 聖地・エルサレム

■ エルサレム

　エルサレムはイスラエル東部にある都市で、イスラエルは、この都市を同国の首都であると宣言していますが、国際的には首都とは言えません。というのは、国際連合と多くの国が、エルサレムを首都と認めていないからです。エルサレムはヘブライ語の「イール・シャローム」(平和の町)からきているという説が主流ですが、他説もあり、その名前の由来ははっきりしていません。

　地中海から内陸部に入った標高800mの丘の上に位置する町で、ユダヤ人が住む西エルサレムとアラブ人が住む東エルサレムから成り立っています。125.1km^2に732,100（2007年現在）人の人たちが住むイスラエル最大の都市です。

■ 西エルサレム

　新市街と呼ばれる近代的な地域で、国会や各省庁、ヘブライ大学やイスラエル博物館があり、イスラエルの政治と文化の中心地です。国防省は、軍事的な観点から、テルアビブに位置しています。

Section 1

The Holy City Jerusalem

■ Jerusalem

Jerusalem is a city in the eastern part of Israel, which Israel declares is the capital city of Israel, though not internationally recognized as such. The United Nations and many countries do not regard this city as the capital city. The theory that the word "Jerusalem" is said to have come from a Hebrew word meaning a peaceful town is prevalent; however, there are other theories. Therefore, the roots of the name of the city are impossible to prove beyond only theories.

The city, which is located on an 800 meter-high hill a good distance inland from the Mediterranean Sea, consists of two parts: West Jerusalem, where Jews live, and East Jerusalem, where Arabs live. The city with a population of 732,100 (as of 2007) living over an area of 125.1 km² is the largest in Israel in both its population and area.

■ West Jerusalem

This is a modern city area called the New City, where buildings for the national assembly, ministries and government offices, Hebrew University and the Israel Museum are located; therefore, this area is Israel's political and cultural center. The Ministry of Defense is situated in Tel Aviv for military reasons.

第1節　ユダヤ教の基礎知識

■ 東エルサレム

　エルサレムはユダヤ教・キリスト教・イスラム教の聖地と言われますが、正確には、これら3つのアブラハムの宗教の聖地とみなされているのは、エルサレムの中でも東エルサレム（厳密には旧市街の地域）です。

　東エルサレムは、エルサレム東部のヨルダン川西岸地区に位置する地域で、エルサレムの旧市街がここにあります。旧市街には、ユダヤ教の「嘆きの壁」、キリスト教の「聖墳墓教会」、イスラム教の「岩のドーム」があります。

　「嘆きの壁」の上は、神殿の丘と呼ばれる、かつてエルサレム神殿が存在していた丘です。ここには、現在、イスラム建築の傑作とされる「岩のドーム」が建っています。

　旧市街は、「エルサレムの旧市街とその城壁群」という名前で、1981年に世界文化遺産に登録されました。

....

注1：エルサレム神殿は、紀元前587年にバビロニアに滅ぼされた。その後、紀元前515年に第2神殿が再建されるが、西暦70年にローマ帝国により、再び破壊された。そのとき残った城壁の一部が「嘆きの壁」である。
注2：遺産の登録申請は、ヨルダンが行った。

■ 嘆きの壁

　エルサレム旧市街の西境の城壁の一部に嘆きの壁という場所があり、ユダヤ人の間では『詩編』に歌われたソロモンの神殿の城壁の跡と伝わっていて、神聖な場所と考えられています。毎週金曜日にユダヤ人は、この壁の前に集って、神殿の破壊を嘆き、聖地の回復を祈って、涙を流すといった伝統があります。この慣習は中世に始まったと考えられています。

Section 1

■ **East Jerusalem**

It is often said that Jerusalem is a holy city to Judaism, Christianity, and Islam, but more exactly, the holy area to these three Abrahamic religions is limited to East Jerusalem, more precisely the Old City area.

East Jerusalem is an area corresponding to the western district of the Jordan River in the eastern part of Jerusalem, which contains the Old City, where you see the Judaism-related "Western Wall (Wailing Wall)," Christianity-related "Church of the Holy Sepulchre (Church of the Resurrection)," and the Islamic "Dome of the Rock."

Above the Western Wall is a hill called the Temple Mount, on which the Temple in Jerusalem (Holy Temple) stood in the past. However, at present, the Dome of the Rock stands on the sacred hill.

The Old City of Jerusalem was registered as a World Heritage Site in 1981 under the name of the Old City and its Walls.

....

Note 1 : The Temple in Jerusalem was destroyed by Babylonia in 587 B.C. In 515 B.C. the Second Temple in Jerusalem was constructed but it was demolished by the Roman Empire in 70 A.D. Part of the wall that remained from that time is the Western Wall.

Note 2 : The application for the registration was conducted by Jordan.

■ **Western Wall**

The Western Wall, regarded as part of the wall located on the west of the Old City of Jerusalem, is believed among Jews to be the remains of the Holy Temple of Solomon depicted in Psalms; therefore, they consider the area a sacred place. Tradition states that every Friday the Jews get together in front of this wall, wailing about the destruction of the Temple and praying for the recovery of its sanctuary.

第1節　ユダヤ教の基礎知識

■ 聖墳墓教会

エルサレム旧市街にある、キリストの墓とされる場所に建っている教会です。新約聖書において、イエスが十字架に磔にされたとされるゴルゴダの丘は、この場所にあったと考えられています。

■ 岩のドーム

エルサレム旧市街にある、メッカのカアバ、メディナの預言者のモスクに次ぐ、イスラム第3の聖地です。この「岩のドーム」は、イスラム教の開祖、ムハンマドが昇天したと言われる場所に建っています。

ここには、アブラハムが息子のイサクを神に捧げるための台であったとされている「聖なる岩」が祀られています。

建設に際して、刻まれた総延長240mに及ぶ碑文があり、そこには、イエスについて、神性を否定するものの、彼を預言者として認めています。

「岩のドーム」の地下には、最後の審判の日にすべての魂が集結すると言われている「魂の井戸」があります。

....

注：「岩のドーム」は、聖なる岩を守るために、八角形の形になっています。

Section 1

■ Church of the Holy Sepulchre

This is a church located in the Old City of Jerusalem, which is considered to stand on the site of Jesus' tomb. Golgotha, or Calvary, where Jesus was crucified, is considered to have been in this area.

■ Dome of the Rock

The Dome of the Rock is the third most important holy spot for Muslims, the first and second most important sites being the Kaaba in Mecca and the Prophet's Mosque (Al-Masjid al-Nabawi) in Medina respectively. This dome stands in the area where Muhammad, founder of Islam, is said to have passed away.

In this dome, "The Foundation Stone," which is said to have been the altar where Abraham placed his son Isaac as a sacrifice to God, is enshrined.

In this area is a 240 meter-long monument in its total length, which was carved at the time of the construction of the dome. The epitaph says that Jesus is accepted as a prophet and not a divinity.

Under the ground of the Dome of the Rock is the Well of Souls, into which it is said all the souls will get together on the Day of the Last Judgment.

Note : The Dome of the Rock is made octagonally so that it can protect the Foundation Stone.

第2節　ユダヤ教の影響

学問・芸術分野：ユダヤ人学者と芸術家

■ 優秀なユダヤ人

　現在、世界中にユダヤ人は約1,500万人いると言われています。ユダヤ人とはユダヤ教徒と同義で、ユダヤ教は民族宗教であり、布教活動を行いません。そのため必然的にユダヤ人の数が急激に増えることはありません。それにもかかわらず、歴史上、優秀なユダヤ人が多く存在し活躍してきました。

　世界人口のわずか0.2%ほどを占めるに過ぎないユダヤ人であるにもかかわらず、ノーベル賞受賞者の約20%がユダヤ人であると言われています。

■ 近代以降に活躍した主なユダヤ人

　以下に、近代以降に活躍した著名なユダヤ人を紹介します。最初の4人はみんなドイツ系ユダヤ人、最後の1人はユダヤ系アメリカ人です。

ユダヤ人	分野	一言説明
1.アインシュタイン	物理学者	相対性理論を提唱した20世紀最大の物理学者。1921年にノーベル物理学賞を受賞。
2.カール・マルクス	経済学者	共産主義を提唱し、1864年の第1インターナショナル（国際労働者協会）創設にもかかわった。
3.キッシンジャー	政治学者 政治家	ニクソン大統領の安全保障問題担当補佐官を務め、1973年にノーベル平和賞を受賞。
4.フランツ・カフカ	作家	20世紀を代表する作家と言われ、シュルレアリスム（シュールリアリズム）にも影響を与えた。
5.スピルバーグ	映画監督	1993年公開の「シンドラーのリスト」では、ナチスの手からユダヤ人を救ったドイツ人シンドラーを描き、7部門でアカデミー賞を受賞した。

Section 2

The field of academics and art : Jewish scholars and artists

■ **Brilliant Jews**

It is said that there are now about 15 million Jews around the world. The term "Jew" refers to a person of the Jewish faith. As Judaism is an ethnic religion, Jews don't do missionary work. Therefore, it's natural that the number of Jews does not rapidly increase. Nevertheless, many smart and talented Jews have taken an active part in history.

It is said that about 20% of the Nobel Prize winners are Jews though the number of Jews accounts for only about 0.2% of the world population.

■ **Jews who played an active role after modern times**

Let me introduce the famous Jews who played an active role in contemporary culture. The first four people are all German Jews and the last person is a Jewish American.

A Jew and his field with a brief explanation
1. Einstein is regarded as the greatest physicist of the 20th century. He discovered the theory of relativity and received the 1921 Nobel Prize in Physics.
2. Karl Marx was an economist who advocated communism and was involved in the founding of the First International (International Working Men's Association) in 1864.
3. Kissinger is a political scientist and politician who served as President Nixon's national security advisor and won the 1973 Nobel Peace Prize.
4. Franz Kafka is said to be one of the 20th century's leading writers and influenced surrealism.
5. Spielberg is a movie director whose movie "Schindler's List" released in 1993 depicts a German Schindler who saved Jews from the Nazis. This movie won 7 Academy Awards.

第2節　ユダヤ教の影響

> TIPS：そのほかの有名なユダヤ人
> 　　バールーフ・デ・スピノザ（1632～77）哲学者
> 　　ジークムント・フロイト（1856～1939）心理学者
> 　　マルク・シャガール（1887～1985）画家
> 　　ジョン・ロバート・オッペンハイマー（1904～67）物理学者、原爆開発者
> 　　ボブ・ディラン（1941～）ロック歌手
> 　　セルゲイ・ブリン（1973～）グーグル共同創設者

■ 優秀なユダヤ人の背景

　ユダヤ人に優秀な学者や芸術家が多いことは一般に知られていますが、これは、職業選択の幅が狭められたことが遠因であると言われています。歴史的に定住の地を奪われた経験を持つユダヤ人にとって、経済的には金融、精神的には知識を武器にせざるを得ない事情も、優秀なユダヤ人を生み出す要因と考えてよいでしょう。

アルベルト・アインシュタイン　　　フランツ・カフカ　　　アンネ・フランク

Section 2

> TIPS：Reference：Other famous Jews
> Baruch De Spinoza（1632～77）Philosopher
> Sigmund Freud（1856～1939）Psychologist
> Marc Chagall（1887-1985）Painter
> John Robert Oppenheimer（1904～67） Physicist and developer of the atomic bomb
> Bob Dylan（1941～）Rock singer
> Sergey Brin（1973～）Co-founder of Google

■ The background of the remarkable Jews

It is generally known that Jews count amongst their numbers many brilliant scholars and artists. This may be due to the Jews having to adapt and survive no matter where they found themselves. It is thought that as Jews have the historical experience of having been continuously forced to relocate, they developed a habit of being economical and acutely knowledgeable and aware of their surroundings.

●Useful Usage● SURVIVE

1. She survived her children.
   （彼女は子供に先立たれた）
2. He survived the operation.
   （彼は手術を持ちこたえた）
3. The play does not survive in its original form.
   （その劇は当初の形式を伝えていない）
4. Even if I fail the entrance examination, I will survive.
   （たとえ入試に落ちても、くじけずやっていくよ）

第5章

イスラム教を知る

第1節　イスラム教の基礎知識

❶ イスラム教とは?

■ イスラム教とは?

　イスラム教は、7世紀にムハンマドが創始した一神教です。唯一神アラーを信奉し、コーラン（クルアーン）を聖典とします。

　全世界で15億人の信者を有する世界宗教で、発祥地である中東のアラブ世界を中心に世界各地に信者がいます。サウジアラビア・イラク・オマーン・カタール・シリア・アラブ首長国連邦・バーレーン、そしてエジプト・リビア・アルジェリア・チュニジア・モロッコなど北アフリカなどのアラブ世界のみならず、イラン・パキスタン・アフガニスタンといった国、カザフスタン・ウズベキスタン・トルクメニスタンなどの中央アジア諸国、トルコ・インドネシア、それからインドや中国に至るまでイスラム教が浸透しています。

■ 日本人が感じるイスラム教

　日本は、明治になってようやくヨーロッパから多くを学び、戦後、アメリカから多くを学びましたが、日本にとって同じアジアにありながらイスラムは遠い存在で、イスラム教は中世の宗教というイメージがあるかもしれません。

　しかし、年1回のメッカへの大巡礼を見ても、現代に生きる世界宗教としてのすごい求心力が窺えます。というのは、出身国100カ国以上、200万人から300万人の信者が、大巡礼に参加しているからです。

　大巡礼は、ハッジと呼ばれ、イスラム世界のメッカへの巡礼を意味し、ヒジュラ（イスラム）暦第12月のズー・アル＝ヒッジャ月の8日から10日に行われます。

Section 1

What is Islam?

■ What is Islam?

Islam is a form of monotheism founded by Muhammad in the 7th century. Islam embraces one god, Allah, with the Koran (Quran) as the Islamic Bible.

Islam is a world religion with 1,500,000,000 followers all over the world but largely centered around its birthplace, the Arabic Middle East. Islam has spread not only throughout Middle Eastern countries like Saudi Arabia, Iraq, Oman, Qatar. Syria, United Arab Emirates, and Bahrain, but also North Africa with Egypt, Libya, Algeria, Tunisia, and Morocco, as well as Persian countries like Iran, Pakistan, and Afghanistan. Central Asiatic countries such as Kazakhstan, Uzbekistan, Turkmenistan, together with Turkey, Indonesia, India, and China have also been subjected to Islam.

■ Japanese feelings about Islam

It was not until the Meiji Era that Japan learned a lot from Europe and it was after the war that it learned a great deal from the U.S. Even though Islam is found in Asia, it still seems to exist far from Japan and has an image of being a medieval religion.

When we see the pilgrimage to Mecca held each year, we can feel the overwhelming centripetal force of this modern world religion. To clarify, 2 to 3 million followers from over 100 national origins participate in the pilgrimage to Mecca.

The pilgrimage is called the Hajj meaning a pilgrimage to Mecca and is held from the 8th to the 10th of Dhu Al-Hijjah, Hegira the 12th month (the 12th month of the Hijri calendar).

第1節　イスラム教の基礎知識

❷ イスラム教の教祖：ムハンマドとその生涯

■ イスラム教の教祖

　イスラム教の教祖はムハンマドです。彼はキリスト教のイエスのような救世主ではなく、また、仏陀のように悟りを開いた超越者でもありません。彼は、神と交信できるという一預言者に過ぎないのです。

　但し、これが世界三大宗教の教祖として、他の2者に比べて重要度が低いということには決してならないでしょう。というのは、アラーの神の啓示を受けた彼は、旧来のアラビアの宗教だけでなく、社会体制のすべてを急激に変化させた画期的な変革者と言えるからです。

■ ムハンマドの生い立ち

　西暦570年ごろ、アラビア半島のメッカで、ムハンマド・イブン＝アブドゥッラーフは生まれました。父親は彼の誕生前に亡くなり、母親も彼が6歳のころ死去しました。その後、祖父が引き取って育てましたが、2年後祖父も亡くなり、叔父に育てられることになりました。偉大な宗教家には、得てして孤独が付きまとうものですが、ムハンマドもその例外ではなかったようです。

　当時のアラビア半島は、商業が盛んでした。叔父も商売人で、ムハンマドも、内気ではありましたが、商業にかかわりつつ、確実に見聞を広げていきました。

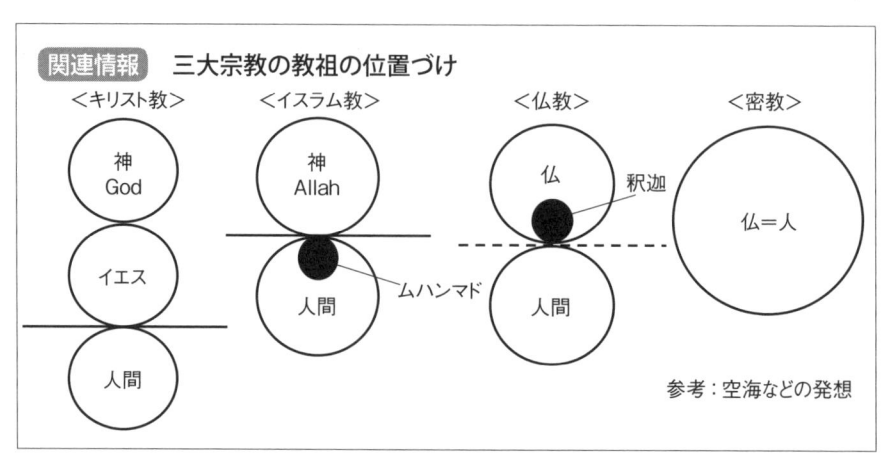

関連情報　三大宗教の教祖の位置づけ

<キリスト教>　　<イスラム教>　　<仏教>　　<密教>

神 God / イエス / 人間

神 Allah / ムハンマド / 人間

仏 / 釈迦 / 人間

仏＝人

参考：空海などの発想

Section 1

The founder of Islam, Muhammad, and his life

■ The founder of Islam

The founder of Islam is Muhammad. He is not considered the Savior like Jesus, or an enlightened being like Buddha. He is only a divine prophet who can communicate with Allah (or Islamic God).

This does not mean that Muhammad is inconsequential compared with the other two, as his revelations from Allah set him on the path to becoming a revolutionary innovator who changed not only the old Arabic religions but also the social systems.

注目：Muhammadは、かつて西洋での表記（Mohammed, Mahomet）に従い、「モハメッド」「マホメット」などと呼ばれることが多かったが、現在ではアラビア語の発音に近い「ムハンマド」と表記される。

■ Muhammad's background

Muhammad was born about 570 in Mecca located in the Arabian Peninsula. His father died before he was born and his mother died when he was six years old. After that, his grandfather took in him, but he also died two years later resulting in his being brought up by his uncle. Great persons of religion are apt to have an air of loneliness and he seems to have been no exception.

In the Arabian Peninsula at that time, business was prosperous. Muhammad was shy, but with his uncle being a merchant, he broadened his business knowledge.

●Useful Usage●　**BROADEN**
1. Each job she undertook broadened her experience.
   （彼女は仕事を受けるたび、経験を積んでいった）
2. The river broadens at its mouth. （その川は河口で広くなっている）

第1節　イスラム教の基礎知識

■ 神の啓示

　ムハンマドは25歳のとき、15歳年上の裕福な未亡人ハディージャと結婚します。結婚後、しばらくしてヒラー山の洞窟に籠もり瞑想を行うようになりました。そして、40歳のある日、運命的な出来事が彼の身に降りかかりました。突然、全身を押しつぶすような超自然の力に見舞われ、気がつくと、そこには天使ジブリール（ガブリエル）がいました。

　ジブリールは有無を言わさず「読め」と命令し、これを三度繰り返し、「汝は神の使徒」と言い渡したのです。これがアラーの最初の啓示でした。アラーは天使を通じ、こういう形で啓示を繰り返すことになります。これらの啓示は、のちにコーランとしてまとめられますが、その元来の意味は「読まれるもの」で、最初の啓示の「読め」に由来しています。

■ 布教と迫害

　異常な出来事に戸惑うムハンマドを落ち着かせ、彼の使命を気づかせたのは、ほかならぬ妻のハディージャでした。彼女は、信徒第1号となりました。彼は613年ごろから、メッカ周辺で説教を開始しました。しかし、アラビアの商人たちにとって、偶像崇拝を禁止するイスラム教は、これまでの伝統を覆す邪魔な宗教で、ムハンマドは様々な迫害に見舞われました。

　数々の迫害にもめげず、裕福な商人から黒人奴隷まで入信し、身分の上下や血縁や地縁に捉われない新しい信仰集団が誕生することになりました。

　自分に対する殺害計画から逃れるため、彼は622年メディナに活動の舞台を移しました。彼のメディナでの最初の仕事はモスク建築でした。メディナでのムハンマドは、もはや預言者だけでなく、政治家・裁判官・立法者の役割を併せ持つ指導者になっていました。このことで、人徳も手伝って、彼は宗教的権威を高めることになりました。

　彼はメッカの無血征服に成功し、カアバ神殿に安置されていた360体の偶像を破壊しました。これにより、カアバ神殿はイスラム教のアラーの館となりました。彼は632年にこの世を去りましたが、彼の実績とカリスマ性からして、彼自身が神格化されなかったのは不思議だと言えるでしょう。しかし、この事実がイスラム教が純粋な一神教であることを示しています。

Section 1

■ Revelation of God

Muhammad married at 25 a wealthy widow, Khadijah bint Khuwaylid, who was 15 years older than he. Shortly after their marriage, he began the habit of going into the cave of Mt. Hira and meditating. One day when he was 40, a fateful incident occurred. He was overwhelmed by supernatural power and found the angel Gabriel standing before him.

Gabriel peremptorily ordered him to 'read' three times and said, "You are a messenger of God." This was the first revelation of Allah. Allah repeated the revelation through the angel. This revelation was compiled into the Koran, the meaning of which was originally 'what is read' which comes from the first revelation 'read.'

■ Propagandism and persecution

Muhammad's wife consoled Muhammad, who was bewildered by the abnormal incident and it was his wife, Khadijah bint Khuwaylid, that made him realize his mission. She joined his first congregation, being his first devotee. He began preaching around Mecca in about 613.

Because Muhammad's preaching defied old traditions such as the worshipping of idols, which is considered evil in Islam, he was heavily persecuted by the establishment.

Despite the persecution, wealthy merchants and even black slaves converted and a new religious movement free from social classes, blood ties, and territorial relationship was born.

To escape from the assassination attempt, Muhammad transferred his base of operations to Medina. His first job in Medina was to build a mosque. Muhammad in Medina was no longer just a prophet, but had become a leader who acted as a politician, judge, and lawmaker, which enhanced his religious authority with the help of his virtue.

He succeeded in a bloodless conquest and destroyed 360 statues of icons placed in the Kabah (Kaaba). By this action, the Kabah became the house of Allah in Islam. He passed away in 632. We may say it's a wonder that he wasn't deified judging from his accomplishments and charisma; however this very fact highlights Islam's pure monotheism.

第1節　イスラム教の基礎知識

❸ イスラム教の教えとコーラン

■ シャリーアとは?

　イスラム世界では、あらゆる人間活動、すなわち、日常生活から宗教儀礼、さらには国家の政治に至るまで、行動規範を示したものがあります。それはシャリーア（イスラム法）と呼ばれています。シャリーアはアラーが定めた改定不可能な法律と言えます。

　シャリーアは、コーランを第1とする4つの法源（最初の2つが主要法源、残り2つが副次的法源）から構成されています。

法源	名称	一言説明
第1法源	コーラン	神（アラー）の言葉
第2法源	スンナ	ムハンマドの慣行
第3法源	イジュマー	共同体（ウンマ）の合意
第4法源	キャース	法学者の類推

注1：第1法源に具体的な規定がない場合、第2法源へ、第2法源に規定がなければ、第3法源へという具合に、下位の法源へ規範を求めることになる。

注2：イスラムには聖職者がいない（→p.104参照）が、その代わりを法学者など知識人が行う。新聞報道などでイスラム指導者というのは、彼らのことである。

注3：イスラム最高指導者をイマームというが、厳密にはイマームすら聖職者ではない。

Section 1

The teaching of Islam and Koran

■ What is Shariah?

In the Islamic world, there exists a certain code of conduct on which any human activity, from daily life to religious ceremonies, should be based and which even covers national politics. It is called Shariah (Islamic law), which is considered to be absolute in the Islamic world.

Shariah (Sharia) consists of four sources with the Koran on top, of which the first two are primary sources, the remaining two being secondary sources.

Source	name	Explanation at a word
The First Source	Koran	Allah's Words
The Second Source	Sunna	Muhammad's Sunna
The Third Source	Ijma	agreement of community (Ummah [Umma])
The Fourth Source	Qiyas	analogy of maulvis

Note 1 : You should refer to the second source if there is not a specific rule in the first source. If there still isn't a specific solution, you should go to the third source. Like this the sub sources are put into play.

Note 2 : There is no clergy in Islam, but instead, there are intellectual persons like the maulvis. The Muslim leaders we see in the news are usually of the group.

Note 3 : Islam's most prominent leader is called an imam, but strictly speaking, even an imam isn't a member of the clergy.

第1節　イスラム教の基礎知識

■ シャリーアの行為5範疇

シャリーアが規定する行為の具体的内容は、5つの範疇に分類されます。

範疇	一言説明
義務行為	「五行」、配偶者の扶養など、行わなければならない行為
推奨行為	「喜捨」や結婚など、行うことが勧められる行為
許容行為	飲食や売買、旅行や趣味など、行っても許される行為
忌避行為	離婚や中絶など、行うことを勧められない行為
禁止行為	殺人・窃盗・姦淫・飲酒・豚肉食や偶像崇拝など、行ってはいけない行為

注1：「五行」とは、イスラム教における義務行為の代表的なもので、信仰告白・礼拝・断食・喜捨・巡礼の5つを言う（詳しくはp.248以降参照）。
注2：喜捨は五行の1つで、財産の2.5%を寄付する行為。

■ シャリーアの内容5項目

シャリーアは、具体的には以下の5項目に分類できます。

項目	一言説明
信条	保つべき「六信」。
道徳律	神への帰依、満足・寛大・忍耐などの道徳上の徳を積むこと。
勤行	「五行」および「聖戦」を実践すること。
和解事項	結婚・離婚・親子関係・相続・契約・売買・裁判などに関する規定。
刑罰	コーランおよび伝承に規定された刑罰。

注1：「六信」とは神・天使・啓典・預言者・来世・天命の6つを信じることを言う。（詳しくはp.244以降参照）
注2：「聖戦」とはジハードとも言い、現在では「イスラム世界を防衛・拡大するための戦い」とされる。
注3：刑罰には盗みに対する片手切断の刑、飲酒に対する80回のムチ刑などがある。

Section 1

■ Sharia's conduct: 5 categories

Specific conduct of Sharia rules are classified into 5 categories.

Category	Explanation
Obligatory activity	'Five Pillars,'obligatory activity such as supporting one's spouse
Recommended activity	Recommended activity such as 'Alms-giving' and marriage
Acceptable activity	Accepted activity such as eating and drinking, buying and selling, traveling, and hobbies
Evaded activity	Evaded activity such as divorce and abortion
Prohibited activity	Prohibited activity such as murder, thievery, fornication, drinking, eating pork, and idol worship

Note 1 : "Five Pillars," which is typical of obligatory activity in Islam, means Testimony, Prayer, Fasting, Alms-giving, and Pilgrimage.
Note 2 : Alms-giving is one of the Five Pillars.

■ Five items of Sharia's contents

Specifically Sharia is classified into the following 5 items.

Items	Explanation
Creed	'The Six Articles of Belief' to keep
Moral code	submission to God, accumulating moral virtues such as satisfaction, generosity, and patience
Devotion	practicing 'the Five Pillars of Islam' and holy war
Conciliation items	rules of marriage, divorce, relationship between parents and children, inheritance, agreement, buying and selling, and judgment
Punishment	punishment as ruled in the Koran and its tradition

Note 1 : It means belief in God, Angels, Revelations, Prophets, Resurrection and judgment and Predestination.
Note 2 : It is also called Jihad, which is now 'the war to defend and extend Islam throughout the world.'
Note 3 : Amputating the hand of a thief and being flogged 80 times for drinking are included in Punishment.

第1節　イスラム教の基礎知識

■ コーランとは?

　コーランとは、唯一全知全能である神アラーの啓示を受けた者である預言者を通して人々に伝えられたという啓典です。コーランは「クルアーン」とも呼ばれ、イスラム世界を束ねるイスラム法（＝シャリーア）の第1法源として絶対的な地位を保っています。

　コーランの特徴として、ストーリー性がない点があげられます。それは人間的な意図を排除するほどコーランは神聖だということを示しています。この観点では、キリスト教の聖書にはストーリー性があり、人間味あふれると言えます。

　また、コーランの中身は預言者ムハンマド1人に与えられたものである点も特徴的です。キリスト教の聖書は、多くの預言者の様々な文書から成っています。

■ コーランの意味

　コーランの元来の意味は「アル・クルアーン（＝読誦されるもの）」です。ムハンマドが最初に神から「読め」という言葉を受けましたが（p.234参照）、そのように読まされた内容がコーランというわけです。

■ コーランの不思議

　コーランは、全114章から成り、基本的に章の大きいものから小さいものへと並べられています。日常生活の細かなことまでカバーするため、神や信仰におよそ関係なさそうなタイトルの章も存在します。

　中には、「18.洞窟章」「27.蟻章」「58.言いがかりをつける女章」「111.腐ってしまえ章」など、これ啓示なの?と思わせるものまであります。人為的な力により脚色することをあえてしないのが、コーランのすごさと言えそうです。

Section 1

■ **What is the Koran?**

The Koran is a revelation which is said to have come down to people through prophets who had a spiritual epiphany of Allah, the one true god. Koran is also spelled 'Quran,' and holds the highest post as the first source in Islamic law (Sharia) which unifies the Islamic world.

Characteristically, the Koran has no story, which means the Koran is sacred and divine as it is not tainted by humanity. In this regard, the Bible of Christianity is made of stories about people, so it is more rooted in humanity.

One characteristic is that the content of Koran was given to only one prophet, Muhammad. The Bible of Christianity holds the prophecies as told by a number of different prophets.

■ **The meaning of Koran**

The original meaning of Koran is 'al-Quran (what is read).' Muhammad was ordered to read at first and the content he was made to read is the Koran.

■ **The mysteries of the Koran**

The Koran consists of 114 chapters. Basically, longer chapters appear earlier in the Koran, while shorter ones appear later. There are parts which seem to have no relationship with God and faith as the Koran covers all things even those related to daily living.

Not all of them seem to be revelations at first glance. Among such revelations are Chapter 18: The Cave, Chapter 27: The Ants, Chapter 58: The Woman Who Pleads, and Chapter 111: Perish (the hands of the Father of Flame). The splendor of the Koran may lie in the fact that it is NOT embellished or elaborated by human efforts.

第1節　イスラム教の基礎知識

　そんなコーランですが、人間がまねできない美しい言葉を連ねている側面が豊富で、単なる宗教書ではなく、文学としても第1級品であると言われています。内容のみならず読まれたときの音の響きにも息を呑むようなものがあります。事実、コーランの中身が高級で何を書いているのかわからない者でも、そのアラビア語の美しさで入信したという人も多いのです。

TIPS：聖戦とは?

　コーランに「イスラムの教えを広め、それを拒む異教徒は排斥すべし」と述べている箇所があり、これを受けて、イスラムに対抗する者に対して行う聖なる戦いを「聖戦」と呼ぶのが一般的です。

　しかし、聖戦を意味する「ジハード」の本来の意味は「戦い」ではなく「努力」（＝イスラムの道を全うするための努力）です。

　弱い自分との内なる戦いを大ジハード、外部からの圧力に屈しない努力を小ジハードと呼びます。

Section 1

The Koran is said to be an example of the highest form of literature, not just a religious book, in that it is written in a beautiful prose that most people would have a difficult time imitating. Not only its contents, but the rhythm of the sound when they are read is breathtaking. In fact, some adherents to the Muslim faith were roped in by the beauty of the Arabic chant even though they can't understand what is written in the Koran, because the language is so sophisticated.

TIPS : What is a holy war?

In the Koran, there is a part saying, 'spread the teachings of Islam and reject the pagans who disobey it,' In this connection, the holy war against those who oppose Islam is called 'jihad' in general.

But the original meaning of 'jihad,' is not just a holy war, but an effort to fulfill the teachings of Islam.

The struggle against the weakness of self is called the Greater Jihad, while the effort not to yield to outside pressure is called the Lesser Jihad.

●Useful Usage● YIELD

1. My investments yield about $3,000 a year.
   (私の投資は年に約3,000ドルの利益を生み出している)
2. She yielded that point in the argument.
   (彼女は議論の中で、その点は認めた)
3. The apple trees did not yield well last year.
   (そのりんごの木は昨年はあまり実がならなかった)

第1節　イスラム教の基礎知識

❹ イスラム教の六信五行

■ イスラムの教えの根本：六信五行

　イスラム法の内容の5項目のトップにくる「信条」の中核である「六信」と、イスラム法の5範疇のトップを占める義務行為の中核である「五行」の2つは、ムスリム（＝イスラム教徒）にとっては守るべき非常に大切な教えです。

■ 六信とは？

　六信は、その絶対的真実性を信じなければならない6つの対象のことで、神（アラー、アッラーまたはアッラーフとも呼ばれる）、天使（マラーイカ）、啓典（キターブ）、預言者（ナービー）、来世（アーヒラ）、天命（カダル）の6つです。

(1) 神

　「アラー」は固有名詞ではなく、神を意味する一般名詞です。名前をみだりに呼ぶことや、偶像化は禁止されています。

....

注1：コーランの112章（信仰ただ一筋章）では、神は「子もなく親もなく、並ぶものなき御神ぞ」と述べられている。つまり誰から生まれたのでもなく、また神的存在の子を産んだのでもないとされる。これは、キリスト教における神の子であるイエスの否定をも意味する。但し、イエスを預言者としては認めている。

(2) 天　使

　神が光から創ったとされる超自然的存在です。イスラム教では、ジブリール（旧約聖書のガブリエルに相当）、ミーカール（旧約聖書のミカエルに相当）、アズラーイール、イスラーフィールが著名です（以上「イスラム四大天使」）が、他にも、墓の中の死者を尋問して信仰の有無を問うムンカルとナキール、地獄で責苦担当のザバーニーヤなど多くの天使を認めています。

Section 1

Six Articles of Faith and Five Pillars in Islam

■ **The basic idea of the teachings of Islam: Six Articles of Faith and Five Pillars**

The "Six Articles of Faith" serve as the backbone for the 'creed,' which ranks first in the five items of Sharia's contents, while the "Five Pillars" function as the core of the 'obligatory activity,' which tops the five categories of Sharia's conduct. These two principles form the fundamental obligations in Islam; therefore, they are considered most sacred and worthy of protection.

■ **What are the Six Articles of Faith?**

The Six Articles of Faith must be believed in: God (called Allah or Allahu), Angels (Malaika), Revelations (Kitab), Prophets (Nabi), Resurrection and Judgment (Akhira), Predestination (Kadaru).

(1) God

'Allah' is not a proper noun but a general noun which means god. Taking the name of God in vain and idolizing him is prohibited.

Note 1 : In Chapter 112, God says, 'I am an unparalleled god with no child or parent.' In short, it means God was born from nobody and bore no child of spiritual presence. This means the denial of Jesus, the child of God in Christianity. However, Jesus is recognized as a prophet.

(2) Angels

Angels are supernatural beings that are said to have been created by God with light. In Islam, Jibril (corresponding to Gabriel in the Old Testament), Mikal (corresponding to Michael in the Old Testament), Azrael, and Israfil (Israfel) are widely known and collectively called "the four Islamic archangels." Munkar and Nakir, or angels of death and judgment, and Zabaniya, who is in charge of the torture in hell, are also recognized.

245

第1節　イスラム教の基礎知識

(3) 啓　典

　啓典はコーランのみではありません。旧約聖書の一部と新約聖書の一部も啓典に含まれます。しかし、コーランは啓典中の啓典と呼ばれ、定冠詞アルをつけて、アル・キターブと呼ばれます。

注2：キリスト教の場合、英語でthe Bookと言えば「聖書」のことになる。

(4) 預言者

　預言者とは神の言葉を人々に伝える人間で、超越者ではありません。神性を帯びているわけではないのです。コーランには25人の預言者が出てきます。ムハンマドが最終預言者で一番重要ですが、彼とてキリスト教のイエスのような救世主というわけではありません。まして、神の子ではありません。もちろん、信仰の対象にもなりません。

参考：「六信」の4番目は「使徒」（ラスール［Rasul］）とされる場合もある。

(5) 来　世

　この世はイスラーフィールという天使が吹くラッパの音とともに突如として終末を迎え、来世がスタートするとされています。神による最後の審判では、人々は「先頭組」（特に優れた神の使徒）と「右組」（善行を積んだ使徒）と「左組」（悪徳を積んだ不信心者）に分けられます。前2者は楽園、後者は煉獄（期限付き）と地獄（無期限）に振り分けられます。

注3：先頭組は神の玉座近くにゆったりとくつろぎ、悪酔いしない酒を楽しみ、美女が
　　　周りを取り囲み、鳥の肉などが食べ放題の別天地を享受するという。

(6) 天　命

　100％の運命説（はじめから運命は決まっているので努力が全く無駄であるという発想）ではなく、「人事を尽くして天命を待つ」ということがイスラムの本義であるとの解釈も可能です。

Section 1

(3) Revelations

Revelations are not exclusive to the Koran. Some parts of the Old Testament and the New Testament are included in Revelations. The Koran is, however, considered second to none in terms of revelations and is called Al Kitab adding the definite article Al.

Note 2 : In Christianity, the Book means "Bible."

(4) Prophets

Prophets are mere mortals who spread the word of God to the people and not possessing of supernatural powers. They are never deified. A total of 25 prophets appear in the Koran. Muhammad is the last prophet and most import, but even Muhammad isn't a Savior like Jesus in Christianity, much less the child of God. Of course, he isn't supposed to be worshipped.

(5) Resurrection and Judgment

It is said that this world will end suddenly with the sound of the trumpet of the angel, Israfil. In the Final Judgment by God, people are divided into 'the top group' (exceptional messengers of God), 'the right group' (the messengers who did good deeds) and 'the left group' (unbelievers who behaved poorly). The former two groups go to Paradise and the latter goes to purgatory (on a temporary basis) and to hell (for an indefinite term).

Note 3 : It is said that the top group will enjoy their afterlife in a different world where they can relax near the throne of God, drink alcohol without becoming sick from drinking and eat chicken as much as they like, surrounded by beautiful virgin girls.

(6) Predestination

It is not to be mistaken as absolute predestination, the idea that one's fortune is determined from the beginning and therefore there is no use making efforts in life. It may be possible to interpret it as "Use the means Allah gave you in order to receive His blessing."

第1節　イスラム教の基礎知識

六信一覧表

六信	専門語	信じるべき内容
神	アラー	創造主であり、全知全能の神。
天使	マラーイカ	天啓の天使ジブリール、戦士の天使ミーカール、死を司るアズラーイール、終末のラッパを吹くイスラーフィールなど。
啓典	キターブ	コーラン、旧約聖書の一部である「モーセ五書」と「ダビデへの詩編」、および新約聖書の「福音書」の4種。
預言者	ナービー	アダム、ノア、アブラハム、モーセ、イエス、ムハンマドなど。
来世	アーヒラ	来世で、死んだ人間が復活し、神による最後の審判を受け、生前の行いと信仰により、天国と地獄に振り分けられる。
天命	カダル	この世界で起こることはあらかじめ神によって定められている。と同時に生前の信仰や努力により報いもある。

■ 五行とは？

　五行とはムスリムがイスラム教の信徒として具体的にとらなければならない行動のことで、信仰告白（シャハーダ）、礼拝（サラート）、喜捨（ザカート）、断食（サウム）、そして巡礼（ハッジ）の5つを指します。六信が完全でも五行ができていないと、信仰は完全とはみなされません。それだけ、五行は大切なのです。

(1) 信仰告白

　信仰告白とは、「アラーの他に神はなし。ムハンマドはアラーの使徒なり。」という言葉（カリマ）を唱えることで、1日5回の礼拝の度に必ず唱えることになっています。

(2) 礼　拝

　礼拝は、1日5回行うのですが、病気のときや旅行中は3回でもよいとされています。礼拝の1単位をラクアといい、これを何単位行うかは、礼拝時間によって異なります。夜明けが2ラクア、正午過ぎと午後と夜半が4ラクア、日没が3ラクアです。

Section 1

The list of Six Articles of Faith

Articles of Faith (Jargon)	Brief explanation
God (Allah)	Creator; Omniscient and Omnipotent.
Angels (Malaika)	Jibril, Mikal, Azrael, who presides over one's death, and Islafil, who blows the trumpet of the end of the world.
Revelations (Kitab)	Koran, parts of the Old Testament ("the Five Books of Moses" (Torah) and "Psalm to David") and Evangel in the New Testament.
Prophets (Nabi)	Adam, Noah, Abraham, Moses, Jesus, Muhammad, and so on.
Resurrection and Judgment (Akhira)	In the afterworld, the dead come back to life and are judged by God, then dispatched to either heaven or hell according to their faith and deeds during life.
Predestination (Kadaru)	What goes on in this world is destined beforehand. Simultaneously, people are rewarded by their faith and effort made during life.

■ What are the Five Pillars?

The Five Pillars refer to the activities that Muslims must take perform, including Testimony (Shahada), Prayer (Salat [Salah]), Alms-giving (Zakat), Fasting (Sawm), and Pilgrimage (Hajj). If people live according to the Articles of Faith but their Five Pillars are insufficient, their faith is regarded as imperfect.

(1) Testimony

Testimony means reciting a set statement called 'Kalima,' 'There is no other god but Allah and Muhammad is Allah's messenger.' Believers must recite this in prayer five times a day.

(2) Prayer

Prayers are offered five times a day, but praying three times (a day) is considered acceptable for those who are ill or traveling. One unit of prayer is called a rakaat and how many units people pray varies according to the time of the day; 2 rakaat at dawn, 4 rakaat in the afternoon, in the evening and in the middle of the night, and 3 rakaat at sunset.

第1節　イスラム教の基礎知識

(3) 断　食

　断食は、ラマダーン月（イスラム暦9月）は日の出から日没まで飲食を断つという修行です。ただし、日没後の飲食は許されます。この月に病気または旅行中なら、別のときにそれだけの日数分断食すればよいとされています。しかし、昼間の断食修行によるフラストレーションはかなりのものらしく、ラマダーン月の消費が年間最大になり、この時期に体重が増える人が多いと言います。

(4) 喜　捨

　喜捨とは、いわゆるお布施に当たる修行です。1年以上所有している財産の何％を寄付すべきかが決められており、その率が物によって異なります。
　① 通貨 2.5％
　② 家畜 0.8～2.5％（家畜の種類により率が異なる）
　③ 果実・穀物 10％（自然に採れるもの）、5％（人力によるもの）
　④ 商品 5％（金）、20％（埋蔵財貨）、2.5％（通常の物品）

注：集まった喜捨の用途は（次の人たちに限って）次の順番に使用される。
　(i)　貧者
　(ii)　税を徴収して回る人
　(iii)　心を協調させた人（あとからイスラム教に入信した人）
　(iv)　奴隷の身請けや借金などで困っている人
　(v)　アラーの道を行く人（伝道活動をする人）
　(vi)　旅人

(5) 巡　礼

　巡礼とは、ズー・アル＝ヒッジャ月（イスラム暦12月）の8日から10日にかけて、決められた方法と順路で、メッカのカアバ神殿に参詣することを言います。カアバ神殿は、コーランの第3章に「人類のために建てられた最初の聖殿、生けとし生けるものの祝福の場所」とされています。

Section 1

(3) Fasting

Fasting is the religious training of abstaining from food and drink from sunrise to sunset during the month of Ramadan (in the year of Hijra, September). However, people are allowed to eat and drink after dark. If they are ill or traveling during this month, it is considered acceptable that they fast for the same number of days at another time. It is said that stress caused by the hardships of fasting in the daytime is overwhelming, so consumption is highest each year during the month of Ramadan and a lot of people are said to put on weight at this time.

(4) Alms-giving

Alms-giving is the practice of what is called charitable giving. The percentage of wealth people have to donate varies according to what is being donated.

① Money 2.5%
② Livestock 0.8%〜2.5% (depending on the kind of the livestock)
③ Fruit. grain 10% (natural), 5% (artificial)
④ Goods 5% (gold), 20% (buried goods), 2,5% (normal goods)

Note: Donated things and money are distributed to the following persons in the following order of importance: (i) Poor people (ii) Those who collect tax (iii) Those with enlightened minds (those who came to believe in Islam later) (iv) Those who have trouble with redemption of slaves and debt (v) Practitioners of Allah (those engaged in mission work) (vi) Travelers.

(5) Pilgrimage

Pilgrimage means making the pilgrimage to the Kaaba in Mecca from the 8th to the 10th during the Islamic month of Dhu al-Hijjah (December) in a predetermined manner and through a predetermined route. The Kaaba shrine itself is said to be 'the first place built for the human race and the most blessed place for all living things.'

第1節　イスラム教の基礎知識

　世界各地から集まった巡礼の大集団は、まず、カアバ神殿を7回まわることになります。その後、決まったコースを決まった手順で回ります。

注：五行で言う「巡礼」は、カアバ神殿への参詣を指すが、これは特に「大巡礼」(ハッジ)と呼ばれます。他にも個人的なカアバ神殿参詣である「ウムラ」やムハンマドやその他の聖者の墓参りである「ジャーラ」もあり、これも「巡礼」の一種とされる。
　＊「ウムラ」は12月以外に行い、「小巡礼」と呼ばれる。

五行一覧表

五行	専門語	行うべき内容
信仰告白	シャハーダ	「アラーのほかに神なし」と「ムハンマドはアラーの使徒」という2つを信じ、公言すること。
礼拝	サラート	1日に5回、つまり、夜明け(日の出前)、正午、午後、日没時、夜半に、メッカの方向(カアバ神殿の方角)に向いて祈ること。
断食	サウム	年に一度、イスラム暦9月(ラマダーン月)の新月から次の新月まで約29日間、昼間の飲食を禁止すること。
喜捨	ザカート	所有通貨の2.5%を寄付するのを含め、様々な施しをすること。財産のある人が貧乏な人を救うことになる。
巡礼	ハッジ	メッカのカアバ神殿へ巡礼すること。イスラム暦12月に行い、一生に一度訪れるのが義務とされる。

> **関連情報**　**イスラム暦**
>
> 　イスラム暦とは、イスラム社会で使用されている暦で、ヒジュラ暦とも言います。英語ではIslamic calendar (Hijri calendar)と翻訳されます。預言者ムハンマドがマッカ(=メッカ)からマディーナ(=メディナ)へ聖遷(ヒジュラ)したユリウス暦622年が、ヒジュラ暦元年とされています。ヒジュラ(聖遷)があった正確な日付は、ユリウス暦622年7月16日です。
>
> 　イスラム暦は太陰暦で、約29.5日である月の公転周期に合わせ、1カ月が29日の小の月と30日の大の月をおおむね交互に繰り返します。したがって、1年は約354日になるので、太陽暦とは1年に11日ずれてきます。ちなみに西暦2000年はヒジュラ暦1421年に相当します。

Section 1

First a large group of pilgrims who gather from all over the world walk around the Kaaba seven times, and then they walk a designated course following an established procedure.

Note : The 'Pilgrimage' in Five Pillars' means the pilgrimage to Kaaba, which is especially called the 'Hajj.' The 'Umrah,' the private pilgrimages to Kaaba and 'Jara,' and those to Muhammad's and other saints' graves are also included in this category.'

List of Five Pillars

Five Pillars	*jargon*	What ought to be done
Testimony	Shahada	To believe andtwo sentences, repeat the 'There is no other god but Allah and Muhammad is His messenger.'
Prayer	Salah (Salat)	To pray towards Mecca five times a day, that is, at dawn, in the morning, in the afternoon, after sunset, and at midnight.
Fasting	Sawm	To prohibit eating and drinking in the daytime for about 29 days from the new moon in the Islamic month of Ramadan (September) to the next new moon.
Alms-giving	Zakat	To give various charities including donating 2.5 % of one's income to serve the poor.
Pilgrimage	Hajj	To make the pilgrimage to Mecca. Obligatory to visit Mecca once in a lifetime.

第1節　イスラム教の基礎知識

❺ イスラム教徒の風習と生活

■ モスクに欠かせないミナレットには鐘がない

　イスラム教の礼拝所であるモスクには、ミナレットと呼ばれる細長い塔があります。これは、礼拝の時間を知らせる役目を持っていますが、鐘がありません。アザーンと呼ばれる朗唱を行って時を知らせるからです。これは、イスラム教では、アラーが創った人間の声が最も神聖であるという発想があるからです。人間の作った鐘はレベルが低いというわけです。このようにイスラム教では、徹底的に人工的要素を排除し、神の偉大さを称えるのです。

■ イスラム教徒になるには?

　イスラム教徒（＝ムスリム）に入信する方法は実に簡単です。2人以上のムスリムの前で、イスラムの信仰を受け容れることを表明すれば、その時点でイスラム教徒となります。つまり、イスラム教には、仏教における受戒やキリスト教における洗礼のような儀式は存在しないのです。人間的なもの（＝厳かな儀式を執り行うこと）を一切排除するイスラムの特徴がここにも表れています。

■ イスラム教徒の一生

　イスラム教徒は、コーラン（イスラム教の中核となる啓典）とハディース（第2の啓典と言われるムハンマドの言行の伝承を記したもの）に従って、幼児期から通過儀礼を行います。

　子供が生まれたら、まず右耳、次に左耳に「アラーは偉大なり」で始まる「アザーン」(＝1日5回の礼拝開始の呼びかけ)の言葉がささやかれます。次に、7日目に「アキーカ」と呼ばれる命名行事が行われ、羊が供えられます。多くはこののち、割礼を行います。

Section 1

Custom and life of Muslims

■ **Minarets being indispensable while Islamic mosques have no bells**

Mosques, places of worship of Islam, have tall spires called minarets. The main function of the minarets is to let people know the prayer time. They have no bells because the prayer time is informed by recitation called "adhan." This is because of the idea that as Allah created the human voice, it is far more sacred than the synthetic sound of bells. In this way, Islam eliminates everything artificial thoroughly in praise of the grandeur of God.

■ **How can we become Muslims?**

It is quite simple to come to believe in Islam. If people announce that they accept Muslim beliefs before two or more Muslims, they are considered Muslims. In short, there are no ceremonies such as receiving the ordination in Buddhism and baptism in Christianity. We can see in this the Islamic characteristic which eliminates everything artificial including solemn ritual.

■ **Muslims' lives**

Muslims take part in an initiation ceremony from childhood according to the Koran (the revelation which is the core of Islam) and Hadith (the second revelation that describes what Muhammad said).

When babies are born, they are whispered the words of "Adhan" (the announcement to begin praying five times a day), which begins with 'Allah is great' first in their right ear and next in their left ear. Then on the seventh day, a naming ceremony called 'akika' is performed and sheep are offered. Then the children are circumcized in many cases afterwards.

第1節　イスラム教の基礎知識

7歳から礼拝ができるようにと、4〜5歳で「クッターブ」という学校に通い、コーランやイスラムの基本を学びます。成人までにイスラム教徒としての生活ができるようにさせるのが、親の義務とされています。

■ イスラムの葬儀

葬儀はモスクで行われ、女性は故人宅でコーランを読み、男性は礼拝を行います。遺体は右わき腹を下にして、頭をメッカに向けて葬ります。土葬が堅く守られています。火葬は、地獄に落ちる者に対し神が与える厳罰とされるので、執り行われることはありません。

■ イスラム教の祭日

イスラムには大きな祭日が2つあります。これらは、スンナ（預言者ムハンマドの言行録）で定められています。

(1) 断食明けの祭り

　断食が行われるラマダーン月（イスラム暦9月）を過ぎた次の日、すなわち、イスラム暦10月1日に行われます。

(2) 犠牲祭

　大巡礼の終わった翌日、すなわちイスラム暦12月10日に行われ、通例13日の日没まで続きます。家畜を神に捧げる日で、具体的には1家族につき羊か山羊を1頭、7家族につき牛1頭を捧げます。肉の3分の1は自分たちが用い、残り3分の2は貧しい人たちや友人や縁者に分け与えます。

■ 集団礼拝の金曜日

毎日の礼拝は、集団で行うのが望ましいが義務ではありません。しかし、毎週金曜日の礼拝は、男子にとっては義務とされています。女子の集団礼拝は本人の気持ち次第とされています。

Section 1

They attend a school called a 'Kuttaab' at the age of 4 and 5 and learn the basics of the Koran and Islam so that they can pray at the age of seven. It is said to be a parent's duty to make them learn to live as Muslims before they come of age.

■ Funeral ceremonies in Islam

Funeral ceremonies are held in mosques. Women read the Koran in the house of the deceased and men pray. The bodies are buried with their right side downward and their head toward Mecca. Interment is strictly observed. Cremation is prohibited because the act of a dead boy being burned is reserved as a heavy punishment exclusively for those who are doomed to hell and only Allah can pass that judgment.

■ High days of Islam

There are two important days. These are established in Sunna (the sayings of Muhammad).

(1) Eid al-Fitr

It is held on the first day of the month after Ramadan, or October (Shawwal) 1st.

(2) Eid al-Adha

It is held on December (Dhu Al-Hijjah) 10th A.H., the next day of the Pilgrimage, and usually continues until sunset of the 13th of Dhu Al-hijjah. It is at this time people are expected to dedicate livestock to God. To be specific, one family dedicates one sheep or goat and seven families devote one cow. People eat a third of the meat and give the remaining two thirds to the poor, their friends, and relatives.

■ Group prayer on Fridays

It is desirable to pray in a group every day, but not mandatory. It is mandatory for men every Friday, while Women engage in group prayer depending on their feelings.

第1節　イスラム教の基礎知識

　この金曜日は、キリスト教の日曜日やユダヤ教の土曜日のような安息日の発想とは全く異なります。創造主が創造の仕事ののち、7日目に休んだことを受けて安息日が制定されていますが、イスラム教では、創造主アラーは、いわば純粋に全知全能で、休息を全く必要としないので、安息日の制度が不要と考えるのです。だから、この金曜日は、仕事に励んでも一向に構わないのです。

TIPS：イスラムの3つの生活時間
イスラムの生活時間は次の3つに分けられます。

生活時間の3分類	どんな時間か？	具体的内容
ショグル	仕事をする時間	生活を営む上で不可欠であるが、必要悪という感覚がある。ユダヤ教やキリスト教と同じで、労働は神からの罰という発想がある（→p.124関連情報参照）。
ラアブ	遊びの時間	子供がすることだと認識され、日本人のように大人が漫画を読んでいたり、コンピュータゲームに興じることは軽蔑される。
ラーハ	くつろぎの時間	この時間が最も重視されている。休息のほか、礼拝・瞑想、家族や友人との語らい、趣味の充実、旅行により見聞を広げることも含まれる。

■ イスラム教徒の食生活

　イスラムの食事は、パン・乳製品・野菜・果物、それに羊を中心とした肉料理、さらに、コーヒー・紅茶などの嗜好品があります。中世よりインド洋交易でもたらされた香辛料により、食生活は豊かなものになっています。

　豚肉を食べるのは禁止されています。これは、コーラン第2章（雌牛章）に「食べることを禁じられるものは、死肉・血・豚肉、およびアラー以外に供えられたもの」とあるからです。包丁もそのままでは「豚肉を切った可能性がある」として疑われるので「この包丁は豚肉を切ったことがない」という証明が必要な場合もあるほどです。しかし、何が何でも食べてはいけないということはなく、それ以外に口にするものがなかったり豚肉だと知らなかった状況では許されます。

Section 1

This idea of a holy Friday is quite different from that of the Sabbath of Sundays in Christianity and Saturdays of Judaism. The Sabbath was established because it is said that the Creator rested on the 7th day after completing Creation, but in Islam, the Creator Allah is not considered a feeble god, so he needs no rest, which is why the Sabbath is thought to be unnecessary. It doesn't matter whether people work or not on Fridays.

Tips : Three living hours in Islam

Type of Living (What kind of hours?)	More specific explanation
Time to work	It is indispensable to live, but also considered an unnecessary evil. The idea that labor is punishment from God is similar to Jewish and Christian beliefs.
Time to play	It is what children do, and if adults read comic books and indulge in computer games like Japanese do, they are despised.
Time to relax	It is most valued. It includes prayer, meditation, talking with family members and friends, fullfilment of hobbies, broadening one's knowledge by traveling, and resting.

■ Dietary habit of Muslims

An Islamic diet consists of bread, milk products, vegetables, fruit, meat (usually mutton), and their favorite drink, coffee and tea. They enjoy a rich and varied diet thanks to spices brought during the Middle Ages by trade through the Indian Ocean.

Eating pork is prohibited. This is because the second chapter in the Koran "Al-Baqarah" says, 'You must abstain from eating carrion, blood, pork and what was offered to other persons but Allah.' There are some cases in which people have to prove that 'they have never cut pork with their knife' for fear that people suspect that 'they may have cut pork with the knife.' This doesn't mean people absolutely can't eat pork. For example if they didn't know it was pork or if faced with starvation, it is forgivable.

第1節　イスラム教の基礎知識

注：ハラールとハラーム

　ハラールとは食べてよいもので、ハラームは食べてはいけないもののこと。だから食べてもよい肉はハラール肉と呼ばれる。イスラム教徒によって頚動脈を切断された肉がハラール肉なので、この手続きを得ていない肉は、豚肉に限らず、羊や鳥肉も食べてはいけないことになる。

> **TIPS：なぜ豚肉がだめなのか?**
>
> 　コーランに書いてあるとはいえ、なぜ豚肉がだめなのか？　については、はっきりしません。一般には、気温の高い中東では、油の多い豚肉は腐りやすいからであるとか、豚は不潔なエサでも平気で食べるので病気に感染しやすい穢［けが］れた動物からなどの理由があります。次のような珍説まであります。
>
> 　「ムハンマド率いるイスラム軍が、ある村を占領した。そこには豚肉があり、それを食すと、これまで硬い羊やラクダの肉しか知らなかった兵士たちは、そのうまさにたいそう驚いた。新たな進撃命令を下しても、兵士たちはピクリとも動こうとはしない。豚肉を食べたい気持ちが勝ったということだ。そこで、ムハンマドは「豚肉は禁止だ!」という啓示があったとみんなに告げ、ようやく進軍が開始できた」

■ イスラム教徒の婚姻・女性観

　コーラン第4章（女章）に、「4人まで女を娶［めと］れるが、公正にできないなら1人だけにしなさい」とあり、一夫多妻が認められています。一般人はコーランに書かれている通り4人が上限ですが、実際には、ほとんどが一夫一婦の状況です。

　孤児の保護・養育のため、また、戦いが多かった時代には寡婦の救済のため、多妻制が認められたという経緯があります。

　イスラムの女性は、外出の際、チャドルやブルカという黒い衣装で全身をすっぽりと覆います。夫や家族以外に、顔や髪、肌を見せないのが常識になっているからです。

Section 1

Note : "Halal" refers to food that is safe to eat and "haram" is used to describe prohibited foods. Meat that is okay to eat is called halal meat. Meat from the beasts which have their carotid artery cut by Muslims is halal meat. This applies not only to pork but to other meats. If even sheep and chicken are not bled correctly, they are not to be eaten.

TIPS : Why is pork prohibited?

The reason why Muslims are prohibited from eating pork is not clear even though it is written in the Koran. There are some logical reasons though: fatty pork goes bad easily in the Middle East where the temperature is high, and pigs can carry disease as they eat indescriminately. The following novel idea exists ,too:

'Islamic soldiers led by Muhammad occupied a village. There they came across pork. The soldiers who knew nothing but the tough meat of sheep and camels were surprised by how good pork tasted. Even though Muhammad ordered them to attack their next military target, they would not budge. They could not help but to yield to temptation and continue eating pork. Muhammad told them that he had received the revelation, 'You must not eat pork.' Then, they put down the pork and renewed their attack.

■ Muslims' marriage : Their philosophy about women

Chapter 4 (an-Nisa) of the Koran says, 'If you cannot treat them fairly, marry one, though you are allowed to marry 4 women' and so polygamy is admitted. Generally men can marry up to 4 women, but in fact, most of them establish a monogamous relationship.

Polygamy was allowed in order to provide nurture for orphans and give widows shelter in times when there were many wars.

Muslim women cover their entire bodies with chadors and burqas when they go out because they are not supposed to show their faces, hair, or skin to people other than their husbands and family.

第1節　イスラム教の基礎知識

　男性は、同じ啓典の民であるキリスト教徒やユダヤ教徒とは結婚はできますが、女性はイスラム教徒の男性としか結婚ができないとされています。これは「男性は異教徒の女性をイスラム教徒に改宗できる力があるから」という理由です。

注：妻に不都合がある場合、男性は「お前は離婚された」(アンティターリカ)を3度言えば一方的に離婚が成立する。(この制度を悪用して、取っかえ引っかえ妻を娶っては離婚するという男性もいるであろうが、そんな男とはさっさと別れたほうが女性も幸せということになるのでは……?)

■ イスラム教の死生観

　イスラム教では、死後の扱いは、以下の3種類です。
　(1) 非イスラム教徒……墓の中で天使から罰を受け続ける。
　(2) イスラム教徒……天国の記録簿に名前を書いたのち、墓の中で復活を待つ。
　(3) 殉教者……聖戦での死者は、復活の必要なく、天国が約束される。

　イスラム教もキリスト教やユダヤ教と同じで、終末が訪れます。終末は、天使イスラフィールの吹くラッパで突然始まります。天変地異が起き、死者は生前の姿で復活するとされています。そして、神による最後の審判が下されます。但し、殉教者は、すでに天国が約束されているので、最後の審判を受けません。復活した人間はみんな、広場に集められ、生前の信仰や善行・悪行を秤にかけられます。
　不信仰者や罪人は地獄に落とされ、永遠に火で焼かれます。一方、イスラム教徒で善行を行った者は天国に行き、緑豊かな地で幸福に暮らします。

注：コーランによると「蓄財した金銀は焼かれ、それで体に烙印を押される。それを自分の蓄財の罰として味わうがいい」とあり、不当な蓄財に対しては、手厳しい。

Section 1

Men can marry Christians and Jews who are People of the Book, but women can marry only Muslims. This is because 'Men have the power to convert heathen women into Muslims.'

Note: When it becomes impossible to keep a marriage together, a divorce is granted unilaterally after the husband says the words "you are dismissed" anti taliq three times (the triple talaq). (It seems there may be some men who marry women one after the other and divorce them, but I kind of feel women will be happier if they leave such men.)

■ Islam's view of life and death

In Islam, the fate of the dead is described in three ways:
(1) Non-Muslims ...... They are punished eternally in their graves by angels.
(2 Muslims .... They have only to wait for their resurrection after being registered in heaven.
(3) Martyrs .... The dead in the holy war need no resurrection and are promised eternity in heaven (paradise).

In Islam, the end-times will come as in Christianity and Judaism. It suddenly begins with the trumpet of Israfil. It is said that extraordinary natural phenomena will occur and the dead will rise in their original bodies. Then the Last Judgment is passed by God. Martyrs are already promised an eternity in heaven so they are not subject to the Last Judgment. The resurrected will gather around and weigh their faith and good deeds with their bad deeds.

Unbelievers and criminals will descend to hell and burn forever; those who are Muslims and did good deeds will go to the heaven and live in peace in paradise.

Note : The Koran says 'accumulated gold and silver are burnt, and are branded into the bodies of the deceased as a form of punishment for excessive and ummerited wealth.'

第1節　イスラム教の基礎知識

TIPS：モスクの中はどうなっているのか？

　イスラム教の礼拝施設であるモスクの中には、絵も彫刻もそして像もなくガラーンとしているのに驚くでしょう。ただ、絨毯を敷き詰めた広い空間となっているのが、モスクの特徴と言えます。

　礼拝は立つか、ひれ伏す姿勢で行われるので、机や椅子の必要もありません。但し、ミンバルという説教台がつましく置かれている程度です。

　大切なのは、壁にアーチのような飾りがついたくぼみがありますが、これはミフラーブといい、メッカの方向を示す印です。礼拝はメッカに向かって行われるからです。

　モスク内がシンプルなのも、人間的な手を加えること（内部のインテリアや偶像を置くことなど）を排除するイスラム教の特徴と言えるでしょう。

イスラム教の清め（ウドゥー）の方法

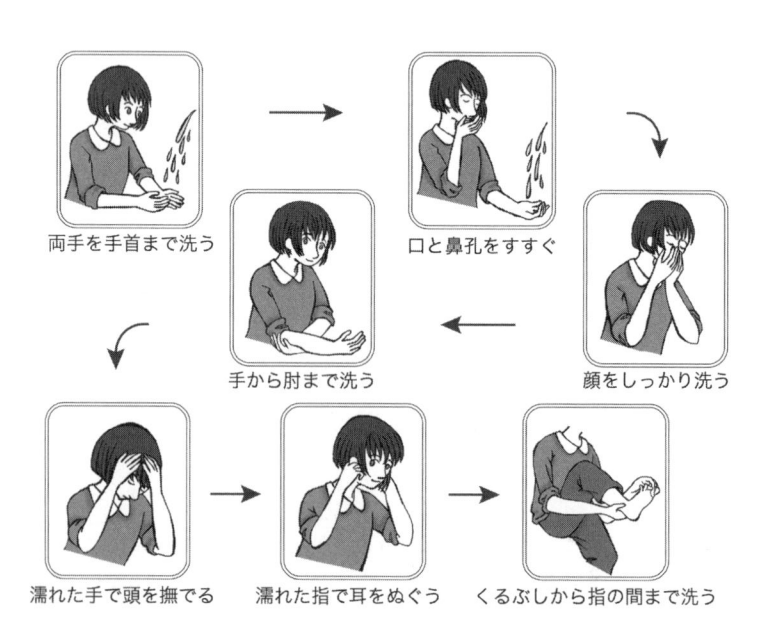

両手を手首まで洗う　→　口と鼻孔をすすぐ　→　顔をしっかり洗う　→　手から肘まで洗う　→　濡れた手で頭を撫でる　→　濡れた指で耳をぬぐう　→　くるぶしから指の間まで洗う

Section 1

> **TIPS：What is the inside of a mosque like?**
>
> Surprisingly, there are no pictures, sculptures, or images inside mosques. Characteristic of all mosques is its wide-open floor plan with carpeting.
>
> When people pray, they stand or go down on their knees, so desks and chairs are unnecessary. A raised preaching lectern called a minbar sits humbly in the main hall.
>
> There is also a decorated arch-shaped niche in the wall, which is called a Mihrab and indicates the direction of Mecca. Prays are made towards Mecca.
>
> The inside of the Mosque shares the same simple characteristics that make up most of the physical parts of Islam without any human influence.

イスラム教における礼拝（サラート）の方法

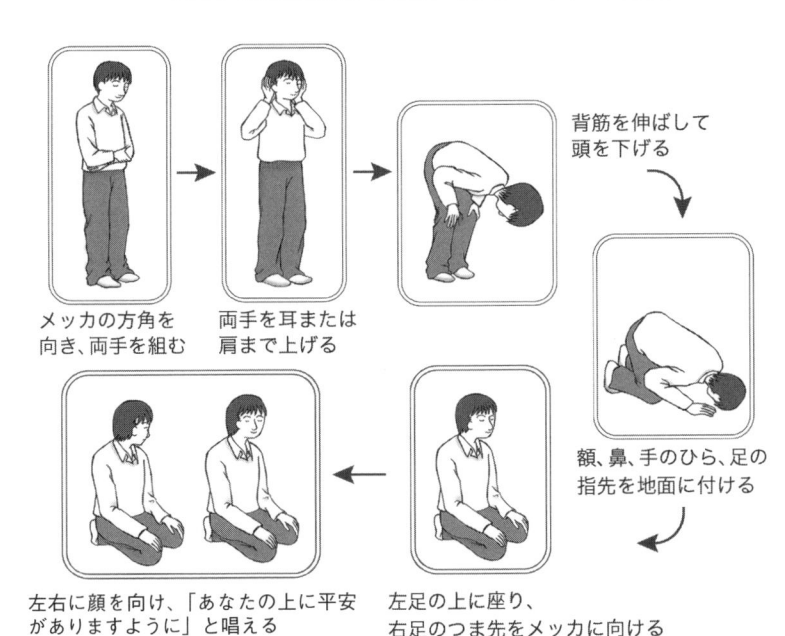

メッカの方角を向き、両手を組む

両手を耳または肩まで上げる

背筋を伸ばして頭を下げる

額、鼻、手のひら、足の指先を地面に付ける

左足の上に座り、右足のつま先をメッカに向ける

左右に顔を向け、「あなたの上に平安がありますように」と唱える

第1節　イスラム教の基礎知識

関連情報　図の簡単解説

　イスラム教では、殉教者は最後の審判を受けず、そのまま天国に入ります。ムスリムや非ムスリムもともに終末を迎え、最後の審判で審理されて、神を信じる者は天国へ、そうでない者は地獄へ振り分けられます。

　イスラム教においては、最後の審判の日には、天変地異を伴い、すべての人々やジン（鬼神）が審判の座の前に召集されることになっています。そして、それぞれの言行が秤［はかり］で量られ、「嘉［よみ］された者」（＝よしとして褒め称えるべき者）には右手に、永劫［えいごう］の罰を受ける者には左手に、それぞれ生前の行為が記された書が手渡されると言います。

　キリスト教では、通例、死後は、天国かよみ（黄泉または陰府）に振り分けられます。「よみ」(Hades［ハーデース］)と呼ばれる死後の世界は「地獄」(Gehenna［ゲヘナ］)とは別のものです。「よみ」に行った人々は、そこで最終的な審判である最後の大審判を待つのです。カトリック教会では煉獄（purgatory）という場所があります。煉獄とは、小罪を犯した死者の魂が、その浄めを受けるために赴く場所です。死後の浄化の信仰は、プラトンやベルギリウスなどにも言及されており、早くから知られていましたが、アウグスティヌス他の教父を通じ、次第に教義として定着し、また、典礼として死者のための祈りやミサなどが行われるようになりました。ダンテの『神曲』はその芸術的描写として有名です。

　ヨハネの黙示録によると、最後の審判の前に、キリストが再臨して地上に王国を打ち立てることになります。この王国は1000年続き、このとき、殉教者や義［ただ］しいキリスト教徒は復活します。これが第一の復活で、1000年間の至福を味わいます。この間悪魔は鎖につながれていますが、王国の終わりにあたりふたたび活動を許されます。激しい闘いののち、最後の審判において悪魔は決定的に敗北します。その後、罪人たちもよみがえります。これを第二の復活といい、彼らは審判を経て、火の池に投げ入れられる可能性があります（第二の死）。一方、義しい人々は天国（神の国）の永遠の至福の中に入り、終末は完成するのです。

　仏教では、死後の魂は、地獄・餓鬼・畜生・修羅・人間・天上の6つの世界のいずれかに生まれます。また、そこで死に、また、この6つの世界のいずれかに生まれます。これを繰り返すのを「六道輪廻」と言って、悟っていない状態です。仏教の目指す、この循環から自らを切り離す（＝解脱［げだつ］する）ことが重要となってきます。そして、菩薩や仏（＝悟った存在）の世界へ向かう（＝すなわち仏陀になる）ことが最終目標です。その仏陀のいる場所が極楽浄土ということになります。仏教は、イスラム教やキリスト教とは全く異なる発想を持ってい

Section 1

ると言えます。イスラム教やキリスト教では、復活は説きますが、魂の輪廻転生は説いていないからです。

関連情報 キリスト教とイスラム教、そして仏教の死生観および天国と地獄の発想

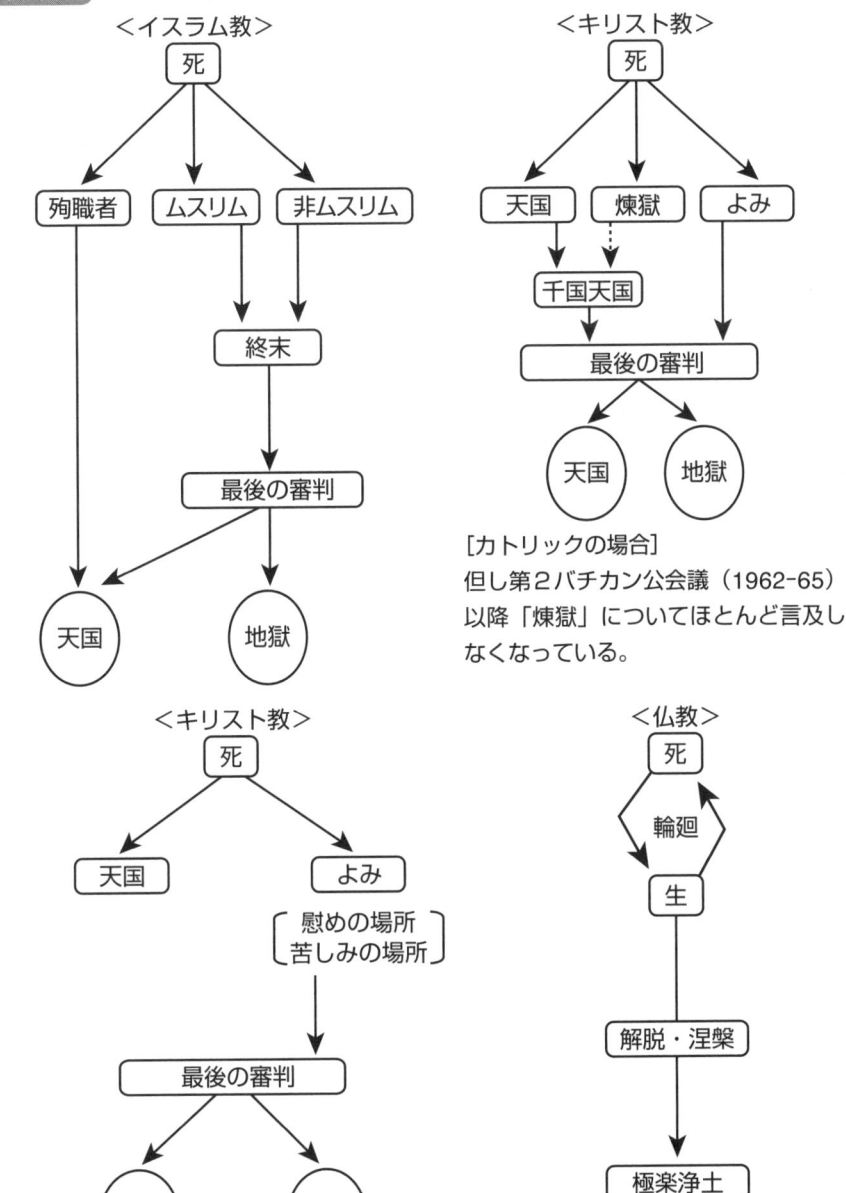

<イスラム教>
死
├→ 殉職者
├→ ムスリム
└→ 非ムスリム
　　ムスリム・非ムスリム → 終末 → 最後の審判
　　最後の審判 → 天国／地獄
　　殉職者 → 天国

<キリスト教>
死
├→ 天国
├→ 煉獄
└→ よみ
天国 → 千国天国
千国天国・よみ → 最後の審判 → 天国／地獄

[カトリックの場合]
但し第2バチカン公会議（1962-65）以降「煉獄」についてほとんど言及しなくなっている。

<キリスト教>
死
├→ 天国
└→ よみ
　　〔慰めの場所／苦しみの場所〕
　　→ 最後の審判 → 天国／地獄

<仏教>
死 ⇄ 輪廻 ⇄ 生
生 → 解脱・涅槃 → 極楽浄土

宗教の基礎知識

キリスト教を知る

聖書を知る

ユダヤ教を知る

イスラム教を知る

267

❻ イスラム教史

■4代正統カリフ時代

　メディナに移住したイスラム教の開祖ムハンマドは、信仰によって結ばれるウンマという共同体を作りました。ウンマは、血縁や民族や国家を超えて存在する共同体です。

　632年6月にムハンマドが亡くなり、指導者を失ったウンマは、メッカ時代からムハンマドを支えたアブー・バクルを後継者に選びました。彼は、預言者の代理としてカリフを名乗るようになりました（「カリフ」とは代理人を意味する言葉が訛ったものとされています）。

　アブー・バクルは在位2年で死亡しましたが、後任（第2代カリフ）は、異教徒から敬虔なイスラム教徒になったウマルでした。彼は軍才に優れ、イスラムの領土を拡大しました。

　第3代カリフは、ウマイヤ家出身のウスマーンで、彼の時代には、コーランがまとめられ、聖典となりました。のちに、不満分子によってウスマーンは暗殺されました。

　第4代カリフは、ムハンマドの娘婿アリーでしたが、661年に暗殺され、正当カリフは4代で終焉を迎えました（「正当カリフ」とは、正しい手続きを経てウンマの承認を得た後継者という意味です）。

注：第4代カリフであるアリーが暗殺されたのち、ウマイヤ家がカリフを独占するようになったが、ムハンマドの血統にこだわる人々はウマイヤ家に強く反発し、アリーの息子を指導者とする党派である「シーア・アリー」（アリーの党）を設立した。これがシーア派の起こりである。それ以外の多数の人々は、スンニ派と呼ばれ、慣行（スンナ）に基づいて共同体を運営した。

Section 1

Islam history

■ Rightly Guided Caliphs

Muhammad, the founder of Islam, who migrated to Medina, made a community called an Ummah, which are united in their faith. An Ummah is a community that transcends blood relationships, people, and nations.

Muhammad died in June, 632. The Ummah, suddenly having become a leaderless community, chose Abu Bakr to take Muhammad's place as their next leader. He had advised Muhammad's since Mecca period and was appointed his successor. He came to call himself Caliph as a representative of a prophet. ('Caliph' is said to have been derived from the corruption of a word meaning representative.)

Abu Bakr died after two years in office, but his successor (the second Caliph) was Umar, who had managed to successfully convert a number of heathens into pious Muslim. He excelled in military matters and expanded Islam territories.

The third Caliph was Uthman from Umayya, and in his days the Koran was organized and became the Muslim Bible. Eventually Uthman was assassinated by discontented rebels.

The fourth Caliph was Muhammad's adopted son-in-law, Ali, but he was assassinated in 661 and the Rightly Guided Caliphs came to an end after four generations. ('Rightly Guided Caliphs' mean successors approved by Ummah through proper procedures.)

Note : After the fourth Caliph, Ali was assassinated, the Umayya clan came to monopolize the office of Caliphate but those who are particular about Muhammad's blood objected to the Umayya strongly and established a party, the 'Shih-Ali' (Ali's party) with Ali's son as its leader. This was the beginning of Shia Islam. The people who wouldn't affiliate with the Shih-Ali are called the Sunni and they ran the community based on traditional practices (Sunnah).

第1節　イスラム教の基礎知識

■ ウマイヤ朝カリフ時代とアッバース朝カリフ時代

　ウマイヤ家がカリフを独占する時代が、正当カリフ時代ののちに起こってきます。ウマイヤ朝は、ダマスカスを首都とし、イスラム史上最大の地域を領有する一代帝国を築き上げました。

　ムハンマドの叔父の子孫に当たるアッバース家は、ウマイヤ家に反発するシーア派の支持を受け、750年にウマイヤ朝を倒し、政権を樹立しました。アッバース朝は、バグダードに首都を建設し、「平安の都」と名づけました。9世紀から10世紀の最盛期には、人口は150万人にも達しました。

■ スルタン制度の成立

　1055年には、中央アジアから南下しながら勢力を増していたトルコ人セルジュークのセルジューク朝が侵攻しました。スンニ派を保護し、同時に形骸化しつつあったシーア派の政権であるアッバース朝の承認を得て、スルタン制が始まりました。セルジュークの孫のトゥグリル・ベグが初代スルタンを名乗りました。

　セルジューク朝は、さらに遠征し、イラン・イラク・シリア・サウジアラビアなど西アジアを統一しました。この時点から、イスラムの中心はアラブ人に代わって非アラブ人が担っていくことになりました。

■ イスラム教の戦い

（1）十字軍との戦い

　　エルサレムをも占領したセルジューク朝に戦いを挑んできたのが、キリスト教の十字軍です。1095年に、セルジューク朝がエルサレムを破壊しているとローマに報じられ、ローマ法王ウルバヌス2世はエルサレム奪還を呼びかけ、十字軍が結成されました。その翌年1096年から、約200年にわたり、キリスト教による聖戦を掲げた遠征は続きました。

　　この遠征は、仕組まれた政治的・経済的な戦いで、そもそも発端からして、イスラム教徒はキリスト教徒を迫害していなかったのです。キリスト教に対抗するイスラムのジハードをようやく旗揚げしたのは、1127年のザンギー朝からでした。

Section 1

■ Umayya Caliphate and Abbasid Caliphate

The Umayya monopolized the Caliphate after the Rightly Guided Caliphs. They created a huge Empire, the largest in Islam's history, the capital of which was Damascus. The Abbasid clan, the descendent of Muhammad's uncle, defeated the Umayya clan in 750 with the support of Shias who had acted against Umayya control and established their own government. The Abbasid dynasty built a capital in Baghdad and named it 'peaceful city.' At its peak from the years 900 through 1000, the population reached as many as 1,500,000.

■ The establishment of the Sultanate

In 1055, Seljuk of Turkey had gained strength and started to invade countries in Central Asia. It supported Sunnas and thus began the sultanate with the approval of the Abbasid Empire which was then collapsing under the administration of the Shias. Seljuk's grandson, Tughril Beg, named himself the first sultan.

The Seljuq Empire kept gaining ground and unified areas of western Asia including modern day Iran, Iraq, Syria, and Saudi Arabia. From then on, non-Arabs played a central role in Islam.

■ Islamic war

(1) Fights against the Crusades

The Crusades threw down the gauntlet against the Seljuq Empire, which had occupied the holy city Jerusalem. In 1095, it was reported to Rome that the Seljuq Empire was destroying Jerusalem. The Pope, Urbanus II, urged the people to recapture Jerusalem and so the Christian Crusade to take back the Holy Land was formed. These series of campaigns against Islam continued for about 200 years.

This expedition was a premeditated political and economic war against Muslims who had in large not persecuted Christians until this point. It was not until the Zangid (Zengid) dynasty in 1127 that Islam declared jihad against Christianity.

第1節　イスラム教の基礎知識

(2) モンゴル帝国の侵攻

　　十字軍との戦いや内部分裂などで政情が不安定になっていたイスラム世界は、モンゴル帝国の侵攻により、セルジューク朝から独立したホラズム・シャー朝が1231年に、アッバース朝が1258年に滅ぼされました。

　　占領地域には、モンゴル帝国の傘下に、チャガタイ＝ハン国（中央アジア）、オゴタイ（オコディ）＝ハン国（現在の中国ウイグル自治区北西部）、イル＝ハン国（現在のイランの地）が建設されました。イル＝ハン国は国ごとイスラム教に改宗しました。

....

注１：モンゴル帝国傘下にもう１つ、キプチャク＝ハン国という国があるが、中央アジア以西のロシアの地に建国され、イスラム世界を占領したわけではない。中国にある元朝と、チャガタイ、オゴタイ、イル、キプチャクの４ハン国を合わせると、モンゴル帝国は、当時の世界人口のおよそ半分近くを支配したことになると言われる。

注２：モンゴル帝国の侵略を退けた国
　マムルーク朝（現在のシリア・エジプト一帯）
　陳朝（現在のベトナム）
　鎌倉幕府（日本）
　マジャパヒト王国（現在のインドネシア）
　神聖ローマ帝国（現在のドイツ）

注３：世界の人口（西暦何年に何人を超えたか?)
　1802年・・・・・・・・10億人
　1927年・・・・・・・・20億人
　1961年・・・・・・・・30億人
　1971年・・・・・・・・40億人
　1987年7月11日・・・・50億人
　1999年10月12日・・・60億人
　2010年・・・・・・・・約69億人
　＊過去6000年間に存在したすべての人口の約5分の1が現在の人口であると言われる。

Section 1

> ●Useful Usage● **DECLARE**
> 1. I hereby declare the opening of the Olympic Games.
>   (ここにオリンピックの開会を宣言いたします)
> 2. I declare myself against the project.
>   (私はその計画に反対であることを表明します)

(2) Invasion of Mongol Empire

As the Islamic world became politically unstable, the Khwarezmian dynasty became independent from the Seljuq, but was destroyed in 1231 by the Mongol Empire. Following that, the Abbasid Caliphate was obliterated in 1258 by the invasion of the same Empire.

In the occupied territories, Chagatai Khanate (Central Asia), Ogedei Khanate (the northwest of the Uigur Autonomous Region of current China), and Il Khanate (now Iran) were incorporated into the Mongol Empire. In Il khanate, the whole nation converted to Islam.

Note 1: The Mongol Empire founded a country called Kipchak Khanate, which stretched throughout a large part of western Russia. This territory was not under the influence of the Islamic world. It is said that the Mongol Empire ruled nearly half of the world of those days if the four Khanates, the Yuan Dynasty in China, Chagatai Khanate, Ogedei Khanate, Il Khanate and Kipchak Khanate are put together.

Note 2: Countries that resisted the invasion of the Mongol Empire
Mamluk Sultanate (the whole areas of current Syria and Egypt)
Tran dynasty (current Vietnam)
Kamakura Shogunate (Japan)
Majapahit Empire (current Indonesia)
The Holy Roman Empire (currently Germany)

第1節　イスラム教の基礎知識

■ イスラム3帝国が西南アジアを支配

　1299年にオスマン1世が建国したオスマン帝国は、スルタン（君主）による専制国家を築き上げ、1453年には東ローマ帝国（ビザンツ帝国）を滅ぼすなどして、勢力を拡大していきました。オスマン帝国は、その辺境地域（バルカン半島など）において、ユダヤ教徒・ギリシャ正教徒・アルメニア教徒などの異教徒に対し、人頭税を払うことで自治を認めるなど寛大な政策を採りました。

　一方、1501年、現在のイランの地に、トルコ系シーア派スーフィー（イスラム神秘主義者）教団を率いたイスマイル（イスマーイール）1世が、サファヴィー朝を建設しました。この王朝は、シーア派を国教としましたが、このことが、イランのシーア派化を促進することにつながりました。

　さらに、現在のインドの地では、1526年に、テュルク・モンゴル系の遊牧貴族バーブルを始祖とし、彼が現在のアフガニスタンからインドに移ってムガル帝国を建国しました。寛大な宗教政策により、イスラム教とヒンドゥー教を融合させたシク教なども生まれました。

　以上のように、16〜17世紀ごろの西南アジアでは、3つのイスラム帝国……西から順にオスマン帝国、サファヴィー朝、ムガル帝国がイスラム世界を代表しており、今日につながるイスラム世界が形成されていきます。

Section 1

Note 3 : The population of the world (the year and the number)
1802 ....10 billion
1927 .... 20 billion
1961 .... 30 billion
1971 .... 40 billion
1987, July 11th .... 50 billion
1999, October 12th .... 60 billion
2010 .... about 69 billion
  ＊about one-fifth of the whole population which existed for the past 6000 years is said to be the current population

■ Islam's three empires rule southwest Asia

In 1299, the Ottoman Empire founded by Osman I established a dictatorship ruled by a Sultan (ruler) and extended his influence by destroying the Eastern Roman Empire (Byzantine Empire) in 1453. The Ottoman Empire adopted generous policies like granting political autonomy to the tax-paying heathen like Jews, members of the Orthodox Church, and Armenians who lived in the empire's lands such as the Balkans.

On the other hand, in 1501 Ismail I, who led the Turkish Shia and Sufi (Islamic mystics), founded the Safavid dynasty in modern day Iran. This dynasty made Shia the state religion, leading to the complete conversion to Shia in Iran.

What is more, a nomadic aristocrat of Turk-Mongolian (Chaghatay-Turkic) peoples, Babur moved to India from what is now Afghanistan and established the Mughal Empire in 1526. By his generous policy, Sikhism was born combining Islam and Hinduism.

As stated above, in Southwest Asia from the 16th to the 17th century, three Islamic Empires in the order from the west, the Ottoman Empire, the Safavid dynasty, and the Mughal Empire, represented the Islamic world and played a big part in what became today's Islamic world.

第1節　イスラム教の基礎知識

■ イスラムの近現代

　18世紀になって、オスマン帝国はヨーロッパ文化を取り入れる欧化政策を打ち出しますが、これに対し、「ムハンマドの時代のウンマに戻れ」をモットーに、アラビア半島内陸部を拠点とするワッハーブ派が起こりました。1932年には、イスラム教ワッハーブ派を国教とするサウジアラビアが建国されました。

　近代から現代にかけてのイスラム世界は、いち早く近代化に成功したヨーロッパ諸国の帝国主義政策や、2度の世界大戦、東西の冷戦などといった世界情勢に翻弄されてきましたが、現在のイスラム世界は、世界の政治・経済・社会で大きな存在感を示しています。21世紀に入って、イスラム教は影響力を拡大しており、やがて世界最大の宗教になる可能性があると予測されています。

Section 1

■ Modernization of Islam

In the 18th century, the Ottoman Empire adopted measures to modernize by embracing European culture, while Wahhabism based in the inland areas of the Arabian Peninsula arose with the motto 'Return to Ummah, the times of Muhammad.' In 1932, Saudi Arabia whose state religion is Wahhabi, was founded.

From the early-modern age through the modern age, the Islamic world was bombarded by the imperialistic policies of European and other foreign countries which were rapidly becoming modernized, as well as two world wars and the Cold War between the East and West. However, Islam stood strong and persevered and now has a great presence in the world's politics, economy, and society. In the 21st century, Islam extended its influence and is predicted to possibly become the largest religion in the world.

第1節　イスラム教の基礎知識

TIPS：イスラムの近現代の諸問題

年代	事象	一言説明
1947年	インド・パキスタン分離	イスラム教徒が多数を占めるインド東部（現バングラデシュ）と北西部がパキスタンとして独立した。
1948年〜	パレスチナ戦争	ユダヤ人のイスラエル建国をきっかけに4度の中東戦争が勃発した。
1979年	イラン革命	シーア派法学者ホメイニ（ホメイニー）師による王政打倒とイスラム主義革命。イランは欧米のみならず周辺のイスラム国とも距離を置くことになった。
1991年	湾岸戦争	1990年8月2日にイラクがクウェートに侵攻したのを機に、1991年1月17日にイラクを空爆したことに始まる。
1992〜95年	ボスニア紛争	ユーゴスラビアからの独立を目指すイスラム教徒とそれに反対するセルビア人との対立が紛争に発展した。
1994年〜	チェチェン紛争	スンナ（スンニ）派が大半を占めるチェチェン共和国がロシアからの独立を目指したが、石油パイプラインが通る重要な地域なので、ロシアが独立を認めず、紛争に発展した。
1996〜2001年	タリバン（ターリバーン）政権	アフガニスタンで台頭したイスラム主義組織で、2001年米軍の攻撃により政権が倒れたが、近年また影響力を持ち始めている。
2003年	イラク戦争	アメリカが大量破壊兵器保持疑惑を理由に、フセイン率いるバース党政権を打倒した。イラク国内の治安の悪化が問題となっていたが、2010年8月31日に、オバマ大統領は正式にイラク戦争の終結を宣言した。

Section 1

TIPS：Various problems of the modern and present-day Islam

What happened when?	Brief explanation
Indo-Pakistan war in 1947	The east（currently Bangladesh）and the northwest of India where a majority of people were Muslims became independent as Pakistan.
Israeli-Palestinian conflicts since 1948	War in the Middle East broke out four times after the creation of Israel.
Iranian revolution in 1979	This was the ousting of the monarchy under the name of pan-Islamic revolution by the religious leader and politician of the Shi'ites, Ruhollah Khomeini. Iran came to have an arm's length relationship with its peripheral Islam countries as well as Europe and the United States.
Gulf war in 1991	As a result of the Iraqi invasion of Kuwait on Aug. 2, 1990, air strikes were initiated against Iraq on Jan. 17, 1991.
Bosnian conflicts from 1992 to 1995	Opposition between Muslims who aimed at becoming independent from Yugoslavia and the Serbians who opposed them developed into a war.
Chechen war since 1994	The Chechen Republic（informally, Chechnya）, where the Sunnites hold a majority, tried for independence from Russia, but Russia refused due to the fact that important oil pipelines run through Chechnya. Conflict ensued.
Taliban regime from 1996 to 2001	It is a pan-Islamic group that came to the fore in Afghanistan. Its administration was overthrown by the attacks of American forces in 2001, but it has become influential in recent years.
Iraq war in 2003	The United States defeated the Baathist regime led by Saddam Hussein under the suspicion that Iraq had weapons of mass destruction. Security deterioration in Iraq became a problem, but President Obama announced officially that the Iraq war was over on Aug. 31, 2010.

注目：independent ofとindependent fromの違い

　この違いに関する見方に次の説がある。A is independent of Bは、Aについての話題で、Bとは関係がないことを強調するのに対し、A is independent from Bは、AとBの関係を話題にし、お互いに独立していることを暗示する。だからA is independent from BはA and B are independentと置き換えられる。さらに、fromはbecomeと結びつくと、独立への動きを暗示する。→A becomes independent from B（AはBから独立する）

❼ 現在のイスラム教

■ 在家の宗教であるイスラム教
　イスラム教は日常の仕事を持ちながら信仰を実践する「在家の宗教」として発展しました。これは普通の人間として人生を全うしたムハンマドを模範としたためとされています。

■ 利子を禁止するイスラム金融
　イスラム社会では、金銭の貸借に利子は存在しません。それはコーランに利子の禁止がうたわれているからです。実際には、利子は禁止であるが、利潤は認めています。イスラムの金融機関では、貸し付けるのに金額・期間・定率などを定める利子の支払いは必要ありませんが、手数料が要求される可能性があります。手数料は利潤とみなされているわけです。

■ イスラム教の刑罰
　イスラム教では、刑罰が厳しいと批判されている面があります。ハッド刑と言ってコーランに内容が明記されている刑罰があります。例えば、コーランの第5章38節を根拠に「窃盗を行った者は指または腕を切断する」罰が存在します。

Section 1

Current Islam

■ Islam as a lay religion

Islam has developed as a 'lay religion,' which means people put their faith in practice performing daily tasks. Muhammad is said to have been a role model, who lived out his life as a normal person.

■ Islam finance prohibits interest

There is no interest in borrowing and lending of money. The prohibition of interest is outlined in the Koran. In fact, interest is prohibited but profit is accepted. In Islamic financial institutions, interest payments establishing the amount of money, period of payment, and fixed rate are unnecessary in loan procedures, but charges may be requested, since charges are recognized as profit.

■ Islamic punishment

Islamic punishment is criticized for its severity. The Hudud defines the methods of punishment in the Koran. For example, the punishment 'cutting off fingers or hands for those who committed a theft' exists in the 5th chapter, verse 38 in the Koran.

注目：聖書などの「節」はverseという単語を用いる。

第1節　イスラム教の基礎知識

　イランでは、初犯で指4本の切断、2回目で左足の指の切断、3回目で終身刑、4回目で死刑になると定められています。しかし、実際にはタージール刑（ハッド刑が適用されない場合の刑罰、裁判官の裁量を重視）として5年以下の懲役刑が科されています。現在では、ハッド刑の縮小廃止に伴い、タージール刑が実質上の刑事罰になっているイスラム国がほとんどです。これは、原理主義の傾向が強いサウジアラビアにおいても言えます。

■ イスラム教の2大宗派

　イスラム教は、スンナ（スンニ）派とシーア派に大別できます。表にして比べてみましょう。

	スンナ派（スンニ派）	シーア派
信者数	約90%	約10%
聖典 イスラム法の法源	コーラン ムハンマドの言行 法学者の見解	
	共同体の合意	歴代イマームの言行
聖地	メッカ、メディナ、エルサレム	
		カルバラー、歴代イマームの廟

注：シーア派は「タキーヤ（信仰隠し）」と言って、シーア派であることがわかると身に危険が及ぶような場合、スンナ派を装ってもよいとされるなど、教義にいろいろ違いがあるが、互いに異端とはしていない。

Section 1

Removing 4 fingers for first offenders, cutting off toes of the left foot for the second, life imprisonment for the third, and the death penalty for the fourth offense are the norm in Iran. However, less than five years, imprisonment is given under the Tazir (in cases of punishments where Hudud can't apply, in which the discretion of judges is taken into account). Tazir is the more practical system of punishment that abolishes the practices of the Hudud and is followed in most Islam countries. This applies even to Saudi Arabia, where the tendency of fundamentalism is strong.

> ●Useful Usage● APPLY
> 1. He applied his savings to the purchase of a convertible.
>   (彼は貯金をオープンカーの購入に充てた)
> 2. She applied her mind to learning Spanish.
>   (彼女はスペイン語の勉強に専念した)

■ The two large sects

Islam can be broadly divided into Sunna and Shia. Let's compare them in tabular form.

	Sunni	Shia
Followers	About 90%	About 10%
Holy book Source of Islamic law	Koran Muhammad's words and deeds Views of jurists	
	Agreement within the community	Words and deeds of imams throughout history
Holy places	Mecca, Medina, and Jerusalem	
		Karbala, mausoleums of the past imams

Note: There are various differences in creed. For example, Shias are allowed to pretend to be Sunnites in cases where their identity as a Shia may endanger their lives. However, both branches don't regard each other as heretical.

第1節　イスラム教の基礎知識

TIPS：イスラムの宗派一覧

宗派	分派と特徴			代表的な国
スンナ派	イスラムの多数派			東南アジア、アラブ諸国
	ワッハーブ派（18世紀のイスラム改革運動から）			サウジアラビア
シーア派	12イマーム派：シーア派の多数派			イラン イラクとレバノンの一部
	イスマーイール派： シーア派の第2勢力	7イマーム派 （7人目のイマームから分岐）		インド、パキスタン
		[分派]ドルーズ（ドゥルーズ）派 （カリフのハーキムの神格化）		レバノンを中心に シリア・ヨルダンなど
		[影響]アラウィー派 （シリアの土着宗教と融合）		シリアの山岳地帯
	ザイド派（5人目のイマームから分岐）			イエメン
ハワーリジュ派	イバード派（ハワーリジュ派の穏健な一派）			オマーン

注：イマームとは、アラビア語で「指導者」の意味で、文字通り「指導者」を意味する。
スンナ派では宗教共同体の統率者を、シーア派では宗教共同体の最高指導者を指す。

■ イスラム原理主義

　現代のイスラム世界はコーランの教えに従うイスラム共同体（ウンマ）の本来あるべき姿ではないと考えて、イスラムの原点に回帰しようとする運動をイスラム原理主義と言います。

Section 1

TIPS : Table of Islamic Sects

Sect	Sub-sect and its characteristics		Typical countries
Sunni Islam	Islam majority		Southeast Asia and Arab countries
	Wahhab (arose from the Islam reform movement in the 1700s)		Saudi Arabia
Shia Islam	Twelver (Imami Shia Islam) : Shia majority		Iran and parts of Iraq and Lebanon
	Ismailism : the 2nd most powerful Shia group	7-imam sub-sect (divergence from the 7th imam)	India and Pakistan
		[derived from Ismailism] the Druze (deification of the caliph, Al-Hakim)	Mainly in Lebanon and parts of Syria and Jordan
		[influenced by Ismailism] the Alawis (fused with Syrian native religion)	Mountainous regions of Syria
	Zaidiyya (Zaydism) (divergence from the 5th Imam)		Yemen
Khawarij (Kharijites)	Ibadi (Ibadism) (a moderate group of Khawarij)		Oman

Notes : "Imam" means 'leader' in Arabic' and is applied literally to a leader. An Imam indicates the ruler of the religious community in Sunna and indicates the supreme religious leader in Shia.

■ Islamic fundamentalism

It is said that the struggle to bring Islam back to its roots is the driving force behind Islamic fundamentalism. As fundamentalists see it, the Islam of present day is not true to its original teachings.

第1節　イスラム教の基礎知識

　イスラム原理主義は、過激派やテロリストであるというイメージがありますが、この運動全体が必ずしも戦闘的であるわけではありません。イスラム原理主義が戦闘的であるという発想は、欧米ジャーナリズムによるレッテルと言えます。このようなイメージを避けて、イスラム研究者の中には、原理主義という言葉を使わず、イスラム復興主義やイスラム主義という言葉を使う人もいるほどです。

　また、イスラム原理主義の戦闘的な性格を表現する際に、ジハード（聖戦）という言葉がよく使われますが、もともとこの言葉は神のために努力することを意味します。

　イスラム原理主義は、18世紀にアラビア半島で起こったワッハーブ運動を始めとする復興運動の流れとして理解することができます。19世紀以降は、ヨーロッパの植民地支配に対抗する反植民地主義・反帝国主義を掲げるイスラム原理主義が急速に展開することになります。イラン革命などを通じて、イスラム原理主義が世界的な注目を浴びました。

関連情報　イスラム教徒は穏やか

　原理主義者やテロリストなどの存在があったり、中東でよく戦争が起こったりするので、イスラムは怖いというイメージがありますが、実は全然そんなことはありません。イスラムから戦争を仕掛けるということはあまりなく、むしろ、攻められた場合に応戦する、命が危ない状況には対応するということで、その意味ではジハード（聖戦）も緊急避難的な側面があります。つまり正当防衛ということです。

　かつて、私の知人のイスラム教徒が、国有テレビで映画を見ていたとき、お祈りの時間に切り替わり、テレビが元に戻ったとき、映画のクライマックスが終わっていたことがあるという話を、私にしてくれました。「ショックじゃないの？」と聞いたら「いいえ、さっさと諦めるよ」と穏やかに言っていたのが印象的でした。もし映画をお祈りの最中に止めていたら、神よりも人工の映画を重視することになるからということのようですが、「あまり納得いかないかも」と言ってみたら、「あなたの国（＝日本）では太陽を拝むでしょ。日曜日にピクニックに行く計画を立てても、雨が降ったら諦めるでしょ。それと同じことだと思う」と切り返されたのには驚きました。日本は、「アマテラス」の信仰があるから、太陽崇拝と言えば太陽崇拝ですが、雨が降ってピクニックを諦める、悪天候なら仕方ないと諦めるのと、イスラムの積極的な諦めとは、質的に違うような気がしますが、当たっているような気もします。

Section 1

We tend to think that Islamic fundamentalism is represented by fringe groups or terrorists. However, most efforts to return to the original Islam are peaceful in nature. It can be said that labeling Islamic fundamentalism as a thing of violence is a product of western journalism. Some of the researchers of Islam use the words such as Islamic Principle of Reconstruction or Islamism to avoid such negative imagery.

In order to express the warlike property of Islamic fundamentalism the word "jihad" (a sacred war) is often used. But intrinsically this word means to struggle for the good of the Creator.

All this said, Islamic fundamentalism is actually a step in the evolution of Islam under the framework of its reconstruction movement centering on Wahhabi, which sprouted in the Arabian Peninsula in the 18th century. Since the 19th century, Islamic fundamentalism, with its tenets of anti-colonialism and anti-imperialism against European encroachers, has developed and spread rapidly. Through the Iranian Revolution and other high profile events, Islamic fundamentalism became noticable on a global mass scale.

注目：fringeに「過激派」の意味がある。

●Useful Usage● SPREAD

1. She spread a piece of toast with butter. [=... spread butter on a piece of toast.]
   （彼女はトースト1切れにバターを塗った）
2. The economic crisis spread over the better part of a decade.
   （経済危機がほぼ10年は続いた）
   ＊He spends the better part of his earnings on drink.
   （彼は収入の大部分を酒に費やす）

第2節　イスラム教の影響

建築・美術分野：イスラム建築と三大聖地

■ イスラム建築の起こり

　代表的なイスラム建築は、礼拝の場であるモスクです。モスクは地域ごとに若干異なる特徴が見られますが、基本的な構造は、イスラム教の開祖である預言者ムハンマドがメディナ移住後に暮らした住居（礼拝堂と中庭からなる）に由来すると言われています。

■ イスラム建築の特徴　その1　ミフラーブ

　礼拝堂には「ミフラーブ」と呼ばれる窪みがあり、それが礼拝の方角であるメッカの方向（キブラ）を示しています。ミフラーブがモスクの中で最も装飾される場所です。

参考：「宇宙空間でのギブラは宇宙飛行士に任せる」というガイドラインがある。

■ イスラム建築の特徴　その2　アラベスク

　モスクの内装にアラベスクと呼ばれる曲線模様や連続した幾何学模様による装飾が見られますが、これは偶像崇拝を拒否したイスラム教ならではの装飾です。つまり、人格のある像を想像させない模様が強調されているのです。

■ イスラム建築の特徴　その3　ミナレット

　モスクに付設されるバルコニーのある高い塔をミナレットと呼びます。1日5回の礼拝を呼びかけるために用いられます。モスクの格によって数が異なり、最大6基まで建てられます。古くは単純な円塔または角塔でしたが、時代が下るにつれ、円塔と角塔を繰り返すパターン、つまり土筆状の構造となりました。

Section 2

The field of architecture and art: Islamic architecture and the three major holy sites

■ The origin of Islamic architecture

The building most typical of Islamic architecture is the mosque, a place of worship. The mosque has slightly different characteristics from region to region. However, it is said that the basic structure originated in the house (consisting of a chapel and a courtyard) where the founder of Islam, the prophet Muhammad, lived after his migration to Medina.

■ The first characteristic of Islamic architecture: Mihrab

There is a hollow called a "Mihrab" in a chapel which shows the direction of worship or the direction of Mecca (Qibla). The Mihrab is the most decorated place in the mosque.

■ The second characteristic of Islamic architecture: Arabesque

Decoration with a pattern of curved lines or a consecutive geometric pattern called Arabesque can be seen in the interior of the mosque. Since Islam prohibits idol worship, this complex design is necessary, as it shows no images suggestive of human characteristics.

■ The third characteristic of Islamic architecture: Minaret

A tall tower with balconies that is attached to a mosque is called a minaret. It is used for the call to prayer five times a day. The number of minarets a mosque has differs depending on the rank of the mosque though it's possible to have up to six. It was a simple round or square tower in ancient times. However, as time went by, it came to take the form of alternating round and square towers, or a horsetail-like form.

第2節　イスラム教の影響

参考：イスラム建築のその他の特徴
(a) ミフラーブの隣あたりにミンバル（Minbar）という説教台がある。
(b) 中庭には祈りの前に身を清めるためのミーダーアという泉亭や水槽がある。

■ 有名なイスラム寺院

主なイスラム寺院について、表にしてまとめます。

	イスラム寺院の名称	所在地	一言説明
1	タージ・マハル*	インド北部　アーグラ	ムガル皇帝シャー・ジャハーンが愛妻の第3夫人ムムターズ・マハルのために建設した総大理石造りの墓廟。
2	聖なるモスク	サウジアラビア　メッカ（マッカ）	中心にカアバ神殿があり、巡礼時には200万人以上の信者が集う。このモスクでの礼拝の方向はカアバ神殿自体になる。
3	預言者のモスク	サウジアラビア　メディナ	生前のムハンマドの住居のあった場所。中央にムハンマドの墓廟がある。
4	岩のドーム*	イスラエル　エルサレム	ムハンマドが昇天の奇跡体験をした場所に建てられた記念碑的な建物。イスラムのドーム建築の原点。
5	イマーム・モスク*	イラン　イスファハーン（エスファハーン）	サファヴィー朝の最盛期、アッバース1世により建てられた。イランにおけるイスラム建築の最高峰。
6	ウマイヤ・モスク*（ウマイヤド・モスク）	シリア　ダマスカス	ウマイヤ朝第6代カリフ、ワリードがキリスト教の聖堂をモスクに改装。カアバ、預言者のモスク、岩のドームに次ぐ第4の聖地とされる。
7	アルハンブラ宮殿*	スペイン　グラナダ	スペイン最後のイスラム王朝であるナスル朝時代に建造。スペインのイスラム文化を代表する。
8	トプカプ宮殿*	トルコ　イスタンブール	東ローマ（ビザンツ）帝国のビザンツ様式を継承したイスラム建築。オスマントルコの君主が居住した宮殿。
9	西安大清真寺（せいあんだいせいしんじ）	中国　西安	742年、玄宗皇帝時代の唐の長安に建てられた。ミフラーブやミナレットはあるが、木造瓦葺の中国風建築。

*印=世界遺産に登録されている建物
参考：イスラム建築で、あと1つ世界遺産に登録されているものがあるが、それは「サーマッラーのミナレット」という独特のらせん状のミナレットである。

Section 2

■ Famous Islamic temples and palaces

The main Islamic temples and palaces are arranged in a table below:

The name of the Islamic temple/palace with its location and brief explanation
1 Taj Mahal*, which is located in Agra, India, is a marble mausoleum built by Mughal emperor Shah Jahan in memory of his beloved third wife Mumtaz Mahal.
2 Sacred Mosque, which is located in Mecca (Makkah), Saudi Arabia, has the Kaaba (the Cube) in its center where over 2 million believers gather while on pilgrimage. The direction of worship in this mosque is the Kaaba itself.
3 Prophet's Mosque, which is situated in Medina, Saudi Arabia, is the site where Muhammad lived during his lifetime. The mausoleum of Muhammad is located in the center of the mosque.
4 Dome of the Rock*, which is situated in Jerusalem, Israel, is a monumental building built in the place where Muhammad experienced the miracle of ascension. It is regarded as the origin of Islamic dome architecture.
5 Imam Mosque*, which is located in Isfahan, Iran, was built by Abbas I at the peak of the Safavid dynasty. It is considered to be the greatest of all Islamic architecture in Iran.
6 Umayya Mosque (Omayad Mosque)*, which is situated in Damascus, Syria, is the mosque remodeled from a Christian church by the 6th Umayyad caliph, Al-Walid. It is regarded as the 4th holiest place after the Kaaba, the Prophet's Mosque, and the Dome of the Rock.
7 Alhambra Palace*, which is located in Granada, Spain, was constructed during the Nasrid Dynasty, the last Muslim dynasty of Spain. It represents Islamic culture in Spain.
8 Topkapi Palace*, which is situated in Istanbul, Turkey, is an example of Islamic architecture which succeeded the Byzantine style of the Eastern Roman Empire, or the Byzantine Empire. It is a palace where the monarch of the Ottoman Turks resided.
9 Qingzhens, which is located in Xian, China, was built in 742 in Changan of the Tang dynasty during the time of Emperor Xuanzong. It has a mihrab and minarets but is Chinese style architecture with wooden tile-roofing.

*The buildings which are designated as World Heritage sites.

●●●図書紹介●●●

◎監修者お勧めの本
★世界の宗教全般の本
図解 世界の宗教〔渡辺和子著〕(西東社)
世界の三大宗教がわかる本〔一校舎社会研究会編〕(永岡書店)
世界の宗教が面白いほどわかる本〔加藤智見著〕(中経出版)
★キリスト教関連の本
図解 いま聖書を学ぶ〔曽野綾子著〕(ワック)
旧約聖書の智慧〔ピーター・ミルワード著〕(講談社現代新書)
「聖書」名表現の常識〔石黒マリーローズ著〕(講談社現代新書)
イラスト早わかり聖書ガイドブック〔ブランケンベイカー他著〕(CS成長センター)
聖書の旅〔山本七平著〕(文春文庫)
(入門)わかるキリスト教〔久保有政著〕(レムナント出版)
聖書の思想〔秋田稔著〕(塙新書)
キリスト教思想史入門〔金子晴勇著〕(日本基督教団出版局)
聖書の概説〔尾山令仁著〕(羊群社)
キリスト教の人生論〔桑田秀延著〕(講談社現代新書)
旧約聖書物語〔犬養道子著〕(新潮社)
新約聖書物語〔犬養道子著〕(新潮社)
聖書をどう読むか〔佐古純一郎著〕(大和書房)
ヨハネの黙示録がわかりますか〔小石豊著〕(いのちのことば社)
歴史と終末〔久保有政著〕(レムナント出版)
聖書ハンドブック〔ヘンリー・ハーレイ著〕(聖書図書刊行会)
★辞典類
宗教学辞典〔堀一郎他監修〕(東京大学出版会)
聖書辞典〔浅見定雄他著〕(新教出版社)
キリスト教大事典〔石原謙他編著〕(教文館)
聖書大事典〔荒井献他編〕(教文館)
新キリスト教辞典〔宇田進他編〕(いのちのことば社)
★文学・思想関連の本
キリスト教文学事典〔佐藤泰正他編〕(教文館)
知と信の構造:科学と宗教のコスモロジー〔稲垣久和著〕(ヨルダン社)
文学における神探究〔高木幹太著〕(日本之薔薇出版社)
近代日本の文学と宗教〔久山康〕(国際日本研究所)
ドストエフスキーと現代〔滝沢克己著〕(三一書房)

死と愛の季節:現代日本文芸の実存的諸問題〔水谷昭夫著〕(ヨルダン社)
パウロ、親鸞*イエス、禅〔八木誠一著〕(法蔵館)
現代の事としての宗教〔滝沢克己著〕(法蔵館)
英米文学にみる現代人の意識の変容〔柳生望著〕(ヨルダン社)
実存主義〔松浪信三郎著〕(岩波新書)
ドストエフスキー〔吉村善夫著〕(新教出版社)
★日本文化と宗教関連、その他の本
人間と宗教〔北森嘉蔵著〕(東海大学出版会)
聖書と日本人〔浅見定雄著〕(晩聲社)
日本経済の深層心理:なぜ原子炉起工式にお祓いをするのか〔金山宣夫著〕(光文社)
日本の中のユダヤ〔久保有政著〕(学研)
「日本」らしさの再発見〔浜口恵俊著〕(講談社文庫)
仏教とキリスト教〔久保田周著〕(いのちのことば社)
異文化間コミュニケーション入門〔L.A.サモーバー他著〕(聖文社)
講座 日本思想1〔相良享他著〕(東京大学出版会)
★DVD
天地創造(20世紀フォックス・ホームエンタテインメント・ジャパン)
十戒(パラマウント・ホームエンタテインメント・ジャパン)
ベン・ハー(COSMIC PICTURES)

◎**参考文献(監修者お勧めの本を除く)**
★**世界の宗教全般の本**
図解宗教史(成美堂出版)
仏教とキリスト教 [ひろさちや著] (新潮社)
キリスト教とイスラム教 [ひろさちや著] (新潮社)
★**キリスト教関連の本**
キリスト教の本(学習研究社)
面白いほどよくわかるキリスト教 [宇都宮輝夫・阿部包著] (日本文芸社)
図解聖書(西東社)
あらすじと解説で「聖書」が一気にわかる本 [大城信哉著] (永岡書店)
不思議なキリスト教 [橋爪大三郎・大澤真幸共著] (講談社現代新書)
キリスト教英語の常識 [石黒マリーローズ著] (講談社現代新書)
★**ユダヤ教関連の本**
ユダヤ教の本(学習研究社)
★**イスラム教関連の本**
イスラム教の本(学習研究社)

日本人が知らなかったイスラム教［佐々木良昭著］（青春出版社）
★道教関連の本
道教の本（学習研究社）
★ヒンドゥー教関連の本
ヒンドゥー教の本（学習研究社）
★比較文化関係の本
水性文化と油性文化［熊山晶久著］（大修館書店）
ふろしき文化のポストモダン［李御寧著］（中央公論社）
シンボル辞典［水之江有一著］（北星堂）
日欧対照イメージ辞典［宮田登・深沢俊共編］（北星堂）
日米ギャップ辞典［C・フィールド監修］（毎日新聞社）

　本書は英語と宗教の入門的な概要を学ぶための教養書として監修されています。神学、信仰、歴史上の論争の対象となりうる事項についても、できるだけ公平で一般的な記述を試みているつもりですが、教派、神学者、歴史学者の間で意見の異なる解釈、表記、見解や、各項目のさらに詳しい専門的知識については、本書の最後にあげた参考文献や論文等を、ご参照いただければ幸いです。

世界の宗教制覇表

第1章 宗教の基礎知識	第1節	宗教とは？ ☐				
	第2節	宗教の分類 ☐				
	第3節	日本の宗教 ☐	世界の代表的宗教 ☐	日本の宗教と世界の宗教の比較 ☐		
第2章 キリスト教を知る	第1節 理由	日本にキリスト教徒が少ない10の理由 ☐				
	第2節 キリスト教の基礎知識	定義 ☐	宗派 ☐	教義 ☐	歴史(世界編) ☐	歴史(日本編) ☐
		教祖と聖典 ☐	弟子 ☐	影響 ☐	生活 ☐	習俗 ☐
	第3節 比較	仏教との比較 ☐	ユダヤ教との比較 ☐	イスラム教との比較 ☐		
第3章 聖書を知る	第1節 聖書	聖書とは？ ☐	旧約聖書の構成 ☐	新約聖書の構成 ☐		
	第2節 旧約聖書の世界	天地創造 ☐	エデンの園 ☐	原罪と追放 ☐	ノアの箱舟 ☐	バベルの塔 ☐
		民族の祖 ☐	出エジプト ☐	約束の地 ☐	士師記 ☐	サムエル記 ☐
		ダビデなど ☐	王国の分裂 ☐	ユダの興亡 ☐	人生の教訓 ☐	
	第3節 新約聖書の世界	聖誕前夜 ☐	受胎告知 ☐	イエス誕生 ☐	ヨハネ ☐	荒野の誘惑 ☐
		十二弟子 ☐	奇跡と救い ☐	山上の説教 ☐	たとえ話 ☐	受難 ☐
		最後の審判 ☐	復活と昇天 ☐	聖霊降臨 ☐	黙示録 ☐	

第4章 ユダヤ教を知る	第1節 ユダヤ教	ユダヤ教とは？ ☐	ユダヤ教の教義 ☐	聖地・エルサレム ☐	
	第2節 影響	学問と芸術 ☐			
第5章 イスラム教を知る	第1節 イスラム教	イスラム教とは？ ☐	教祖 ☐	教えとコーラン ☐	六信五行 ☐
		風習 ☐	イスラム教史 ☐	現代のイスラム教 ☐	
	第2節 影響	建築と美術 ☐			

注：☐内には、勉強をしたことを示すチェック（レ）を入れてください。
　　☐のあとの空欄は、勉強を終えた日程などを入れてください。

索 引

索引・日本語

あ

アーヒラ	244
哀歌	112
アインシュタイン	224
アウグスティヌス	44, 72
アウグストゥス	164
アキーカ	254
アケネメス朝ペルシャ	154
アザーン	254
アサフ	156
アシュエル族	144
アズラーイール	244
アッカド語	126
アッシュール	148
アッシリア	148
アッバース家	270
アッバース朝	270
アナニア	198
アニミズム	14
アハズ	152
アブー・バクル	268
アフガニスタン	230
油注ぎ	144
アブラハム	130
アモス書	112
アラー	24, 230, 244
アラウィー派	284
アラブ首長国連邦	230
アラベスク	288
アラム語	194
アララト山	124
アリー	268
アリウス派	42
アリストテレス哲学	74
アルジェリア	230
アルテミス	200
アルバート公	84
アルハンゲルス	74
アルハンブラ宮殿	290
アルファイの子ヤコブ	64
安息日	116, 210
アンティオキア教会	68
アンティオコス4世	156
アンデレ	64

い

イースター	90
イエス	24
イエズス会	54
イコン	70
イサク	130
イザヤ書	112
石打の刑	176
イジュマー	236
イシュマエル	130
イスカリオテのユダ	64
イスマーイール派	284
イスマイル1世	274
イスラーフィール	244
イスラエル王国	148
イスラム教	16
イスラム教徒	24
イスラム原理主義	284
イスラム暦	230
イッサカル族	144
一神教	16, 105
一神教的	30
一神崇拝	105
一夫多妻	260
イバード派	284
イマーム	236
イマーム・モスク	290
イラク	230
イラン	230
イル＝ハン国	272
岩のドーム	222, 290
印相	96
インドネシア	230

う

ウィリアム・オッカム	74, 76
ウィンザー宮	84
氏子	24
ウズベキスタン	230
ウスマーン	268
ウマイヤ・モスク	290
ウマイヤ家	268
ウマイヤ朝	270
ウマル	268
ウムラ（小巡礼）	252
ウラマー	24
ウルバヌス2世	270
ウンマ	106, 236, 268

え

エ・テメン・アン・キ	128
エイオストレ	90
エキュメニカル運動	40, 52
エキュメニズム	52
エサウ（兄）	130
エジプト	230
エステル記	110
エズラ記	110
エゼキエル書	112
エッセネ派	162
エドム人	132
エフェソス	66
エフライム（＝ヨセフの子）族	144
エフライム族	138
エリ	144
エリコ	138
エルサレム	24
エレミヤ書	112
エレボス	118
エロス	118

お

オイレンブルク	84
オゴタイ=ハン国	272
オスマントルコ	274
オバデヤ書	112
オマーン	230

か

カアバ神殿	234
ガイア	118
改革派教会	38
改宗させる	54
会衆派教会	38
改心	180
傀儡政権	34
雅歌	112, 156
ガザ地区	140
カザフスタン	230
火葬	256
カタール	230
カタコンベ	70
カダル	244
カトリック	24
カトリック教会	34, 42
ガド族	144
カナ	174
カナン	130
カナン人	140
カノッサの屈辱	50
カファルナウム	66
カフカ	224
ガブリエル	162
神	24
カリオテ	66
カリフ	268
カリマ	248
ガリラヤ	48
ガリラヤ地方	48
カルヴァン	50
カルケドン公会議	42
カルタゴ	42
カルバラー	282
カレブ	138

き

喜捨	248, 250
キターブ	244
北イスラエル王国	148
キッシンジャー	224
キプチャク=ハン国	272
キブラ	288
ギホン川	120
キャース	236
救世主	98, 104
旧約聖書	24
キュロス（初代国王）	154
教育勅語	58
教会	24
教会一致運動	52
教皇	78
キリキア	68
ギリシャ正教	38, 42
キリスト教	16
キリスト教神学	74
キリスト教徒	24
キリスト単性論	44
キリストの再臨	46
禁断の木の実	72

く

悔い改め	180
偶像崇拝	102
クッターブ	256
熊本バンド	56, 58
クラウディウス2世	86
クリスマス	84
クルアーン	230
グレゴリウス7世	50
グレゴリオ聖歌	74

け

啓典	244, 246
契約	208
ゲマラ	208
ケルト人	88
ゲルマン神話	90
顕教	94
原罪	44, 120

原罪説	122
玄宗皇帝	290
原理主義	286

こ

公祈祷	80
コーラン	24, 230, 236
五行	238
告白	72
ゴシック	70
五旬節	194
コダシーム	216
コペルニクス	76
コヘレトの言葉	112, 158
コラ	156
ゴリアテ	146
ゴルゴダ	188
コルネリウス	196
コンスタンツ公会議	50
コンスタンティヌス帝	42

さ

サーウィン祭（サムハイン祭）	88
最後の審判	46, 98
最後の晩餐	186
ザイド派	284
サウジアラビア	230
サウム	248
サウル	144
サウロ	198
ザカート	248
鎖国令	56
悪魔（サタン）	170
札幌バンド	56, 58
サドカイ派	162
悟った	96
ザバーニーヤ	244
サファヴィー朝	274
サマリア	148
サマリア人	180
サマリア人の	176
サムエル	144
サムエル記	110

299

サムソン	142
サラ	130
サラート	248
サン・フェリペ号事件	54
ザンギー朝	270
三十年戦争	52
山上の説教	176
三位一体	36, 42
三位一体説	100

し

シーア派	24, 282
死海	138
司教	78
シク教	16
使徒言行録（使徒行伝）	112
地獄	266
司祭	76, 78
士師	140
士師記	110
7イマーム派	284
ジッグラト（聖塔）	128
失楽園	44, 72
使徒	60
シナイ山	176
シナゴーグ	24, 172
ジブリール	234, 244
詩編	112, 154
シメオン族	144
シモン	64
シャーマニズム	14
ジャーラ	252
釈迦	24
シャニダール遺跡	14
シャハーダ	248
シャリーア	236
シャルトル大聖堂	70
十字架	188
十字軍	270
集中式教会	70
修道院	74
12イマーム派	284
十二弟子	174
12部族	144

宗派	36
終末論	46
宗門改	56
受戒	254
受胎告知	60
出エジプト記	110
十戒	136
受難	184
殉教	54
巡礼	248, 250
小アジア	86
上座部仏教	24
昇天	192
書簡	114
贖罪	80
植民地化	53
植民地化政策	52
ショグル	258
助祭	78
諸書	208
叙任権闘争	50
ジョン・ウィクリフ	50
シラス	200
シリア	230
シンアル（バビロニア）	128
神学	46, 74
『神学大全』	74
進化論	40
神曲	72, 266
箴言［しんげん］	112, 158
信仰告白	248
真言	96
神聖ローマ帝国	272
使徒言行録	62
新バビロニア	148
神父	24
神仏習合	18
申命［しんめい］記	110
新約聖書	24
浸礼	168

す

ズー・アル＝ヒッジャ月	230, 250

スコラ学	74
ステファノ	198
ステンドグラス	70
スピルバーグ	224
スルタン	270
スンナ	236, 256
スンナ派	282
スンニ派（スンナ派）	24

せ

西安大清真寺	290
正教会	42
聖公会	42, 82
聖霊	24
聖職者	104
聖霊の降臨	194
成聖	92
聖戦	238
正当カリフ	268
聖なるモスク	290
聖なる岩	222
聖ニコラス	86
聖バレンティヌス	86
聖墳墓教会	220
世界教会協議会	40, 52
世界教会主義	40
世界宗教	16
ゼカリヤ書	112
ゼパニヤ（ゼファニヤ）書	
	102
ゼファニア書	112
ゼブルン族	144
ゼベダイの子ヤコブ	64
セム	126
ゼライーム	216
セルジューク朝	270
宣教	58
全知全能	96
千年王国	204
千年王国説	205
選民思想	102, 210
洗礼	80, 254
洗礼者ヨハネ	60

そ

造化三神	118
荘厳ミサ曲	74
創世記	110, 116
ゾロアスター教	16
ソロモン	146

た

タージ・マハル	290
タージール刑	282
第1コンスタンティノポリス公会議	44
第1ニカイア公会議	42
第2バチカン公会議	52
大巡礼	230
大乗仏教	24
大日本帝国憲法	58
タキーヤ	282
多神教	16
多神教的	30
タダイ	64
磔刑［たっけい］	48
たとえ話	182
タナハ	208
ダニエル書	102, 112, 156
ダビデ	146
魂の井戸	222
ダマスコ	68, 198
タリバン	278
タルソス	68
タルタロス	118
タルムード	24, 208
断食	248, 250
単性説	44
単性論派	44
単旋律	74
ダンテ	72, 266
ダン族	144

ち

チェチェン紛争	278
チグリス川	120
地中海	138
地動説	76, 77
チャイコフスキー	74
チャガタイ＝ハン国	272
チャドル	260
陳朝	272
チュニジア	230
超教派	40

つ

ツヴィングリ	50

て

ディアーナ	200
ディオクレティアヌス	48
テオドシウス	48
滴礼	168
テモテ	200
寺請制度	56
テルトゥリアヌス	42
天使	244
転生	98
天体	76
伝道	48
伝道する	49
天動説	76, 77
天命	244, 246
典礼	70

と

道教	16
トゥグリル・ベグ	270
冬至祭	84
東方諸教会	42
東方正教会	24, 34, 42
土葬	256
トプカプ宮殿	290
トホロート	216
トマス	64
トマス・アクィナス	74
ドミティアヌス	202
ドルイド教	88
ドルーズ派	284
トルクメニスタン	230
トルコ	230

な

ナービー	244
嘆きの壁	220
ナキール	244
ナザレ	162
ナシーム	216
ナタリス・インウィクティ	84
ナフタリ族	144
ナホム書	112

に

ニコライ・カサートキン	58
西エルサレム	218
二神教	16
日米修好通商条約	56
日本国憲法	58
日本ハリストス正教会	100
ニュクス	118
如来	24

ね

ネズイキーン	216
熱心党	162
ネブカドネザル2世	152
ネヘミア記	110
ネロ	48

の

ノア	124
のどぼとけ	120

は

バーブル	274
バーレーン	230
ハインリヒ4世	50
パウロ	46, 198
パウロ6世	52
パウロ書簡	62
ハガイ書	112
ハガル	130
パキスタン	230
迫害	198
箱舟	124

301

バシリカ式教会堂	70		162	ホセア書	112
ハッジ	248	フィリオクェ問題	48	ホメイニ	278
ハッド刑	280	フィリピ	64	ポモナ	88
バッハ	74	福音書	62, 112	ボルトニャンスキー	74
発布	56	福音派	40		
ハディージャ	234	復活	60, 92, 192	**ま**	
ハディース	254	復活祭	194	マグダラのマリア	176
ハバクク書	112	仏教徒	24	マケドニア	200
バビロン	148	ブッダガヤ	24	マジャパヒト王国	272
バビロン捕囚	152	プトレマイオス	76	マタイ	62, 64
バプテスト教会	38	踏絵	56	マタイによる福音書	112
バプテスマ	168	フランシスコ・ザビエル	54	マタイによる福音書	176
バプテスマのヨハネ	168	ブルカ	260	末法思想	46
バベルの塔	126	ブルックナー	74	マナセ（＝ヨセフの子）族	
ハム	126	フレスコ画	70		144
ハラーム	260	プロイセン	84	マニ教	16
ハラール	260	プロテスタント	24, 42	マムルーク朝	272
バラモン教	16			マラーイカ	244
ハラン	130	**へ**		マラキ書	112
バルトロマイ	64	ベーダ	90	マリア	162
バルナバ	200	ベートーベン	74	マルクス	224
パレスチナ	130	ベタニア	186	マルコ	62
バレンタインデー	86	ベツレヘム	60, 164	マルコによる福音書	112
バロック	70	ペトロ	194	マルティン・ルター	34, 50
ハワーリジュ派	284	ペトロ（ペテロ）	64	曼荼羅	96
汎神教	16	ベニヤミン	144		
万聖節	88	ベニヤミン族	144	**み**	
般若心経	24	ヘブライスト	196	ミーカール	244
		ヘブライ語	126	ミーダーア	290
ひ		ペラギウス主義	46	ミカエル・ケルラリオス	48
東エルサレム	220	ペリシテ人	142	ミカ書	102
非カルケドン派	42	ベルディ	74	ミカル	146
ビザンツ帝国	290	ベルリオーズ	74	ミカ書	112
ビザンティン美術	70	ヘレニスト	196	ミケランジェロ	146
ヒジュラ暦	230	ヘロデ・アグリッパ1世	64	ミサ曲	74
ピション川	120	ヘロデ・アンティパス	170	ミサ曲ロ短調	74
ヒゼキヤ	152			ミシュナ	208
百人隊長	196	**ほ**		密教	94
ピラト	188	放蕩息子	180	ミトラス教（ミトラ教）	84
ヒンドゥー教	16	冒涜	188	ミナレット	254, 288
		牧師	24	ミフラーブ	264, 288
ふ		法華経	24	ミラノ勅令	48
ファラオ	132	菩薩	24	ミルトン	72
ファリサイ（パリサイ）派		ボスニア紛争	278	民数［みんすう］記	110

民族宗教	16
ミンバル	264

む

ムガル帝国	274
ムハンマド	24
ムンカル	244

め

メガチャーチ	40
メソジスト教会	38
メッカ	24, 230, 234
メディナ	24, 234
免罪符	50

も

モエード	216
モーセ	24, 136
モーセの十戒	98
黙示録	200
黙認	56
モスク	24
モテット	74
樅（もみ）の木	84
モリヤ山	130
モロッコ	230
モンゴル帝国	272

や

八百万の神	24
ヤコブ（弟）	130
ヤハウェ	24
ヤフェト（ヤペテ）	126
ヤン・フス	50

ゆ

ユーフラテス川	120
ユール	84
ユグノー戦争	52
ユダヤ	48
ユダヤ教	16
ユダヤ教会堂	172
ユダヤ教徒	24
ユダヤ地方	48
ユダ王国	148
ユダ族	138, 144
ユニテリアン	42
ユノ	86

よ

ヨエル書	112
預言者	104, 168, 208, 244, 246
預言者のモスク	290
横浜バンド	56
ヨシア	152
ヨシュア	138
ヨシュア記	110
ヨセフ	132, 162
ヨナ書	112
ヨハネ	62, 64
ヨハネ23世	52
ヨハネス・ケプラー	76
ヨハネによる福音書	112
ヨハネの黙示録	62, 114
ヨブ記	112, 154
よみ	266
ヨルダン川	138, 168
ヨルダン川西岸地区	140

ら

ラーハ	258
ラアブ	258
来世	244, 246
ライプニッツ	82
ラクア	248
ラザロ	174
ラバン	132
ラビ	24, 210
ラフマニノフ	74
ラマダーン	250

り

リキニウス	48
律法	208
リビア	230
リベカ	130
領主	170
両性論派	44
輪廻	98
輪廻転生	98

る

ルーテル教会	38
ルカ	62
ルカによる福音書	112, 166
ルツ記	110
ルネサンス	70
ルペルカリア祭	86
ルベン族	144
ルンビニー	24

れ

礼拝	248
レオ9世	48
歴代誌	110
レクイエム	74
列王記	110
レビ記	110
煉獄	266

ろ

ローマ教皇	34
ローマ帝国	34, 42
六信	238, 244
六動輪廻	266
ロマネスク	70

わ

ワッハーブ派	276, 284
ワリード	290

索引・英語

A

a myriad of deities	25
a plate with a crucifix	57
Abraham	131
Abu Bakr	269
Acts of the Apostles	113
Adam's apple	120
adhan	255
Afghanistan	231
Ahaz	153
Akhira	245
akika	255
Akkadian	127
Algeria	231
Alhambra Palace	291
Ali	269
All Saints' Day	89
Allah	25, 231, 245
alms-giving	249
Al-Walid	291
Amos	113
Ananias	199
Andrew	65
angel	245
Anglican Church	82
animism	15
anointing	145
Antiochia	69
Antiochus IV	157
apostle	61
Arabesque	289
Aramaic	195
Arianism	43
Aristotelian philosophy (Aristotelianism)	75
ark	125
Arkhangelsky	75
Artemis	201
Asaph	157
Asher	144
Asia Minor	87
Assur	149
Assyria	149
atonement	81
Augustinus	44, 73
Augustus	165
Azrael	245

B

Babur	275
Babylon	151
Bach	75
Bahrain	231
baptism	169, 255
baptism by affusion	169
Baptists	39
baptize	81
Barnabas	201
Baroque	73
Bartholomew	65
Beda	91
Beethoven	75
Benjamin	144, 145
Berlioz	75
Bethany	187
Bethlehem	61, 167
bishop	79
bitheism	17
blasphemy	189
Bodhgaya	25
Bodhisattva	25
Book of Lamentations	113
Book of Revelation	115
Books of Chronicles	111
Books of Kings	111
Borutonyansuki	75
Bosnian conflicts	279
Brahmanism	17
Bruckner	75
Buddha	25
Buddhist	25
burka	261
Byzantine art	71

C

Caleb	139
Caliph	269
Calvin	51
Cana	175
Canaanites	141
Cannan	131
Capernaum	67
Carthage	43
catacombs	71
catholic	38
Catholicism	25
(Catholic) priest	77, 79
celestial body	77
Celts	89
centurion	197
chador	261
Chagatai Khanate	273
Chartres Cathedral	71
Chechen war	279
Christian	25
Christian theology	75
Christianity	17
Christmas	85
church	25
Church of the Holly Sepulchre	221
Cilicia	69
Claudius II	89
clergy	105
clergyman	25
colonialism	53
colonization	53

Confession	73	Egypt	231	geocentric theory	77
consecration	92	Einstein	225	Germanic mythology	91
conserate	92	Eli	145	God	25
Constantine the Great	43	elitism	102	God the Father	43
Constitution of the Empire of Japan	59	Emperor Xuanzong	291	God the Holy Spirit	43
		Eostre	91	God the Son	43
Copernican System	77	Ephesus	67	Golgotha (Calvary)	189
Copernicus	77	Ephraim	139, 144	Goliath	147
Cornelius	197	Epistle	115	Gospel	63, 113
covenant	209	Erebos	118	Gospel of John	113
cremation	257	Eros	118	Gospel of Luke	113
crucifixion	49	Esau	131	Gospel of Mark	113
crucify	189	eschatology	47	Gospel of Matthew	113
Crusades	271	Essenes	163	gospelize	49
Cyrus	155	Esther	111	Gothic	73
		Etemenanki	129	Grand Inquest	99
D		ethnic religion	17	Gregorian chant	75
Damascus	69, 199	Eulenburg	85	Gregorius VII	51
Dan	144	Evangelicalism	40		
Daniel	103, 113, 157	evangelize	49	**H**	
Dante	73	evolutionism	40	Habakkuk	113
Daoism (Taoism)	17	exist dualistically	19	Hades	266
David	147	Exodus	111	Hadith	255
deacon	79	exoteric Buddhist teaching	95	Hagar	130
Decalogue	137			Haggai	113
deluge	125	Ezekiel	113	Hajj	231, 249
denomination	37	Ezra	111	halal	261
Deuteronomy	111			Ham	127
Dhu al-Hijjah	231, 251	**F**		haram	261
Diana	200	fasting	249	Haran	131
Diocletianus	49	Filioque	49	Heart Sutra	25
Dome of the Rock	223, 291	fir	85	Hebraists	197
Domitian	203	Francis Xavier	55	Hebrew	127
druidism	89	fresco paintings	71	Hegira	231
Dyophysite	45			heliocentric theory	77
		G		Hellenists	197
E		Gabriel	163, 235, 245	Henry IV	51
East Jerusalem	221	Gad	144	Herod Agrippa I	65
Easter	91, 195	Gaia	118	Herod Antipas	171
Eastern Church	25	Galilean regions	49	Hezekiah	153
Ecclesiastes	113, 159	Galilee	49	Hinayana	25
ecumenical movements	53	Gautama	25	Hinduism	17
ecumenism	40, 52	Gehenna	266	Holy spirits	25
Edomites	133	Genesis	43, 111, 117	Hosea	113

Hudud	281	Jerusalem	25	Kodshim		217
Huguenot Wars	53	Jesus	25	Korah		157
		Jew	25	Koran	231,	237
I		Jewish elitism	211	Kuttaab		257
Ibadi	285	Jewish houses of worship				
icon	71		173	**L**		
idolatry	103	Jihad	239	Laban		133
Ijma	237	Job	113, 155	labor		124
Il Khanate	273	Joel	113	Lazarus		177
imam	237	Johannes Kepler	77	Leibniz		82
Imam Mosque	291	John	63, 65	Leo IX		49
immersion baptism	169	John the Baptist	61	Leviticus		111
Imperial Rescript on		John the Baptist	169	Libya		231
Education	59	John Wycliffe	51	Licinius		49
Indonesia	231	John XXIII	53	liturgy		71
indulgence	51	Jonah	113	Lotus Sutra		25
interdenominationalism	40	Joseph	133, 163	Luke		63
interment	257	Joshua	111, 139	Lumbini		25
Investiture Controversy	51	Josiah	153			
Iran	231	Judah	139, 144	**M**		
Iraq	231	Judaism	17	Macedonia		201
Isaac	131	Judaistic ethnocentricism		Mahayana		25
Isaiah	113		211	Malachi		113
Ishmael	130	Judas Iscariot	65	Malaika		245
Islafil	245	Judea	49	Manasseh		144
Islam	17	Judean regions	49	Mandala		97
Islamic fundamentalism		Judge	141	Manichaeism		17
	285	Judges	111	Mantral		97
Ismail I	275	Juno	87	Mark		63
Ismailism	285			Martin Luther	35,	51
Issachar	144	**K**		Martyrdom		55
		Kadaru	245	Mary		163
J		Kafka	225	Mary Magdalene		177
Jacob	131	Kalima	249	Marx		225
James the son of Alphaeus		Karbala	283	mass		75
	65	Kazakhstan	231	Mass in B minor		75
James the son of Zebedee		Kerioth	67	Matthew	63,	65
	65	Khadijah bint Khuwaylid		Mecca	25, 231,	235
Jan Hus	51		235	Medina	25,	235
Japheth	127	Khawarij	285	Messiah		99
Jara	253	Khomeini	279	Methodism		39
Jehovah	25	Kissinger	225	Micah	103,	113
Jeremiah	113	Kipchak Khanate	273	Michael Keroularios		
Jericho	141	Kitab	245	(Cerularius)		49

Michal	147	Nezikin	217	prodigal son	181
Michelangelo	146	Nikolai Kasatkin	59	promulgate	57
Mihrab	265, 289	Noah	125	propagate	49
Mikal	245	non-Chalcedon	43	propagation	59
millenarianism	205	Nyx	118	prophet	105, 245
millennialism	205			Prophet's Mosque	291
Milton	73	**O**		Protestantism	25
Minaret	255, 289	Obadiah	113	Prussian	85
minbar	265	Ogedei Khanate	273	Psalms	155
Missa Solemnis	75	Oman	231	"Ptolemaic System"	77
missionize	49	omnipotent	97	Ptolemy	77
Mithraism	85	omniscient	97	public prayer	81
Moed	217	ordination	255	puppet state	35
monastery	75	original sin	45, 121	purgatory	266
monolatry	105				
monophonic	75	**P**		**Q**	
Monophysite	45	Pakistan	231	Qatar	231
Monophysitism	45	Palestine	131	Qibla	289
monotheism	17, 105	pantheism	17	Qiyas	237
monotheistic	31, 105	parable	183	Quran	231
Morocco	231	"Paradise Lost"	73		
Moses	25, 137	Paul	47	**R**	
mosque	25	Paul	199	rabbi	25, 211
motet	75	Paul VI	53	Rachmaninoff	75
Mount Ararat	125	Paul's Letters	63	rakaat	249
Mount Moriah	131	Pelagianism	47	Ramadan	251
Mount Sinai	177	Pentecost	195	Rebecca	131
Mudra	97	persecution	199	recruit	55
Muhammad	25	Peter	65, 195	redenomination	37
Mumluk Sultanate	273	Pharaoh	133	reformation	183
Munkar	245	Pharisees	163	reincarnation	99
Muslim	25	Philip	65	religious investigation	57
		Philistines	143	Renaissance	73
N		pilgrimage	231, 249	repentance	183
Nabi	245	polygamy	261	requiem	75
Nahum	113	polytheism	17	resurrect	61
Nakir	245	polytheistic	31	resurrection	93
Naphtali	144	Pomona	89	resurrection and judgment	245
Nashim	217	Pontius Pilate	189		
Natalis Invicti	85	Pope	79	Reuben	144
Nazareth	163	prayer	249	revelation	245
Nebuchadnezzar	153	predestination	245	Rightly Guided Caliph	269
Nehemiah	111	priest	25	Romanesque	73
Nero	49	Prince Albert	85	Ruth	111

S

Sacred Mosque	291
Sadducees	163
Salat (Salah)	249
Samaria	149
Samaritan	177
Samaritan	181
Samhain Festival	89
samsara	99
Samson	143, 168
Samuel	111, 145
San Felipe Incident	55
sanctify	92
Sarah	131
Saudi Arabia	231
Saul	145, 199
Sawm	249
scholasticism	75
Seljuk of Turkey	271
7-iman-sub-sect	285
Shahada	249
shamanism	15
Shanidar Cave	15
Shariah	237
Shem	127
Shia	25, 283
Shinar (Babylonia)	129
Shintoist	25
Sikhism	17
Silas	201
Simeon	144
Simon	65
Solomon	149
Song of Solomon	113
Song of Songs	113
Spielberg	225
spiritually awakened	97
St. Nicholas	87
St. Valentinus	87
stained glass	71
Stephen	199
stone	177
sultan	271
"Summa Theologica"	75
Sunna	237, 257
Sunni	25, 283
synagogue	25, 173
Syria	231

T

Taj Mahal	291
Taliban regime	279
Tantric Buddhism	95
Tarsus	69
Tartaros	118
Tazir	283
Tchaikovsky	75
temple gurantee system	57
Tertullianus	43
testimony	249
tetrarch	173
Thaddaeus	65
the Abbasid clan	271
the Abbasid Empire	271
the Achaemenid Empire of Persia	155
the Acts of the Apostles	63
the Alawis	285
the Anglican Church	43
the Annunciation	61
the Ascension	193
the Babylonian Captivity	153
the Baptist Church	39
the basilica style	71
the Bible	25
the Book of Proverbs	159
the Books of Revalation	63
the Byzantine Empire	291
the Catholic Church	35, 43
the central plan style	71
the Congregational Church	39
the Constitution of Japan	59
the Council of Chalcedon	47
the Council of Constance	43
	51
the Dead Sea	139
the Decalog	99
the Decalogue	99
the Descent of Holy Spirit	195
the Devil (Satan)	171
"The Divine Comedy"	73
the Druze	285
the Eastern Orthodox Church	35
the Edict of Milan	49
the Euphrates	121
the First Council of Constantinople	45
the First Council of Nicaea	43
the Five Pillars of Islam	239
the forbidden fruit	73
the Foundation Stone	223
the Gamera	209
the Gaza Strip	141
the Gihon	121
the Gospel according to Matthew	179
the Gospel of Luke	167
the Great Moque of Xian	291
the Greek Orthodox Church	39
the Hijri calendar	231
the Holy Roman Empire	273
the Jordan	139, 169
the Kabah (Kaaba)	235
the Ketubim	209
the Kingdom of Israel	149
the Kingdom of Judah	149
the Koran	25
the Kumamoto Band	57
the Last Judgment	47
the Last Supper	187
the Lupercalia festival	87

the Lutheran Church 39	the Talmud 25, 209	United Arab Emirates 231
the Majapahit Empire 273	the Thirty Years' War 53	UrbanusII 271
the Mediterranean Sea 139	the Tigris 121	Uthman 269
the Methodist Church 39	the Torah 209	Uzbekistan 231
the millennium 205	the Tower of Babel 127	
the Mishnah 209	the Treaty of Amity and	
the Mongol Empire 273, 275	commerce 57	**V**
the national isolation law 57	the Trinity 37, 43	Valentine's Day 87
	the various Eastern	Verdi 75
the Neo-Babylonian Empire 151	Churches 43	vizier 135
the Nevim 209	the Wall of Souls 223	
the New Testament 25	the West Bank 141	**W**
the Northern Kingdom of Israel 149	the World Council of Churches (WCC) 53	Wahhab 285
the Numbers 111	the Yokohama Band 57	Wahhabism 277
the Old Testament 25	Theodosius 49	Wailing Wall 221
the Orthodox Church 37, 43	theology 47, 75	Walk to Canossa 51
the Ottoman Empire 275	Theory of Original Sin 123	West Jerusalem 219
the Passion 185	Thomas 65	Western Wall 221
the Pishon 121	Thomas Aquinas 75	William of Ockham 75
the Pope 35	Timothy 201	Windsor Castle 85
the Protestant Church 43	TNK 209	Winter Solstice Festival 85
the Proverbs 113	Tohorot 217	work to eat 124
the Psalms 113	tolerate 57	world religion 17
the Reformed Churches 39	Topkapi Palace 291	WWC = the World Council of Churches 40
the Resurrection 193	Tran dynasty 273	
the Revelation 203	transmigration 99	**Y**
the Roman Empire 35, 43	Trinitarianism 101	Yule 85
the Sabbath 116, 211	Tughril Beg 271	
the Safavid dynasty 275	Tunisia 231	**Z**
the Sapporo Band 57	Turkey 231	Zabaniya 245
the Savior 105	Turkmenistan 231	Zaidiyya (Zaydism) 285
the Second Coming of Christ 47	twelve disciples 175	Zakat 249
	Twelver 285	Zangid dynasty 271
The Second Vatican Council 53		Zealots 163
	U	Zebulun 144
the Seljuq Empire 271	ulama 25	Zechariah 113
the Sermon on the Mount 177	Umar 269	Zephaniah 103, 113
	Umayya 269	Zeraim 217
the Six Articles of Belief 239	Umayya Caliphate 271	Ziggurat 129
	Umayya Mosque 291	Zoroastrianism 17
The Society of Jesus 55	Ummah 107, 237, 269	Zwingli 51
The Song of Solomon 157	Umrah 253	
	Unitarian 43	

著者略歴

石井　隆之(いしい　たかゆき)

筑波大学大学院修了。専門は、言語学、言語文化論、日本文化論。通訳案内業資格保持。現在、近畿大学名誉教授、京都女子大学非常勤講師、滋賀県立大学非常勤講師。言語文化学会会長、通訳ガイド研究会会長。著書に『日本の宗教の知識と英語を身につける』(ベレ出版)、『魔法のイディオム』(Jリサーチ出版)など多数。英語テキスト、論文多数。

監修者略歴

土井　清孝(どい　きよたか)

関西学院大学文学部卒業。同大学院文学研究科修了。パシフィック・ルセラン大学大学院修了。トロント大学、セント・マイケルズ大学大学院研究員。専門は、英語教育、通訳法、比較文化論。現在、兵庫県立大学教授。著書に『新アメリカ文化事典』(共著)『ネイティブ英語表現辞典』他、英語テキスト、論文多数。

校閲者略歴

Joe Ciunci (ジョー・シウンシ)

米国ロードアイランド州出身。専門は聖書歴史学。現在、関西で大学講師および講師トレーナーを務める。

キリスト教・ユダヤ教・イスラム教の知識と英語を身につける

2011年10月25日	初 版 発 行
2023年12月31日	第3刷発行

著者	石井　隆之(いしい　たかゆき)
カバーデザイン	赤谷　直宣
本文イラスト	杉谷　ふさえ

© Takayuki Ishii 2011. Printed in Japan

発行者	内田　真介
発行・発売	ベレ出版 〒162-0832 東京都新宿区岩戸町12　レベッカビル TEL (03)5225-4790 FAX (03)5225-4795 ホームページ https://www.beret.co.jp/
印刷	三松堂株式会社
製本	根本製本株式会社

落丁本・乱丁本は小社編集部あてにお送りください。送料小社負担にてお取り替えします。

ISBN978-4-86064-299-0 C2082　　　　　編集担当　脇山和美

日本の宗教の知識と英語を身につける

石井隆之 著

A5 並製／定価 2205 円（5% 税込） 本体 2100 円
ISBN978-4-939076-266-2 C2082 ■ 296 頁

日本文化の基礎を形作っているのは、日本の宗教および宗教的発想ですが、いざ外国人に日本の宗教について質問されても説明できないことが多い。本書は第 1 部「宗教と日本人に関する基礎情報」、第 2 部「日本の宗教・基礎編」、第 3 部「日本の仏教に関係する人物」の構成です。英文説明で用いた英語は比較的易しく覚えやすいものばかりです。英語で日本文化を紹介することに関心がある人、通訳ガイドを目指している人の必携の一冊。

日本の都道府県の知識と英語を身につける

石井隆之 著

A5 並製／定価 2205 円（5% 税込） 本体 2100 円
ISBN978-4-86064-227-3 C2082 ■ 352 頁

日本のことを英語で発信する機会が増えています。正しい日本の情報を外国人に伝えるためには日本の都道府県の知識と英語力が必要です。本書は 4 部構成になっています。1 部は日本紹介に使える基本英語表現、2 部は日本の世界遺産について、3 部は北海道から沖縄までの各都道府県の情報で本書の中心部分、4 部は日本の宗教についてです。CD には 1 部、2 部の基本表現を収録。

日本の地理・歴史の知識と英語を身につける

植田一三 著

A5 並製／定価 2205 円（5% 税込） 本体 2100 円
ISBN978-4-86064-161-0 C2082 ■ 368 頁

日本について英語で発信するための基本的な知識とキーになる英単語と英語表現が学べる本。日本の地理、世界の地理、日本の通史、経済史、外交史、文化史、戦後史の 7 章に分かれています。それぞれのテーマごとの流れが簡潔にまとめられており、重要な表現は英語が並列されています。北海道から九州までの観光通訳や日本史テストが CD に収録。